PRACTICAL ENGLISH

Volume One

PRACTICAL
ENGLISH

by
Madeline Semmelmeyer

*Former Supervisor of Languages, Chicago Public Schools,
and Lecturer in Education: Chicago Teachers Review School,
Roosevelt University, and National College of Education.*

Edited by
Donald O. Bolander

Director of Education, Career Institute

A Two Volume Course and Reference Set
Containing 27 Self-graded Units
on GRAMMAR, CORRECT USAGE, and PUNCTUATION

Career Institute

30 East Adams Street • Chicago, Illinois 60603

1965 EDITION
Copyright 1955, 1965, by
CAREER INSTITUTE, Inc.
30 East Adams Street
Chicago, Illinois 60603

Printed in the United States of America
by
Rand McNally & Company

TABLE OF CONTENTS

Note: The twenty-seven units here contained in two volumes were first published as separate booklets. The pages in the volumes, therefore, are not numbered consecutively. Any topic listed in the table of contents may quickly be found by turning first to the specific unit number as given on the handy index tabs and then by referring to the page indicated within the unit. A *Comprehensive Index* and *Glossary of Terms* are contained at the back of this volume.

Contents—Volume One

Contents—Volume Two

A *Glossary of Terms* and a *Comprehensive Index* are contained at the back of Volume One.

Practical English

OUTLINE OF UNIT ONE

THE PARTS OF SPEECH

Page

INTRODUCTION

YOUR ENGLISH IS YOU!

Your English is an integral part of your personality, your character, your real self. You can no more get rid of it than of your shadow. A knowledge of good English gives you poise and confidence. Its employment enables you to take your place in all circles confidently—without fear of ridicule.

A. CHARLES BABENROTH

Your English is *you*. No matter how great your natural ability or intelligence, *you* will always be judged on the basis of how well you speak and write. The use of poor English is a serious handicap in business and social life—a handicap, however, that can be easily overcome.

Yes, you can master perfect English. By following the step-by-step program outlined in these two volumes, you can acquire the ability to converse more interestingly and easily, to write clearly and gracefully, and to express yourself more effectively. This fact has been proved by the thousands who have gone before you in this course.

The twenty-seven units contained in these two volumes were developed after years of testing different methods to determine which system of learning produced the most satisfactory results. Originally, the Practical English classes at Career Institute were attended by mature men and women who, for various business and social reasons, needed a "second chance" at grammar and correct English usage.

Learning for some of these adult students was at first a difficult process. Then, through research conducted by the Institute, a door was opened. It was found that when subject matter was broken down into very small segments, followed by practice exercises that could be self-scored by the student immediately upon completion, most students developed a greater interest in the course. But, even more important, they made much more rapid progress and, in most cases, learned and remembered more. Almost without exception, these adult students, after completing the course, reported highly favorable results in terms of business advancement, increased social benefits, greater poise and self-confidence. As a result of this success — and because of the demonstrated ability of adults to achieve amazingly fast results from the system on a self-graded basis — the *Practical English* course was prepared.

Again, success stories began to come in, not only from adults but also from their sons and daughters who found that they, too, could benefit from the course. These younger students ranged from the sixth grade to college level. They, like their parents, needed a second chance at grammar

5

and correct English usage in order to catch up or to excel in their school work.

Now *Practical English,* tested and proved thousands of times over, stands ready to help you—to rid you of doubts about correct grammatical expression, to help you speak and write clearly, colorfully, and effectively, and to put you at ease in any business or social situation.

YOU WILL MOVE AHEAD IN EASY STEPS

Each unit or chapter of *Practical English* begins with a general *explanation* of the topic to be covered. Read this explanation carefully. Following each explanation you will find one or more *examples.* The examples are included to give you practical applications in a number of everyday language situations.

When you feel that you understand a principle or rule, work out the exercise that follows and check your answers with the *Key to Correct Answers* at the end of the unit. Correct your mistakes.

After you have read the explanatory material and have finished all of the exercises in the unit, read the *Summary* at the end of the lesson and do the *Self-Grading Assignments* which follow. These assignments give you further practice covering the points in the unit. Check your answers for each assignment before going on to the next. If you have made any mistakes, reread the text as necessary to find your errors — and correct them.

Next you are ready for the final test in the unit. This is called a *Progress Test* because it indicates your mastery of all of the principles and rules developed in the unit. Your score on this test will show whether or not you need further review before moving ahead to the next unit.

At the end of Volume I and again at the end of Volume II, you will find a complete set of *Mastery Tests* covering every important phase of the work developed up to that point. These tests will serve as a final evaluation of your progress in the study of English grammar, correct usage, and punctuation.

As you do each exercise or test, be sure to write all the answers in the space provided. The exercises and tests not only allow you to measure your own progress but also enable you to put what you learn into practice at once. You will be delighted at how soon and how easily you will be able to apply each new principle you learn.

Don't worry about technical terms. At the end of Volume One, there is a reference list or glossary of important grammatical terms. These terms or words are also explained in the text. Although these terms are important in the study of English grammar—just as the names of tools are to the auto mechanic — you are not expected to memorize them. You will learn most of them naturally as you progress through the course.

Don't try to memorize all the rules. Deliberate memorizing of the rules of grammar will only waste time and slow your progress through the course. You will gradually acquire a good working knowledge and understanding of the rules simply by doing the practice material in the units.

Remember, always, that learning a rule is not important in itself. The really important thing is the ability to use what you have learned to express yourself effectively without being especially conscious of any rules at all.

Set your own pace—but stay with it. You are the best judge of how much time you can devote to *Practical English.* Some adults who are out of the habit of studying may work best in short periods of time— say 15 to 30 minutes a day. Others may find it easier or more convenient to set aside a longer period, an hour or two, every second or third day. But, whatever time you decide upon, follow it consistently and you will soon find yourself making real progress.

If you have been away from school for some time, you may at first feel that you can't concentrate properly or that you don't remember what you read. Don't worry if you have this experience. Many adults feel this way when they begin a new course.

When reading, pause frequently and, without looking at the book, try to state in your own words the ideas which you have just read. If you do not fully understand a certain section, do the best you can with it, but then move ahead to the next part. Go back in a week or so and reread the section that gave you difficulty. You will be surprised how much easier it will seem the second time.

Develop the "listening habit." Throughout your course, make a practice of listening to the language you hear about you. You will find vast differences.

Television and radio announcers, for example, are usually excellent grammarians, and they normally work with prepared material that conforms to the rules of correct usage. On the other hand, you will detect glaring errors in the language of some persons, errors that were not obvious to you before you began the course. Keep listening and analyzing what you hear. By doing so, you will have a fascinating hobby that will help you change your own speech habits for the better.

Make good English a family game. Share your interest in the *Practical English* course with other members of your family. If two or more persons in the family are taking the course, you will find that discussions of proper usage between study hours can be very helpful and stimulating.

Even if you the the only one directly concerned, you will find it entertaining and useful, to you and your family, to participate in a dinnertime game in which one person analyzes and "criticizes" the speech of another. All criticism and comments should be made in "the spirit of fun." Use your *Practical English* volumes to settle any differences.

You will quickly master good English. As you progress through the course, keep in mind that your goal—a command of good English—is easily within your reach. Unlike some subjects which contain a large body of knowledge and require years of study, English grammar and correct usage can be learned rather quickly because the amount of information you must absorb is limited. Once you have grasped and understood a relatively few simple rules and terms, they are yours for life. Once you understand and properly use these rules, you will have a mastery of English that many people never attain.

Keep Practical English as a permanent reference library. Both as you study and after you have completed the course, use the *Alphabetical Index* at the end of Volume One to find quickly any topic on which you want information. Keep *Practical English* handy at home or at the office. With it, you have an unparalleled reference source on any phase of English usage.

THE PARTS OF SPEECH—I

THE PARTS OF SPEECH—I

LANGUAGE is the expression of ideas by means of words. The grammar of a language is primarily the study of the forms of words and their relationship to each other. We study grammar to find out how to put words together correctly and so that the words express our ideas most clearly and effectively.

When you are trying to put words together in their proper relationships, you are working in much the same way as a mechanic works when he is trying to put together a piece of machinery. Like the mechanic, you must be familiar with the parts that are needed and with the use or purpose of each part.

In dealing with language, *words* are the parts that are used to build up sentences. The English language has thousands of words, but all of them fall into eight groups or classes known as the *parts of speech*. The following names have been given to the *parts of speech:*

Nouns   Pronouns   Verbs   Adjectives   Adverbs

Prepositions   Conjunctions   Interjections

Each group has its special work to do. *Nouns* are the names of persons, places, and things. *Pronouns* take the place of nouns. *Adjectives* and *adverbs* help express the ideas that give color and more definite meanings to nouns, verbs, and other words. *Conjunctions* are joining or connecting words.

Words, then, are the tools of communication. Like any other tool, a word may be used for different purposes at different times. For example, a word might be used as a noun in one sentence and as a verb in another sentence. Another word might be used as a preposition in one sentence and as an adverb in another sentence. All words do not have more than one use, but many words do.

In the first two units you will learn that the most important fact concerning any word is its *function* or use in a particular sentence. If you keep this fact in mind, you will have no difficulty in understanding the simple principles that govern the relationships of words in sentences. The first two units also provide you with an important part of the working vocabulary that you will need as you progress through the course. By thoroughly reviewing or learning the material in these units your study of later units will be greatly simplified.

NOUNS
WORDS USED AS NAMES

You will begin your study of the parts of speech with the noun. A **noun** is one of the most important words that you use when either speaking or writing. It is the word that tells what you are talking about. *A noun is a word that names something.* You have a name. I have a name. Everything that we see, or examine, or talk about must have a name. There are names for *persons, animals, places,* and *objects* that can be pointed out and recognized. There are also names for *substances, qualities, actions,* and *measures* of time or quantity. The following list includes examples of different kinds of nouns.

Persons: soldier—Jane—friend—Englishman
Animals: elephant—mouse—zebra—panda
Places: home—Chicago—camp—factory
Objects: desk—picture—typewriter—hammer
Substances: iron—air—water—food
Qualities: kindness—heroism—beauty—faith
Actions: climbing—cooking—batting—reading
Measures: year—pound—inch—bushel—day

Nouns Used in Sentences

The *soldier* is wearing his new *uniform.*
   noun   noun

Chicago is a great industrial *city.*
 noun   noun

Iron is a useful *metal.*
 noun   noun

**A noun is a word
used as a name.**

EXERCISE 1

On the line to the right of each of the nouns in the following list, indicate whether the noun is the name of a **person, place, animal, object, quality, substance, action,** or **measure.**

1. cup ....

2. pound ....

3. swimming ....

4. lawyer ....

5. home ....

6. courage ....

7. Boston ....

8. guest ....

9. book ....

10. month ....

11. flower ....

12. initiative ....

13. hill ....

14. captain ....

15. France ....

16. century ....

17. library ....

18. zinc ....

19. skiing ....

20. speaker ....

Note: The correct answers to exercises will be found at the end of this unit. Correct your mistakes and, if necessary, reread the text material before going on to the next section.

EXERCISE 2

Underline the **nouns** in the following sentences:

1. Michael bought a canoe from an Indian.

2. Scientists are looking for rare specimens of flowers.

3. The men in the factory signed a petition for higher wages.

4. Visitors filled the balcony of the theater.

5. The book contains pictures of animals and plants.

6. The manager objected to the amount of the bill.

7. The swimmer had courage and endurance.

8. A fugitive escaped through the door of the hotel.

9. My brother is a very efficient salesman.

10. The young aviator piloted his plane skillfully.

11. An automobile skidded on the wet pavement.

12. Oranges and figs grow in California.

13. Signals were put up at the crossings.

14. We enjoyed hunting and fishing in the mountains.

15. Snow and ice covered the trees and fences.

16. Television may displace radio in a few years.

17. Jack and his friends rowed the boat across the stream.

18. The tourists visited the castles along the Rhine.

19. The sailors were on the deck when the shark was sighted.

20. The agent sold several cars and a truck.

PRONOUNS
SUBSTITUTES FOR NOUNS

You will often find it necessary to refer to a *name* a number of times in a single sentence. This repetition usually results in a sentence that is very awkward or monotonous. You can readily see what might happen from the following illustration:

Jack went to *Jack's* closet and took out *Jack's* new suit because *Jack* was going to a dance given by *Jack's* company.

In this sentence the word *Jack* is stated five times. This awkward repetition of the word *Jack* and *Jack's* could be avoided by substituting another part of speech for these words.

Jack went to *his* closet and took out *his* new suit because *he* was going to a dance given by *his* company.

The words *his* and *he* used in the revision of the sentence are called **pronouns.** They are substitutes for the noun *Jack.* The prefix **pro** in the word pronoun means *for.* The word **pronoun** simply means *for a noun,* or *in place of a noun.*

The underlined words in the following illustrations are pronouns. The words to which they refer are underlined twice.

Mary came to America when she was five years old.

The men forgot their tickets.

The officer blew his whistle.

A pronoun is a word used in place of a noun or a name.

Commonly Used Pronouns

You should be familiar with the pronouns in common use. For that reason a list of pronouns is a handy reference guide. Whenever you are not certain whether a word is a pronoun, refer to the following list. In a short time you will be familiar with most of them.

I	you	hers	what	all	none	somebody
my	yours	it	who	any	some	no one
mine	your	its	whose	both	several	someone
me	he	they	whom	each	other	everyone
we	his	their	this	either	another	one
our	him	theirs	that	neither	anybody	whoever
ours	she	them	these	few	everybody	whosoever
us	her	which	those	many	nobody	anyone

EXERCISE 3

A.

Fill in the blank spaces with **pronouns** used in place of nouns.

1. Grace has been ill. _____ will return to work tomorrow.

2. The ink is on the desk. Please bring _____ to me.

3. Ted and Alice are visiting us. _____ will stay a week.

4. I am looking for my skates. Have you seen _____?

5. Good citizens keep _____ sidewalks clean.

6. The man _____ found the money returned _____ to the owner.

B.

Underline the **pronouns** in the following sentences:

1. Mother has house guests. She gave a dinner for them.

2. All of the men went to the meeting. Many stayed for the program.

3. This is the doctor who made the tests.

4. Each of the players brought a uniform which he had worn before.

5. The farmer who helped us would not take the money we offered him.

6. The men heard someone discussing their plans.

Note: Check answers before starting next section.

VERBS

ACTION AND LINKING VERBS

The **verb** is the most important part of speech. *It is the only part of speech that can make a statement about the subject.* The subject is the part of a sentence that names the person, place, or thing that is talked about. If you wanted to write or say something about *a hunter*, you could not complete your statement without the use of a verb. You must have a verb in every sentence. The following illustration will make this clear.

The hunter *shot* the deer. (The verb is the word *shot*.)

If you take the verb *shot* out of the sentence, you have left the words, *the hunter, the deer,* but you do not have a complete thought. You need a verb to state what the hunter did to the deer. When you supply a verb, you have a complete statement.

Most of the verbs in common use express **action.** The action is not always physical action like the action expressed in the sentence, *The hunter shot the deer.* In the sentence, *I solved the problem,* the meaning of the verb *solved* implies both mental and physical activity.

In the sentence, *The engineer built a bridge,* all the types of activity that went on until the bridge was completed are implied in the verb *built.* The same would be true of the verb *made* in the sentence, *The chef made a cake.* All the verbs in the following sentences express action of some kind:

The painter *decorated* the hall.

I *pricked* my finger.

The stenographer *wrote* a letter.

The president *called* a meeting.

The officer *handed* a ticket to the driver.

A small, but very important group of verbs, *do not* express action. The verb **to be** is the most important verb in this group. This verb has many forms which you will learn later in your course. The most common forms of the verb *to be* include *is, are, was* and *were.* Since the verb *to be* does not express action, it must have another function in the sentence. With the help of some other word or words, it makes a statement about the *condition* of the subject, or the person, place, or thing that is talked about.

In the sentence, *Henry is ill,* the verb *is* does not express action of any kind, but it serves two purposes in the sentence. With the help of the word *ill* it makes a statement about the subject, *Henry*. It also serves to connect the word *ill* with *Henry*. The sentence really means *ill Henry,* but you need the verb *is* to make the statement a complete sentence. Because the verb has this connecting function, it is called a **linking verb.**

From the following illustrations, you will see that the verb *to be* with the help of some other word describes or explains the condition of the subject in some way. The verb *is* is a form of the verb *to be.*

My uncle *is* a famous surgeon. (classifies uncle as surgeon)

Mother *is* very happy. (describes the condition of mother)

This cabinet *is* a television set. (identifies the cabinet)

Her dress *is* beautiful. (describes dress)

A number of other verbs are often used in the same way as the verb *to be* is used in the preceding illustrations. You will study these verbs in a later unit. The point to remember is that not all verbs express action. Some verbs have a *linking* function. In defining a verb you must include both functions.

A verb is a word which expresses action, condition, or state of being.

EXERCISE 4

Underline the **verbs** in the following sentences. On the line to the right, indicate whether the verb expresses *action,* or has a *linking* function, by using the initials **A.** or **L.**

1. The automobile skidded on the wet pavement.   1. ....

2. The merchant knows his customers.   2. ....

3. The rain fell in torrents.   3. ....

4. I hung my coat on the rack.   4. ....

5. The lake is very rough.   5. ....

6. The lion roared at the hunter.   6. ....

7. We swam across the tank twice.   7. ....

8. The man accumulated great wealth.   8. ....

9. Charles went to the convention at St. Louis.   9. ....

10. Melvin sold his bicycle to his cousin.   10. ....

11. We spent the summer in the mountains.   11. ....

12. Three men stopped our car.   12. ....

13. The weather is very pleasant.   13. ....

14. Madge complained about the high price of food.   14. ....

15. The secretary read the minutes.   15. ....

16. We opened the door to the secret chamber.   16. ....

17. Refreshing rain fell all night.   17. ....

18. We met a distinguished writer.   18. ....

19. The balloon rose slowly.   19. ....

20. My friend is a costume designer.   20. ....

VERB PHRASES
PRINCIPAL AND AUXILIARY VERBS

A *verb* is not always a single word. *When the verb is composed of two or more words, it is called a* **verb phrase.** The verb form at the end of the verb phrase is always the *principal verb.* It is the verb form that indicates the nature of the action, if the verb expresses action. The other verb forms in the verb phrase are called *auxiliary verbs* or *helping verbs.*

The men *work* in the fields.

The men *are working* in the fields.

The men *have been working* in the fields.

The men *must have been working* in the fields.

In the first sentence the verb consists of one word, the verb *work.* The verb *work* tells the kind of action that is going on. The verb in the second sentence consists of two words. The principal verb is *working.* The auxiliary, or helping verb is *are.* The verb phrase is *are working.* The verb phrase in the third sentence is *have been working.* The principal verb is *working,* and the two helping verbs are *have been.* The verb phrase in the fourth sentence is *must have been working.* The principal verb is *working* and the three helping verbs are *must have been.*

One of the first things you should learn to do in your study of grammar is to be able to identify the verb or the verb phrase in any sentence. Some students have trouble in deciding what words belong in the verb phrase. You will never encounter this difficulty if you become familiar with the commonly used auxiliary verbs. A list of these auxiliary verbs follows. You should refer to this list constantly until you become familiar with the verbs that help make verb phrases.

**A verb phrase is a group of words consisting of
two or more verb forms.**

Commonly Used Auxiliary Verbs

am	have	do	should
is	has	did	must
are	had	does	should have
was	have been	may	would have
were	had been	can	must have
will be	has been	might	should have been
shall be	shall	could	could have been
could be	will	would	must have been

Verb Phrases Used in Sentences

She <u>has said</u> that you <u>will receive</u> the money.
      verb phrase   verb phrase

He <u>was talking</u> with the manager when you came in.
   verb phrase

The new office building <u>was destroyed</u> by fire.
                         verb phrase

The books <u>were inspected</u> by the librarian.
           verb phrase

EXERCISE 5

Draw a line under the **verb phrases** in the following sentences. Write **P.** under the *principal verb*, and **A.** under the *auxiliary verb* or *verbs*.

Example: I <u>have been singing.</u>
           A.   A.   P.

1. The players were resting on the grass.

2. A tree had fallen across the road.

3. Tom has been playing golf all day.

4. You must return to the city at once.

5. Daily talks will be given by the guide.

6. The company is buying a new factory.

7. We should have worn our old clothes.

8. Your report will be sent to the manager.

9. The mountains could be seen from our windows.

10. Many new books have been added to the library.

11. Newton has traveled extensively.

12. I shall go to Italy next summer.

SUMMARY OF GRAMMAR UNIT ONE

Words are classified into eight groups according to the work that they do in sentences. These eight groups are called the **parts of speech.** The parts of speech are known as *nouns, pronouns, verbs, adjectives, adverbs, prepositions, conjunctions,* and *interjections.*

A **noun** is a word that is used to **name** something. Nouns name *persons, places, animals, objects* of various kinds, *substances, qualities, actions,* and *measures,* such as year, pound, quart, etc.

A **pronoun** is a word that is used **in place of a noun** or a name. Pronouns are commonly used to avoid the awkward repetition of nouns.

A **verb** is usually regarded as the most important part of speech because it is impossible to make a statement without using a verb. A verb is a word that expresses *action, condition,* or *state of being.*

Most verbs express **action.** There is a small, but very important group of verbs that do not express action. With the help of some other word, these verbs usually describe the condition of the person, place, or thing that is being talked about. They are called **linking** verbs to distinguish them from action verbs. The verb *to be* is the most important linking verb. The forms *is, are, was,* and *were* belong to the verb *to be.*

A verb is not always a single word. Sometimes it is made up of two, three, and even four verb forms. When the verb is made up of more than one form, it is called a **verb phrase.** The verb form at the end of the phrase is called the *principal verb.* The other verbs forms are called *auxiliary verbs,* or *helping verbs.*

SELF-GRADING ASSIGNMENT 1

Directions: Underline the **nouns** in the following sentences.

1. Engineers dug a tunnel under the river.

2. Our coach was injured Friday.

3. Atlases were placed on the table in the library.

4. The treasurer paid the entertainers.

5. The prisoner had faith and courage.

6. Drawing and painting are his favorite hobbies.

7. Eric bought a new home in Evanston.

8. Our game was interrupted by a messenger.

9. Skiing is a dangerous sport.

10. Coats and hats were piled up on a table.

11. Stephen plans to take lessons in driving.

12. Iron and steel are useful metals.

13. The company made a great many improvements.

14. The doctor ordered penicillin for his patient.

15. A plane will leave the airport in an hour.

16. That man lacks initiative.

17. Two explorers returned from a trip to Africa.

18. My boat sank during the storm.

19. Smoke rose from the tall chimney.

20. Fruit and nuts were served at the dinner.

Caution: Check your answers to each assignment with the answer key at at the end of this unit before proceeding with the next assignment.

SELF-GRADING ASSIGNMENT 2

Directions: Underline the **pronouns** in the following sentences.

1. The man who was injured recovered.

2. These are Jane's medals.

3. She asked me to show them to you.

4. They went to Cuba with us.

5. Robert will not tell me why he quit.

6. We objected to the bill. The company corrected it.

7. Anybody can qualify for the position.

8. That is the hat they featured.

9. The rug that you selected was admired by others.

10. The judge questioned her, but she could not describe the intruder.

11. These are the plans. Those are the sketches.

12. He held the horse for her.

13. The candy was delicious. I ate all of it.

14. That is the book I mentioned to them.

15. We waited for him at the corner.

16. This is the letter that they wrote to her.

17. Many went to the meeting. Several left early.

18. The members did not recognize us.

19. The boy who brought the message is a relative.

20. She will tell you about the parade.

SELF-GRADING ASSIGNMENT 3

Directions: Underline the **verbs** in the following sentences. On the line to the right, indicate whether the verb expresses *action,* or has a *linking* function, by using the initials **A.** or **L.**

1. The ambassador forgot his portfolio.   1. ....

2. Mr. Smith is one of the directors of the bank. 2. ....

3. The bus stops at this corner.   3. ....

4. The legislators passed a bill yesterday.   4. ....

5. The senator is a very interesting speaker.   5. ....

6. The scientist examined the rare specimens.   6. ....

7. The skiers planned a visit to Sun Valley.   7. ....

8. My friend won the award.   8. ....

9. I completed the assignment yesterday.   9. ....

10. We canned several quarts of peaches.   10. ....

11. The conductor signaled with two lanterns.   11. ....

12. The members of the band purchased their   12. ....
    instruments.

13. Loose boards caused the creaking sound.   13. ....

14. The life guards saved the swimmers.   14. ....

15. The Indians gave up their land piece by piece. 15. ....

16. He is responsible for the error.   16. ....

17. The guide led them over the dangerous pass.   17. ....

18. I doubted his sincerity.   18. ....

19. Many wild flowers grow in the forest preserves. 19. ....

20. Italian marble is beautiful.   20. ....

SELF-GRADING ASSIGNMENT 4

Directions: Underline the **verb phrases** in the following sentences. Write **P.** under the principal verb and **A.** under the auxiliary verb or verbs.

Example: The dog <u>was howling</u> last night.
                A.   P.

1. I shall remember that experience for a long time.

2. The necessary supplies were ordered.

3. We are looking for a larger apartment.

4. He did attend the convention.

5. The tourists will visit all the cathedrals.

6. Footsteps were heard on the stairs.

7. The price does cover the excise tax.

8. James has been promoted recently.

9. The weeds in my garden have been growing **rapidly.**

10. He is destroying all the evidence.

11. The masons have been working all night.

12. New mines have been discovered in Africa.

13. The flags are fluttering in the breeze.

14. Several inaccuracies were found in his report.

15. He is making recordings for future use.

PROGRESS TEST ONE

Do not take this test until one or two days after you have completed the assignments. The purpose of this progress test is to check your understanding of all of the points covered in Grammar Unit One. If you do not make a satisfactory grade on this test, you should study the unit again, especially those sections that will help you in correcting your mistakes. A satisfactory grade on the test will show you that you have made a good start on your way toward an effective command of English.

A.

Directions: Underline the **nouns** and the **pronouns** in the following sentences: Write **N.** under a *noun* and **P.** under a *pronoun*. *(35 points)*

Example: I saw you at the opera.
      P.   P.   N.

1. They sat in the balcony during the meeting.

2. The audience applauded the young leader of the orchestra.

3. You will find it in the desk.

4. Everybody bought supplies at the store in the village.

5. Some will receive money. Others will receive medals.

6. She checked the books in the case for them.

7. The law about speeding was changed by the legislature.

8. The dress that she is wearing was made in Paris.

9. All of the members of the committee resigned.

10. These are the paintings which you admired.

PROGRESS TEST ONE

B.

Directions: Underline the **verbs** and the **verb phrases** in the following sentences. Write **v.** under a *verb,* and **v.ph.** under a *verb phrase.* *(15 points)*

1. The inspectors searched every room.

2. You should write more legibly.

3. Television is popular entertainment.

4. The deficit has increased during the year.

5. Chicago is drawing trade from the surrounding area.

6. The theater will be rebuilt next year.

7. The fishermen examined the tracks in the sand.

8. Margaret was preparing the material for her speech.

9. Father will call for us at eight o'clock.

10. Three cans of fruit have been opened.

11. Daisies were growing along the bank.

12. You must solve the problem before tomorrow.

13. He has lost his ticket to the game.

14. Motor boat racing is an exciting sport.

15. The blow affected his hearing.

ANSWER KEY

for

EXERCISES, ASSIGNMENTS, AND PROGRESS TEST

Grammar Unit One

CORRECT ANSWERS TO EXERCISE 1

1. object or measure	8. person	15. place
2. measure	9. object	16. measure
3. action	10. measure	17. place
4. person	11. object	18. substance
5. place	12. quality	19. action
6. quality	13. place or object	20. person
7. place	14. person	

CORRECT ANSWERS TO EXERCISE 2

1. Michael—canoe—Indian	11. automobile—pavement
2. Scientists—specimens—flowers	12. oranges—figs—California
3. men—factory—petition—wages	13. Signals—crossings
4. Visitors—balcony—theater	14. hunting—fishing—mountains
5. book—pictures—animals—plants	15. Snow—ice—trees—fences
6. manager—amount—bill	16. Television—radio—years
7. swimmer—courage—endurance	17. Jack—friends—boat—stream
8. fugitive—door—hotel	18. tourists—castles—Rhine
9. brother—salesman	19. sailors—deck—shark
10. aviator—plane	20. agent—cars—truck

CORRECT ANSWERS TO EXERCISE 3

A.	B.
1. She	1. She—them
2. it	2. All—Many
3. They	3. This—who
4. them	4. Each—which—he
5. their	5. who—us—we—him
6. who—it	6. someone—their

CORRECT ANSWERS TO EXERCISE 4

1. skidded—*action*
2. knows—*action*
3. fell—*action*
4. hung—*action*
5. is—*linking*
6. roared—*action*
7. swam—*action*
8. accumulated—*action*
9. went—*action*
10. sold—*action*
11. spent—*action*
12. stopped—*action*
13. is—*linking*
14. complained—*action*
15. read—*action*
16. opened—*action*
17. fell—*action*
18. met—*action*
19. rose—*action*
20. is—*linking*

CORRECT ANSWERS TO EXERCISE 5

1. The players <u>were resting</u> on the grass.
             A.   P.

2. A tree <u>had fallen</u> across the road.
         A.   P.

3. Tom <u>has been playing</u> golf all day.
       A. A.   P.

4. You <u>must return</u> to the city at once.
        A.   P.

5. Daily talks <u>will be given</u> by the guide.
         A. A. P.

6. The company <u>is buying</u> a new factory.
         A.   P.

7. We <u>should have worn</u> our old clothes.
       A.   A. P.

8. Your report <u>will be sent</u> to the manager.
        A. A. P.

9. The mountains <u>could be seen</u> from our windows.
         A. A. P.

10. Many new books <u>have been added</u> to the library.
          A. A.   P.

11. Newton <u>has traveled</u> extensively.
        A.   P.

12. I <u>shall go</u> to Italy next summer.
       A. P.

CORRECT ANSWERS TO ASSIGNMENT 1

Nouns are printed in **heavy type.**

1. **Engineers** dug a **tunnel** under the **river.**
2. Our **coach** was injured **Friday.**
3. **Atlases** were placed on the **table** in the **library.**
4. The **treasurer** paid the **entertainers.**
5. The **prisoner** had **faith** and **courage.**
6. **Drawing** and **painting** are his favorite **hobbies.**
7. **Eric** bought a new **home** in **Evanston.**
8. Our **game** was interrupted by a **messenger.**
9. **Skiing** is a dangerous **sport.**
10. **Coats** and **hats** were piled up on a **table.**
11. **Stephen** plans to take **lessons** in **driving.**
12. **Iron** and **steel** are useful **metals.**
13. The **company** made a great many **improvements.**
14. The **doctor** ordered **penicillin** for his **patient.**
15. A **plane** will leave the **airport** in an **hour.**
16. That **man** lacks **initiative.**
17. Two **explorers** returned from a **trip** to **Africa.**
18. My **boat** sank during the **storm.**
19. **Smoke** rose from the tall **chimney.**
20. **Fruit** and **nuts** were served at the **dinner.**

CORRECT ANSWERS TO ASSIGNMENT 2

Pronouns are printed in **heavy type.**

1. The man **who** was injured recovered.
2. **These** are Jane's medals.
3. **She** asked **me** to show **them** to **you.**
4. **They** went to Cuba with **us.**
5. Robert will not tell **me** why **he** quit.
6. **We** objected to the bill. The company corrected **it.**
7. **Anybody** can qualify for the position.
8. **That** is the hat **they** featured.

9. The rug *that you* selected was admired by **others.**
10. The judge questioned **her,** but **she** could not describe the intruder.
11. **These** are the plans. **Those** are the sketches.
12. **He** held the horse for **her.**
13. The candy was delicious. **I** ate **all** of **it.**
14. **That** is the book **I** mentioned to **them.**
15. **We** waited for **him** at the corner.
16. **This** is the letter **that they** wrote to **her.**
17. **Many** went to the meeting. **Several** left early.
18. The members did not recognize **us.**
19. The boy **who** brought the message is a relative.
20. **She** will tell **you** about the parade.

CORRECT ANSWERS TO ASSIGNMENT 3

1. forgot—*action*
2. is—*linking*
3. stops—*action*
4. passed—*action*
5. is—*linking*
6. examined—*action*
7. planned—*action*
8. won—*action*
9. completed—*action*
10. canned—*action*

11. signaled—*action*
12. purchased—*action*
13. caused—*action*
14. saved—*action*
15. gave—*action*
16. is—*linking*
17. led—*action*
18. doubted—*action*
19. grow—*action*
20. is—*linking*

CORRECT ANSWERS TO ASSIGNMENT 4

1. shall remember
   A.   P.
2. were ordered
   A.   P.
3. are looking
   A.   P.
4. did attend
   A.   P.
5. will visit
   A.   P.

6. were heard
   A.   P.
7. does cover
   A.   P.
8. has been promoted
   A.   A.   P.
9. have been growing
   A.   A.   P.
10. is destroying
    A.   P.

11. have been working   14. were found
    A.   A.   P.   A.   P.

12. have been discovered   15. is making
    A.   A.   P.   A.   P.

13. are fluttering
    A.   P.

CORRECT ANSWERS TO PROGRESS TEST ONE

A.

1. They sat in the balcony during the meeting.
   p.   n.   n.

2. The audience applauded the young leader of the orchestra.
     n.   n.   n.

3. You will find it in the desk.
   p.   p.   n.

4. Everybody bought supplies at the store in the village.
    p.   n.   n.   n.

5. Some will receive money. Others will receive medals.
  p.   n.   p.   n.

6. She checked the books in the case for them.
 p.   n.   n.   p.

7. The law about speeding was changed by the legislature.
   n.   n.   n.

8. The dress that she is wearing was made in Paris.
   n. p. p.   n.

9. All of the members of the committee resigned.
 p.   n.   n.

10. These are the paintings which you admired.
  p.   n.   p.   p.

B.

1. The inspectors searched every room.
          v.

2. You should write more legibly.
     v.ph.

3. Television is popular entertainment.
      v.

4. The deficit has increased during the year.
      v.ph.

5. Chicago is drawing trade from the surrounding area.
     v.ph.

6. The theater will be rebuilt next year.
     v. ph.

7. The fishermen examined the tracks in the sand.
     v.

8. Margaret was preparing the materials for her speech.
     v. ph.

9. Father will call for us at eight o'clock.
     v. ph.

10. Three cans of fruit have been opened.
     v. ph.

11. Daisies were growing along the bank.
     v. ph.

12. You must solve the problem before tomorrow.
     v. ph.

13. He has lost his ticket to the game.
     v. ph.

14. Motor boat racing is an exciting sport.
     v.

15. The blow affected his hearing.
     v.

How to Obtain Your Score

The test totals 50 points. To obtain your score, divide the number of your correct answers by 50. The answer will be your score on this test. For example, if you have 41 points correct, your score is 41.00 divided by 50 or 82 per cent. In other words, your score on this test is 82. You can obtain your score on any of the exercises or assignments by following the same procedure.

LOOKING FORWARD

If you have made a satisfactory grade on your first progress test, you are on your way toward a thorough knowledge of good English. You are now able to identify the most important parts of speech, *nouns, pronouns,* and *verbs.* In Grammar Unit Two you will learn how *adjectives* and *adverbs* are used to make the meaning of a sentence clearer and more interesting. You will also learn about *prepositions, conjunctions,* and *interjections.*

THE PARTS OF SPEECH

THE PARTS OF SPEECH—II

I N UNIT ONE you learned how *nouns, pronouns, verbs,* and *verb phrases* function in English. With these three parts of speech you can build the framework of any sentence. But it is only a framework. The sentence that contains only a noun or a pronoun and a verb is not a very interesting sentence. It does not give very specific information, or present a very interesting picture. Such sentences become very monotonous if repeated often, as you will readily see from the following illustrations:

Birds fly.	Dogs bark.
Men work.	She knits.
He swims.	They sing.

ADJECTIVES—Modifiers

You will generally find it necessary to add other parts of speech to a skeleton sentence to make the meaning clearer and more exact. You can add words to nouns and pronouns that tell *what kind, what color, which one,* etc. If you wanted to tell about the hat a woman was wearing, you would describe the hat in some way. You might say that it was a *large* hat, an *atrocious* hat, or a *red* hat, depending upon the meaning which you intended to convey.

When you add one or more of these *describing words* to hat, you give a clearer picture of what the hat is like. *Words which add new ideas to nouns and pronouns are called* **adjectives.**

The adjective not only describes by telling what kind or what color, but it may limit the meaning by telling *which* hat, *whose* hat, or the *number* of hats. For example, you might limit the meaning by saying *that* hat, *Fred's* hat, *two* hats, or *several* hats.

In grammar, we say that the adjective *modifies* the meaning of the noun or pronoun. The word **modify** means *to change the meaning slightly* by *describing* or *limiting* the meaning to a certain kind or to a certain number.

When we speak of a hat as an *attractive* hat, we are limiting the meaning because we are leaving out all the hats that are not attractive. If a word describes, limits, or restricts the meaning in any way, it is called a **modifier.** This is an important term that is frequently used in grammar.

The words *a, an,* and *the* are adjectives although in grammar they are called **articles.** The word *the* is called the *definite* article. The words *a* and *an* are called the *indefinite articles.* When we say, *the* book on *the* table, we are pointing out a particular book on a particular table. When we say, *I have a book,* no specific or particular book is indicated.

Adjectives Modifying Nouns

The following examples show how adjectives modify nouns and how their use makes the meaning clearer or more explicit.

long road	*good* friend	*rainy* day
rusty nail	*beautiful* dress	*accurate* accountant
old piano	*worthy* cause	*rapid* typist
five dollars	*steep* hill	*essential* parts
intelligent answer	*difficult* task	*juicy* orange

**An adjective is a word used to modify
a noun or a pronoun.**

EXERCISE I

Directions: Underline the **adjectives** in the following sentences. On the line to the right, indicate the word the adjective *modifies.*

Example: The long planks were placed in a pile.　*planks*
....

1. Eight boxes were left in the truck.　　　1. ....

2. The stock room was used as an office.　　2. ....

3. A valuable gift was presented to the winner.　3. ....

4. I tried to ask an intelligent question.　　4. ....

5. Many famous authors live in New York.　5. ....

6. The scientist gave a complete report.　　6. ....

7. We climbed a steep hill yesterday.　　　7. ....

8. The falling snow covered the trees.　　　8. ....

9. Five editors attended the conference.　　9. ....

10. A long bridge spans the river.　　　　　10. ....

11. Serious mistakes were found in the reports.　11. ....

12. That is a beautiful diamond.　　　　　　12. ....

13. Stylish hats are seen everywhere.　　　　13. ....

14. The speaker recited a favorite poem.　　14. ....

15. The messenger left an important message.　15. ....

Note: *The correct answers to exercises will be found at the end of this unit. Correct your mistakes and, if necessary, reread the text material before going on to the next section.*

ADVERBS—Modifiers

Another interesting group of words that serve as modifiers are **adverbs.** The prefix *ad* in the word adverb means *to, toward,* or *in addition to.* An adverb is a word that you *add to a verb to modify or expand the meaning of the verb.* Adverbs may also modify adjectives or other adverbs. In this unit we shall consider the adverb as a modifier of the verb. A later unit will give you the other uses of an adverb.

Adverbs are easy to identify because they usually answer the questions *when, where, how, in what manner,* or *to what extent* or *degree.* The following illustrations will make this clear:

You must set up the copy *now. (Now* tells when to set it up.)

We put the desk *there. (There* tells where to put it.)

Mary walks *gracefully. (Gracefully* tells how she walks.)

The old man traveled *far. (Far* tells the extent of traveling.)

When we say, *The paper is issued weekly,* the adverb *weekly* introduces an additional idea of *time.* The adverb *weekly* makes the meaning explicit because we know *how often* or *when* the paper is issued. When we say, *Dandelions grow everywhere,* we have introduced the idea of *place,* or we tell *where* the dandelions grow. In the sentence, *We walked farther into the forest,* we have added the idea of *extent* or the *degree to which.* The adverbs in the preceding sentences are called adverbs of *time, place, manner,* or *degree.*

**An adverb is a word used to modify a verb,
an adjective, or another adverb.**

POSITION OF THE ADVERB

Although an adverb often modifies the verb in the sentence, it is not always placed directly after the verb. Sometimes the adverb introduces the sentence. In this position it gives more emphasis. At times the adverb is placed between the parts of the verb phrase. Study the following sentences carefully. Note the position of the adverb.

Sometimes I take a walk in the woods.

Jack *always* leaves the house at seven.

We added a room to our house *recently*.

Tom studies *diligently*.

I have *always* admired him.

In the first sentence, the adverb *sometimes* introduces the sentence. It modifies the verb *take*. In the second sentence, the adverb *always* modifies the verb *leaves*. Instead of following the verb, it is placed before the verb. This is done for emphasis.

In the third sentence, the adverb *recently* appears at the end of the sentence. It modifies the verb *added*. In the fourth sentence, the adverb *diligently* follows the verb *studies*, which it modifies. In the last sentence, the adverb *always* comes between the parts of the verb phrase *have admired*.

EXERCISE 2

Underline the **adverbs** in the following sentences. On the line to the right, indicate the *verb* which the adverb modifies.

Example: He <u>rarely</u> went to the meetings.   *went*
....

1. Our guests arrived early.   1. ....

2. Her house is furnished artistically.   2. ....

3. The judge never loses his temper.   3. ....

4. We treat our customers courteously.   4. ....

5. My cousins go to the theater frequently.   5. ....

6. Silently the crowd left the hall.   6. ....

7. Our class meets daily.   7. ....

8. The climbers finally reached the top.   8. ....

9. He acquired his fortune easily.   9. ....

10. Sometimes the manager helps us.   10. ....

11. The team has seldom practiced here.   11. ....

12. For a beginner, he works skillfully.   12. ....

13. The tailor pressed the suit carefully.   13. ....

14. The tank is emptied often.   14. ....

15. Bill always leaves at eight.   15. ....

Note: Check your answers before going on to the next section.

PREPOSITIONS

Words That Show a Relationship

Another important part of speech is the **preposition.** A preposition is not a modifier. The only parts of speech that are modifiers are adjectives and adverbs. The preposition has a different function to perform in the sentence. *A preposition shows the relationship that exists between certain words in a sentence.*

The word *preposition* comes from two Latin words which mean *placed before.* A preposition is a word that is *placed before some noun or pronoun.* It shows the relationship that exists between that noun or pronoun and some other word in the sentence. When we say "a bag *for* the mail," the word *for* is a preposition. It shows a relationship between *bag* and *mail.* The word *mail* which follows the preposition is called the **object** of the *preposition.*

In the sentence, *The accident occurred on the bridge,* the word *on* is a preposition. The preposition *on* is followed by the word *bridge* which is called its object. The entire group of words, *on the bridge,* is called a **prepositional phrase.** The preposition *on* shows the relation between the noun *bridge* and the verb *occurred.* The entire phrase *on the bridge* tells where the accident occurred.

We might use a number of prepositions to show the relationship between the noun *bridge* and the verb *occurred.* Each preposition would show a slightly different type of relationship, as you will readily see from the following illustrations:

The accident occurred <u>under</u> the bridge.
preposition

The accident occurred <u>near</u> the bridge.
preposition

The accident occurred <u>above</u> the bridge.
preposition

The accident occurred <u>behind</u> the bridge.
preposition

The accident occurred <u>beneath</u> the bridge.
preposition

You should become acquainted with the words that are commonly used as prepositions. A list of these prepositions is given here for your reference. Refer to this list repeatedly until you are able to identify the prepositions that are in common use. The fact that a word is in this list does not mean that it is always used as a preposition. Some of these words often function as other parts of speech. The test of its use as a preposition is to determine whether it shows the *relationship* between its object and some other word in the sentence.

A List of Commonly Used Prepositions

above	at	by	into	toward
about	before	down	like	through
across	behind	during	near	under
after	below	except	of	until
against	beneath	for.	off	up
along	beside	from	on	upon
among	between	in	since	with
around	beyond	inside	to	within

A preposition shows the relationship that exists between certain words in a sentence.

EXERCISE 3

Underline the **prepositions** in the following sentences. On the line to the right, indicate the group of words, or the phrase which the preposition introduces.

Example: He went <u>into</u> the house.   *into the house*
....

1. The hands of the clock did not move.   1. ....

2. We purchased the suit in Paris.   2. ....

3. The girl at the desk is Margaret.   3. ....

4. The chair behind the door is broken.   4. ....

5. A dog was caught between two rocks.   5. ....

6. This box was found under the cabinet.   6. ....

7. That package should be sent by express.   7. ....

8. The picture above the desk is an heirloom.   8. ....

9. John studied until midnight.   9. ....

10. We found the book beneath the table.   10. ....

11. You must leave within an hour.   11. ....

12. Tourists picked flowers along the way.   12. ....

13. We tried to swim across the stream.   13. ....

14. I followed the path near the river.   14. ....

15. We rowed down the stream.   15. ....

Note: Check your answers before going on to the next section.

CONJUNCTIONS—Connecting Words

In many of your sentences you need words that serve to join words or groups of words. In grammar, words that have this connecting function are called **conjunctions.**

The word *conjunction* comes from two Latin words which mean to *join with* or to *join together.* In the sentence, *Jane and Alice are stenographers,* the word *and* connects the two nouns, *Jane* and *Alice.* The word *and* in this sentence is a conjunction. In the sentence, *The manager or his secretary will see you,* the word *or* connects the words *manager* and *secretary.* The word *or* in this sentence is a conjunction. In the sentence, *Her small but attractive apartment is for rent,* the word *but* joins the words *small* and *attractive.*

The conjunctions that were used in the preceding illustrations were *and, but,* and *or.* These conjunctions always connect words or groups of words of equal rank. For the present, we shall limit our discussion to the use of these three conjunctions.

Mark drives too fast *and* too recklessly. (joins two adverbs)
             adverb   adverb

He   *or*   I   will audit the account. (joins two pronouns)
pronoun   pronoun

I fell *and* broke my arm. (joins two verbs)
  verb   verb

He will give the book to Mary *or* Jane. (joins two nouns)
                 noun   noun

They bought a large *but* attractive home. (joins two adjectives)
         adjective   adjective

A conjunction is a word used to connect words or a group of words.

EXERCISE 4

Underline the **conjunctions** in the following sentences. Draw two lines under the words that the conjunction serves to connect.

Example: <u><u>Bill</u></u> <u>or</u> <u><u>Mary</u></u> will go to the airport.

1. The women served cake and sandwiches.

2. You may bring paper or a notebook.

3. James and Harry read the same article.

4. He opened the door and entered the room.

5. The brook ran swiftly, but quietly.

6. He and I will make the plans.

7. The grocer did not have oranges or lemons.

8. Martha dances and sings in a musical revue.

9. The floor was covered with dirt and sand.

10. That child sings and plays all day.

11. His physician ordered rest and nourishing food.

12. Running and jumping are strenuous exercises.

13. The men hunted and fished all summer.

14. The tired but happy vacationers returned to the hotel.

15. We did not wear our coats or our hats.

Note: Check your answers before going on to the next section.

INTERJECTIONS—Exclamatory Words

In English we have a number of words that are used to express strong feeling or sudden emotion. Words that serve this purpose are called **interjections.** The word *interjection* comes from two Latin words which mean *to throw between.* Interjections are really thrown into the sentence to express some type of emotion such as disgust, joy, excitement, enthusiasm, etc.

Interjections have no grammatical relation to any word or group of words in the sentence. In grammar we call words of this type *independent elements.* Sometimes words which are independent elements stand for an entire sentence. The following illustrations show the kinds of words that are commonly used as interjections:

Alas! This is the end of everything! (Interjection is *Alas.*)

Hey! Do you know where you're going? (Interjection is *Hey.*)

Bah! That's humbug. (Interjection is *Bah.*)

Oh, I can't believe that. (Interjection is *Oh.*)

Pshaw! Why did I do that? (Interjection is *Pshaw.*)

The words classified as interjections in the preceding illustrations *are always interjections.* In addition to such words, nouns, pronouns, adjectives, and other parts of speech *are often used* as interjections.

Heavens! I cut my finger instead of the cloth!

Good! I'm glad to hear that.

Horrors! Look at that hat!

Well! When are you going to pay that bill?

Some of the interjections that you use or hear in speech are not even words, although it is possible to represent the sounds expressed. A careful speaker or writer does not use interjections very often, especially expressions like the following:

Whew! What a day!

Um! This soup tastes good.

Humph! I knew that ages ago.

FUNCTION OF WORDS

One of the most important things to learn about the English language is the fact that *the same words are often used as different parts of speech.* A word may perform a certain function in one sentence and an entirely different function in another sentence. This will become more apparent to you as you progress further in the course.

Adjectives are commonly used as nouns, and nouns are frequently used as adjectives. The same word may function both as an adverb and as a preposition. Almost any type of word may be used as an interjection. The following sentences show how words function as different parts of speech:

The *light* in my study is very poor. (*Light* is a noun.)

Please *light* the candles. (*Light* is a verb.)

Her hat is a *light* shade of blue. (*Light* is an adjective.)

Father is a *fast* driver. (*Fast* is an adjective.)

Father drives too *fast.* (*Fast* is an adverb.)

I *fast* one day every week. (*Fast* is a verb.)

**The same words are often used as
different parts of speech.**

SUMMARY OF GRAMMAR UNIT TWO

It is possible to have a sentence with only a noun or a pronoun and a verb. This is the essential framework or skeleton of a sentence. But it is often desirable and necessary to add other parts of speech to make our meaning clearer, or to make our sentences more interesting. *Adjectives* and *adverbs* are used for this purpose.

Adjectives and **adverbs** are *modifiers;* that is, their chief purpose is to modify or change the meaning in some way. Adjectives modify *nouns* and *pronouns.* Adverbs modify *verbs, adjectives,* and *other adverbs.*

The words *a, an,* and *the* are called **articles** although they function just like adjectives. The word *the* is called the *definite article,* and the words *a* and *an* are called the *indefinite articles.*

Another important part of speech is the **preposition.** A preposition has an entirely different function in the sentence. It is used to show the *relationship* between certain words. One of these words is the noun or pronoun which follows the preposition. This noun or pronoun is called the **object** *of the preposition.*

We often need to use words that serve to connect words and groups of words. The part of speech that performs this function is the **conjunction.** The most commonly used conjunctions are *and, but, or.*

There are a number of words whose purpose is to express strong feeling or sudden emotion. Such words are called **interjections.** An interjection is usually independent of the rest of the sentence.

One of the most important facts to keep in mind from the very beginning is the fact that *the same words are often used as different parts of speech.* Adjectives are commonly used as nouns, and nouns are commonly used as adjectives. A word might be a preposition in one sentence, and an adverb in another sentence. The only way to tell the part of speech of a word is to study its *function* in a particular sentence.

HOW TO CHECK YOUR PROGRESS

Through your study of Unit 1 and Unit 2 you have learned how the eight parts of speech function in sentences. By this time you should be able to identify the parts of speech in almost any simple sentence. This knowledge will be very helpful to you in your further study of grammar. You must understand the kind of work that words do in sentences before you can grasp the simple grammatical principles upon which good usage depends.

However, your study of the parts of speech is not yet complete. In later units you will take up a more detailed study of the use of these important tools of communication. Gradually you will become as familiar with the function of the parts of speech as an automobile mechanic is with the function of the various parts of an engine.

Your success with the Assignments and the Progress Test which follow will show you how much progress you have made. If you have studied the explanations given in Units 1 and 2 carefully, you should have no difficulty in giving the correct answers. Since these assignments are self-grading, you will know what phases of the subject are not clear to you when you check your answers with the key.

If you find that you have made any mistakes, study the text again carefully, especially those parts that are related to the questions that you did not answer correctly. Then try the Assignment or Progress Test a *second* time. Check your answers again and note what progress you have made on the second trial. If you follow this plan consistently, you will be well on your way toward a thorough knowledge of good English.

Be sure to use and apply what you learn to your everyday activities. Re-read your social and business letters after they are written. Analyze your own speaking habits and listen to the speech of others. Doing these things will make you conscious of the importance of good English, and will help you eliminate any errors that you now make.

SELF-GRADING ASSIGNMENT 1

Directions: Underline the **adjectives** in the following sentences. On the line to the right, indicate the *noun* the adjective modifies. Do not include the articles *a, an,* and *the.*

Example: He broke the <u>rusty</u> lock.   *lock*
....

1. Ellen lives in a comfortable apartment.   1. ....

2. I have an interesting collection of books.   2. ....

3. A permanent record was made of the speech.   3. ....

4. A group of famous singers presented the program.   4. ....

5. Marge is a skillful designer.   5. ....

6. We sang the national anthem before the game.   6. ....

7. Hot food was served to the refugees.   7. ....

8. He tried to read the faded manuscript.   8. ....

9. Temporary walls were added to the structure.   9. ....

10. I heard an interesting talk on the subject.   10. ....

11. The anxious parents rushed to the scene.   11. ....

12. Adequate plans were made for the pageant.   12. ....

13. That is a beautiful view.   13. ....

14. We talked to a former soldier.   14. ....

15. The cabin was hidden by dense shrubbery.   15. ....

16. The burning building collapsed.   16. ....

17. This is an unusual piece of pottery.   17. ....

18. We went through a very dangerous pass.   18. ....

19. Tall steeples pointed toward the sky.   19. ....

20. Luscious berries are found in the markets.   20. ....

Caution: Check your answers to each assignment with the answer key at the end of this unit before proceeding with the next assignment.

SELF-GRADING ASSIGNMENT 2

Directions: Underline the **adverbs** in the following sentences. On the line to the right, indicate whether the adverb expresses *time, place, manner, degree,* or *extent.*

Example: She will do it <u>later.</u>   *time*
                                                         ....

1. The crowd waited in line patiently.   1. ....
2. John seldom does his reading at home.   2. ....
3. We went farther into the canyon.   3. ....
4. We do not expect to remain here.   4. ....
5. We scattered confetti everywhere.   5. ....
6. The patient soon became stronger.   6. ....
7. The birds came for crumbs daily.   7. ....
8. Suddenly the door opened.   8. ....
9. The machine works noiselessly.   9. ....
10. You may see the doctor now.   10. ....
11. The weeds have grown fast.   11. ....
12. I did not see an officer anywhere.   12. ....
13. Production was curtailed sharply.   13. ....
14. Occasionally you should read in the library. 14. ....
15. I shall speak to you frankly.   15. ....
16. Sometimes we go to the mountains.   16. ....
17. I have not met him lately.   17. ....
18. James is slowly recovering.   18. ....
19. Cautiously the detective opened the door.   19. ....
20. We have often taken that road.   20. ....

SELF-GRADING ASSIGNMENT 3

Directions: Underline the **prepositions** in the following sentences. On the line to the right, indicate the *phrase,* or group of words that the preposition introduces.

Example: We walked <u>down</u> the street.   *down the street*
....

1. She wrote a story about a panda.   1. ....

2. The officers will be elected at the next meeting.   2. ....

3. They found his will in an old book.   3. ....

4. I did not look under the davenport.   4. ....

5. Trees were planted between the houses.   5. ....

6. He plays tennis like a professional.   6. ....

7. The speaker read a passage from his book.   7. ....

8. We wrapped the paper around the gift.   8. ....

9. The nurse sat beside the patient.   9. ....

10. A painting hung above the mantel.   10. ....

11. The sailors walked along the shore.   11. ....

12. The roses in our garden are blooming.   12. ....

13. Word passed through the village.   13. ....

14. My uncle was attacked by two men.   14. ....

15. The water flowed over the fields.   15. ....

SELF-GRADING ASSIGNMENT 4

Directions: Underline the **conjunctions** and the **interjections** in the following sentences. Draw two lines under the words that the conjunctions connect. Write **C.** under conjunctions and **I.** under interjections.

Examples: You may have <u>coffee</u>   or   <u>tea</u>.
                                      C.

Huh! That's what you think.
I.

1. I like cities and people.

2. We walked in and out of the store.

3. Mary or Jane will drive the car.

4. Hurrah! We won the race.

5. The dog was alert but cautious.

6. The dress was simple and elegant.

7. Shucks! Why did I make that foolish move?

8. War and peace were discussed at the meeting.

9. Oh, what a day that was!

10. He must pay his rent or move.

11. The hat is beautiful but extreme.

12. The wind whistled through the trees and bushes.

13. Well! What did he say?

14. You will find him in the library or den.

15. They will serve fish and chicken.

PROGRESS TEST TWO

This progress test should not be taken until a day or two after you have completed the assignments. The score you make on the test will then more clearly reflect your understanding of the material in the unit.

A.

Directions: On the line to the right indicate the **part of speech** of each of the words that are printed in **heavy face.**   (20 points)

Example: The **old** barn collapsed in the storm.   *adjective*
....

1. Heifetz plays the violin **well.**   1. ....

2. They built a wall **around** the town.   2. ....

3. The excavators removed a deposit of **mud.**   3. ....

4. He **shared** his good fortune with others.   4. ....

5. Apples **and** peaches grow in Michigan.   5. ....

6. Everyone admired the **fearless** leader.   6. ....

7. **We** enjoyed the trip to New York.   7. ....

8. **Oh,** look at that beautiful sunset!   8. ....

9. He was not thrifty **but** greedy.   9. ....

10. They were waiting **at** the corner.   10. ....

11. Dan **should drive** more carefully.   11. ....

12. The old law was changed **recently.**   12. ....

13. You should wear a sweater **or** an old coat.   13. ....

14. The **scientist** made a study of insects.   14. ....

15. **Skiing** is a dangerous sport.   15. ....

16. Edith has a very **fair** complexion   16. ....

17. **Everyone** likes the new manager.   17. ....

18. **He** spent his life on the sea.   18. ....

19. The plumber **has been repairing** the pipe.   19. ....

20. Father takes a walk **before** breakfast.   20. ....

PROGRESS TEST TWO

B.

Directions: Name the **part of speech** of each word in the following sentences. Do not include the articles *a, an,* and *the.* Write the abbreviation for the part of speech under the word. (*50 points*)

Abbreviations

noun—pronoun—verb—verb phrase—adjective—adverb
n.   p.   v.   v.ph.   adj.   adv.

preposition—conjunction—interjection
prep.   c.   i.

Example: The parade marched down the avenue.
              n.   v.   prep.   n.

1. You will find him in the library.

2. The crowd watched the game closely.

3. We have placed four tables in the lobby.

4. Nancy is a successful writer and speaker.

5. Heavy storms delayed the trains to Chicago.

6. So! Finally you have been caught.

7. Wood and rubbish blocked the entrance.

8. An announcement was read by the clerk.

9. I shall send Florence a beautiful scarf.

10. A clever detective finally solved the mystery.

ANSWER KEY

for

EXERCISES, ASSIGNMENTS, AND PROGRESS TEST

GRAMMAR UNIT TWO

CORRECT ANSWERS TO EXERCISE 1		CORRECT ANSWERS TO EXERCISE 2	
Adjective	**Modifies**	**Adverb**	**Modifies**
1. eight	boxes	1. early	arrived
2. stock	room	2. artistically	is furnished
3. valuable	gift	3. never	loses
4. intelligent	question	4. courteously	treat
5. Many famous	authors authors	5. frequently	go
6. complete	report	6. silently	left
7. steep	hill	7. daily	meets
8. falling	snow	8. finally	reached
9. five	editors	9. easily	acquired
10. long	bridge	10. Sometimes	helps
11. serious	mistakes	11. seldom here	has practiced has practiced
12. beautiful	diamond	12. skillfully	works
13. stylish	hats	13. carefully	pressed
14. favorite	poem	14. often	is emptied
15. important	message	15. always	leaves

CORRECT ANSWERS TO EXERCISE 3

	Phrase
1. The hands of the clock did not move.	1. of the clock
2. We purchased the suit in Paris.	2. in Paris
3. The girl at the desk is Margaret.	3. at the desk

4. The chair <u>behind</u> the door is broken.

5. A dog was caught <u>between</u> two rocks.

6. This box was found <u>under</u> the cabinet.

7. That package should be sent <u>by</u> express.

8. The picture <u>above</u> the desk is an heirloom.

9. John studied <u>until</u> midnight.

10. We found the book <u>beneath</u> the table.

11. You must leave <u>within</u> an hour.

12. Tourists picked flowers <u>along</u> the way.

13. We tried to swim <u>across</u> the stream.

14. I followed the path <u>near</u> the river.

15. We rowed <u>down</u> the stream.

4. behind the door

5. between two rocks

6. under the cabinet

7. by express

8. above the desk

9. until midnight

10. beneath the table

11. within an hour

12. along the way

13. across the stream

14. near the river

15. down the stream

CORRECT ANSWERS TO EXERCISE 4

1. The women served <u>cake</u> and <u>sandwiches</u>.

2. You may bring <u>paper</u> or a <u>notebook</u>.

3. <u>James</u> and <u>Harry</u> read the same article.

4. He <u>opened</u> the door and <u>entered</u> the room.

5. The brook ran <u>swiftly</u> but <u>quietly</u>.

6. <u>He</u> and <u>I</u> will make the plans.

7. The grocer did not have <u>oranges</u> or <u>lemons</u>.

8. Martha <u>dances</u> and <u>sings</u> in a musical revue.

9. The floor was covered with <u>dirt</u> and <u>sand</u>.

10. That child <u>sings</u> and <u>plays</u> all day.

11. His physician ordered <u>rest</u> and nourishing <u>food</u>.

12. Running and jumping are strenuous exercises.

13. The men hunted and fished all summer.

14. The tired but happy vacationers returned to the hotel.

15. We did not wear our coats or our hats.

CORRECT ANSWERS TO ASSIGNMENT 1		CORRECT ANSWERS TO ASSIGNMENT 2	
Adjective	**Modifies**	**Adverb**	**Expresses**
1. comfortable—apartment		1. patiently—*manner*	
2. interesting—collection		2. seldom—*time*	
3. permanent—record		3. farther—*degree* or *extent*	
4. famous—singers		4. here—*place*	
5. skillful—designer		5. everywhere—*place*	
6. national—anthem		6. soon—*time*	
7. hot—food		7. daily—*time*	
8. faded—manuscript		8. Suddenly—*manner*	
9. temporary—walls		9. noiselessly—*manner*	
10. interesting—talk		10. now—*time*	
11. anxious—parents		11. fast—*manner*	
12. adequate—plans		12. anywhere—*place*	
13. beautiful—view		13. sharply—*manner*	
14. former—soldier		14. Occasionally—*time*	
15. dense—shrubbery		15. frankly—*manner*	
16. burning—building		16. Sometimes—*time*	
17. unusual—piece		17. lately—*time*	
18. dangerous—pass		18. slowly—*manner* or *degree*	
19. tall—steeples		19. Cautiously—*manner*	
20. luscious—berries		20. often—*time*	

CORRECT ANSWERS TO ASSIGNMENT 3

Phrase

1. She wrote a story about a panda.
2. The officers will be elected at the next meeting.
3. They found his will in an old book.
4. I did not look under the davenport.
5. Trees were planted between the houses.
6. He plays tennis like a professional.
7. The speaker read a passage from his book.
8. We wrapped the paper around the gift.
9. The nurse sat beside the patient.
10. A painting hung above the mantel.
11. The sailors walked along the shore.
12. The roses in our garden are blooming.
13. Word passed through the village.
14. My uncle was attacked by two men.
15. The water flowed over the fields.

1. about a panda
2. at the next meeting
3. in an old book
4. under the davenport
5. between the houses
6. like a professional
7. from his book
8. around the gift
9. beside the patient
10. above the mantel
11. along the shore
12. in our garden
13. through the village
14. by two men
15. over the fields

CORRECT ANSWERS TO ASSIGNMENT 4

1. I like cities and people.
   c.

2. We walked in and out of the store.
   c.

3. Mary or Jane will drive the car.
   c.

4. Hurrah! We won the race.
   I.

5. The dog was alert but cautious.
   c.

6. The dress is simple and elegant.
   c.

7. Shucks! Why did I make that foolish move?
   I.

8. War and peace were discussed at the meeting.
      c.

9. Oh, what a day that was!
   I.

10. He must pay his rent or move.
                    c.

11. That hat is beautiful but extreme.
                        c.

12. The wind whistled through the trees and bushes.
                                    c.

13. Well! What did he say?
    I.

14. You will find him in the library or den.
                                c.

15. They will serve fish and chicken.
                        c.

CORRECT ANSWERS TO PROGRESS TEST TWO

A.—(20 points)

1. well—*adverb*
2. around—*preposition*
3. mud—*noun*
4. shared—*verb*
5. and—*conjunction*
6. fearless—*adjective*
7. We—*pronoun*
8. Oh—*interjection*
9. but—*conjunction*
10. at—*preposition*
11. should drive—*verb phrase*
12. recently—*adverb*
13. or—*conjunction*
14. scientist—*noun*
15. Skiing—*noun*
16. fair—*adjective*
17. Everyone—*pronoun*
18. He—*pronoun*
19. has been repairing—*verb phrase*
20. before—*preposition*

CORRECT ANSWERS TO PROGRESS TEST TWO

B.—(50 points)

1. You will find him in the library.
   p.   v.ph.   p. prep.   n.

2. The crowd watched the game closely.
   n.   v.   n.   adv.

3. We have placed four tables in the lobby.
   p.   v.ph.   adj.   n. prep.   n.

4. Nancy is a successful writer and speaker.
   n.   v.   adj.   n.   c.   n.

5. Heavy storms delayed the trains to Chicago.
   adj.   n.   v.   n. prep.   n.

6. So! Finally you have been caught.
   i.   adv.   p.   v.ph.

7. Wood and rubbish blocked the entrance.
   n.   c.   n.   v.   n.

8. An announcement was read by the clerk.
   n.   v.ph. prep.   n.

9. I shall send Florence a beautiful scarf.
   p.   v.ph.   n.   adj.   n.

10. A clever detective finally solved the mystery.
    adj.   n.   adv.   v.   n.

HOW TO OBTAIN YOUR SCORE

The test totals 70 points. To obtain your score, divide the number of your correct answers by 70. The answer will be your score on this test. For example, if you have 63 points correct, your score is 63 divided by 70 which is 90 per cent. In other words, your score on.this test is 90. You can obtain your score on any of the exercises or assignments by following the same procedure.

Practical English Grammar

OUTLINE OF UNIT THREE

THE SENTENCE

THE SENTENCE

IN GRAMMAR UNITS ONE and Two you studied the functions of eight parts of speech: *nouns, pronouns, verbs, adjectives, adverbs, prepositions, conjunctions,* and *interjections.* In this unit you will learn how these eight parts of speech are combined to form sentences.

When a number of words (parts of speech) are put together in such a way that they express a **complete thought,** you have a *sentence.* The sentence may consist of one word, or it may consist of as many as three hundred words. The tendency in modern writing is to use short, effective sentences. Twenty words is about the average length in present-day writing.

Often those who are beginning the study of language find it difficult to understand what is meant by a *complete thought.* Some students punctuate parts of sentences as if they were sentences because they do not realize that some essential element is missing. The following groups of words are not sentences, although they are punctuated as if they were complete.

The officers of our company. (*not a sentence*)

Enjoyed the banquet. (*not a sentence*)

On the top of the hill. (*not a sentence*)

These groups of words are not sentences because they lack something that is necessary in order to express a complete thought. When you examine the first group of words, you will readily see that you know what the writer is talking about. However, the writer did not complete the sentence by telling you what the officers did. The second group of words tells you that somebody enjoyed a banquet. But the author neglected to tell you who it was. The third group of words tells you very little. You have no way of knowing what the writer is talking about.

SUBJECT AND PREDICATE

In order to express a complete thought, a sentence usually must have both a *subject* and a *predicate.* These are two important grammatical terms used to describe the essential elements of a sentence.

The **subject** is the word or group of words that tells us *what or whom the speaker or writer is talking about.* The **predicate** is the part of the sentence *that makes a statement about the subject.* The *predicate* usually tells what the subject is doing, or what is happening to the subject.

Study the following sentences carefully. Note that the subjects have been separated from the predicates so that you will be able to see the relationship between the two parts more easily.

Subjects	Predicates
My friend	lives in New York.
The letter	contained exciting news.
The men in our office	are experienced salesmen.

In the first sentence, I am talking about *my friend.* Therefore, *my friend* is the subject of the sentence. I complete the sentence by making a statement about my friend. I say that my friend *lives in New York.* The predicate is *lives in New York.* This group of words, *My friend lives in New York,* is a sentence because it expresses a complete thought. It has both a subject and a predicate.

The second group of words, *The letter contained exciting news,* expresses a complete thought. It has a subject, *The letter,* and a predicate, *contained exciting news.*

The third group of words, *The men in our office are experienced salesmen,* is also a sentence. It expresses a complete thought. The subject is *The men in our office,* and the predicate is *are experienced salesmen.*

COMPLETE SUBJECT AND COMPLETE PREDICATE

In many sentences the subject or the predicate is only a single word. But more often, the subject consists of two or more words. In grammar, we call the entire subject, regardless of the number of words, the **complete subject**. We call the entire predicate the **complete predicate**.

If the subject of a sentence is a single word, that word is the *complete subject*. If the predicate of the sentence is a single word, that word is the *complete predicate*. In the sentence, *Birds fly,* the word *birds* is the complete subject, and the word *fly* is the complete predicate.

EXERCISE 1

Draw a vertical line between the *complete subject* and the *complete predicate* in each of the following sentences:

Example: A beautiful pin | was given to Alice.
comp. subj.　　　　comp. pred.

1. Many of the tickets were sold at the gate.

2. The secretary of our club read the minutes.

3. A number of planes flew over the lake.

4. Several men were working on the project.

5. Bob met Ruth in the library.

6. The rugs in her living room were sold at auction.

7. The management gave all the men a holiday.

8. Your pronunciation of those words is incorrect.

9. The women in the factory received a bonus.

10. Women's fashions change rapidly.

11. The auditor will have his report ready by noon.

12. Everyone in our club enjoyed the last meeting.

13. The penalty for speeding is very severe.

14. Both trains were delayed by the storm.

15. I sold my grand piano to a friend.

Note: The correct answers to exercises will be found at the end of this unit. Correct your mistakes and, if necessary, reread the text material before going on to the next section.

SIMPLE SUBJECT AND SIMPLE PREDICATE

After you have learned how to identify the complete subject and the complete predicate, you can easily find the **simple subject** and the **simple predicate.**

Somewhere in the complete subject you will find the *particular word* about which something is said. That word is the *simple subject.* It is usually either a noun or a pronoun.

Somewhere in the predicate you will find a word that serves as the *key* to the predicate. That word is the *verb,* the most important word in any sentence. If the verb consists of more than one word, it is called a *verb phrase,* as you learned in Unit One. In the following examples the simple subject is underlined once and the simple predicate is underlined twice:

The American ambassador attended a conference.

The hero of the story had many thrilling adventures.

My friend in Boston has bought a new television set.

The simple subject of the first sentence is *ambassador.* The simple predicate, or the predicate verb, is *attended.* The simple subject of the second sentence is *hero.* The simple predicate is *had.* The simple subject of the third sentence is *friend,* and the simple predicate is the verb phrase *has bought.*

Sometimes you will find only one word in the subject or one word in the predicate. In that case, the single word in the subject is the simple subject. It is also the complete subject. The single word in the predicate is the simple predicate and also the complete predicate.

Pronouns are often used as the simple subject and the complete subject. In the sentence, *We are buying a new home,* the pronoun *we* is the simple subject. It is also the complete subject since there are no other words in the subject.

In the sentence, *The building collapsed,* the verb *collapsed* is the simple predicate. It is also the complete predicate since it is the only word in the predicate.

In the following illustrations, the abbreviations **s.s.** and **s.p.** are used to indicate the simple subject and the simple predicate:

Fast driving is often dangerous.
   s.s.   **s.p.**

The detectives on the case found the jewels.
   s.s.   **s.p.**

The people of the village were listening to the bell.
   s.s.   **s.p.**

The cashier immediately reported the shortage.
   s.s.   **s.p.**

Children play.
   s.s.   **s.p.**

A verb phrase is regarded as a unit. It is the simple predicate and the predicate verb.

EXERCISE 2

Draw a vertical line beween the *complete subject* and the *complete predicate*. Draw one line under the simple subject and two lines under the simple predicate.

Example: The company | has opened a branch in Idaho.

1. The guard shouted at the prowler.

2. The work on the house began yesterday.

3. Someone in the building heard the crash.

4. I shall take the six o'clock plane.

5. The factory was completed in record time.

6. The stormy weather kept us indoors.

7. Tall trees shaded the winding road.

8. A notorious bandit was captured last week.

9. We shall order our supplies from New York.

10. The automobile skidded on the icy road.

11. Bob drives a delivery truck.

12. The price of wool has advanced in the last week.

13. John swims every day.

14. One of the lost tickets was found.

15. You will receive your instructions tomorrow.

COMPOUND SUBJECT AND COMPOUND PREDICATE

A sentence may have two or more simple subjects and two or more simple predicates. In the sentence, *Harry and Fred joined a lodge,* there are two simple subjects, *Harry* and *Fred.* The connecting word is *and.* In grammar we say that the sentence has a **compound subject.**

In the sentence, *The stenographer wrote the letter and mailed it,* there are two predicate verbs, *wrote* and *mailed.* The connecting word is *and.* This sentence has a **compound predicate.**

Some sentences have a compound subject and a compound predicate. In the sentence, *Alice and Jane washed the curtains and ironed them,* there are two simple subjects and two simple predicates. The subject nouns are *Alice* and *Jane.* The two predicate verbs are *washed* and *ironed.* In both cases, the connecting word is *and.*

The following sentences contain either a compound subject, a compound predicate, or both.

Corn and beans | are grown in the valley. (*compound subject*)

I | attended the lecture and took notes. (*compound predicate*)

The boys and girls | sang and danced at the club. (*compound subject and compound predicate*)

EXERCISE 3

Determine whether the subject or the predicate is *compound.* Draw one line under each part of a compound subject. Draw two lines under each part of the compound predicate. On the line to the right, indicate whether the subject or the predicate is compound by using the initials **S.** or **P.**

Compound

Example: Peter raises and lowers the gates.　　　**P.**
....

1. The secretary and the treasurer were present.　　1. ....

2. We heard the noise and hid behind the tree.   2. ....

3. Mother and I attended the concert.   3. ....

4. The men huddled under the tent and shivered
   in the cold.   4. ....

5. German and French were spoken by the delegates. 5. ....

6. Sue made a scarf and sent it to Jean.   6. ....

7. The trucks and the cars are for sale.   7. ....

8. The speaker presented and discussed two plans. 8. ....

9. Meat and potatoes were served every day.   9. ....

10. The company appreciates and values your business. 10. ....

11. We opened the door and entered the room.   11. ....

12. The speaker and his secretary arrived late.   12. ....

SENTENCE FRAGMENTS

If you have studied this unit carefully, you will have a thorough understanding of the essential elements of a sentence. But even persons who have this knowledge often punctuate groups of words as sentences when one or both of the essential elements are missing .

Any incomplete group of words punctuated as if it were a sentence is called a *sentence fragment* or a *fragmentary sentence*. As you know, a fragment is only a piece or a part of the whole. A fragment always refers to something that is incomplete.

A fragmentary sentence always lacks one or both of the essential elements of a sentence. That is, either the subject or the predicate, or both the subject and predicate are missing. Whenever you are in doubt about a particular sentence, apply this test: Does the group of words contain both a subject and a predicate? Does it express a complete thought?

Very often the subject of the sentence is missing. The following group of words is *not* a sentence because it does not tell who it is that the writer is talking about:

Interviewed the candidate. (This is not a sentence.)

The president interviewed the candidate. (This is a complete sentence.)

The sentence was completed by supplying a subject, *The president.*

Sometimes the predicate is missing. The following group of words is *not* a sentence because the entire predicate is missing:

The sound of footsteps. (This is not a sentence.)

The sound of footsteps *alarmed us.* (This is a complete sentence.)

The use of fragmentary or incomplete sentences is an unsatisfactory way of communicating your ideas. Surprising as it may seem, sentence fragments similiar to the following examples can be found repeatedly in letters sent out by reputable business firms. Check the letters of your company. You may be amazed at what you find. Be sure you do not use fragments in your own personal writing.

Received your letter this morning. (*Subject* is missing.)

Will send order at once. (*Subject* is missing.)

Have shipped your order. (*Subject* is missing.)

Hoping this meets with your approval. (*No subject or predicate.*)

With kind personal regards. (No *subject* or *predicate.*)

EXERCISE 4

Study the following groups of words carefully. Check to see whether each group has both a subject and a predicate. If the sentence is complete, write the word **complete** on line to the right. If the sentence is not complete, write the word **subject** or **predicate** on the line to the right to indicate the part that is missing.

Example: Was swimming in the pool.   *subject*
....

1. Went to France last summer.   1. ....

2. A dog barked loudly.   2. ....

3. We mailed your bill last week.   3. ....

4. Was greatly enjoyed by the visitors.   4. ....

5. Crowds of shoppers jammed the streets.   5. ....

6. Several boxes of fruit.   6. ....

7. A new kind of television set.   7. ....

8. This valley is very fertile.   8. ....

9. Met the following day in the lobby.   9. ....

10. The officers of the firm.   10. ....

11. Rushed to the ticket window.   11. ....

12. A seat in the front row was vacant.   12. ....

13. Occurred near the bridge.   13. ....

14. Several men in uniform.   14. ....

15. Father sent Mary a check for ten dollars.   15. ....

DIAGRAMMING THE SUBJECT AND THE PREDICATE

Many students find it easier to see the relations that exist between words in a sentence if they make use of a simple chart or diagram. A **diagram** is a kind of picture representation of the sentence which shows how the various parts of the sentence are related.

In order to make use of this method, you should learn the accepted ways of diagramming. The following illustrations show the method that is generally used in diagramming complete subject and predicate, simple subject and predicate, and compound subject and predicate.

1. Diagramming Complete Subject and Complete Predicate

The first thing to do in making this diagram is to draw a vertical line between the *complete subject* and the *complete predicate*. The next step is to show the *simple subject* and the *simple predicate* in this same diagram. Draw a line under the subject *noun* or *pronoun* and two lines under the predicate *verb* or *verb phrase*. The following diagram will serve as an illustration.

Sentence: The old mansion was sold recently.

Diagram

The old <u>mansion</u> | <u><u>was sold</u></u> recently.

In this diagram, the vertical line divides the complete subject from the complete predicate. A single line is drawn under the word *mansion*, which is the simple subject. Two lines are drawn under the verb phrase *was sold*, which is the simple predicate.

2. Diagramming the Simple Subject and the Simple Predicate

The next step in diagramming is to start with the simple subject and the simple predicate. This gives you the basic structure or framework of the sentence. You can then add other parts of the sentence to this basic structure.

In making this diagram, start with a horizontal or base line. Then draw a vertical line to separate the simple subject from the simple predicate, which is always the verb or the verb phrase. The simple subject is placed to the *left of the vertical line.* The simple predicate, or the verb, is placed to the *right of the vertical line.*

Sentence: Men work.

Diagram

Men	work

Sentence: The president welcomed the new members.

Diagram

president	welcomed

You probably have noticed that there are several words in the preceding sentence which do not appear in the diagram. You will learn how to diagram such words in later units. In this unit, you are diagramming only the subject and the predicate. In this particular diagram, you show only the simple subject and the simple predicate.

3. Diagramming the Compound Subject and the Compound Predicate

The following diagrams show a compound subject, a compound predicate, and a sentence in which both the subject and predicate are compound.

Sentence: Herbert and James built a canoe. *(compound subject)*

Diagram

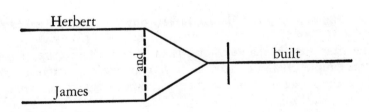

Sentence: The hunter followed the trail and found the deer. (*compound predicate*)

Diagram

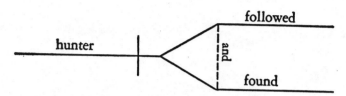

Sentence: The men and the women planned and worked together. (*compound subject and predicate*)

Diagram

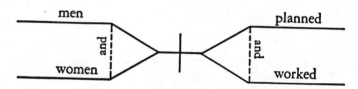

EXERCISE 5

Diagram the following sentences to show *simple subject, simple predicate, compound subject,* and *compound predicate.*

1. Soldiers in uniform were walking down the avenue.

2. My aunt and my uncle are traveling in Spain.

3. The author and the producer met and discussed the play.

4. The farmer and his son planted the seeds.

5. The doctor examined the patient and ordered a complete rest.

SUMMARY OF GRAMMAR UNIT THREE

A **sentence** is a group of words that expresses a complete thought. A sentence must have both a *subject* and a *predicate*.

The **subject** of a sentence is the part that tells what the speaker or writer is talking about.

The **predicate** of a sentence is the part that makes a statement about the subject.

The *simple subject* names the person, place, or thing that is talked about. It is usually a noun or a pronoun.

The *simple predicate* is the verb or verb phrase in the sentence.

The *complete subject* is the simple subject with all its modifiers.

The *complete predicate* is the verb or verb phrase with its modifiers and any other words used to complete the predicate.

A *compound subject* consists of two or more simple subjects.

A *compound predicate* consists of two or more simple predicates.

A **diagram** is a pictorial representation which shows certain grammatical relationships in a sentence.

A **fragmentary sentence** is a group of words that lacks one or both of the essential parts of a sentence, but is punctuated as if it were a complete sentence.

SELF-GRADING ASSIGNMENT 1

Directions: Draw a vertical line between the *complete subject* and the *complete predicate*. Draw one line under the *simple subject* and two lines under the *simple predicate*.

Example: The <u>dancers</u> | <u>wore</u> Spanish costumes.

1. Magazines were sent to the veterans.

2. Skiing in the mountains is a popular sport.

3. The Indians distrusted the white men.

4. The president of the company has a private secretary.

5. Temporary houses sheltered the refugees.

6. Your telephone has been ringing.

7. Beautiful trees have been planted along the road.

8. Mike took his sleeping bag with him to camp.

9. The ambassador was educated in France.

10. Some left the meeting early.

11. Lilacs bloom in the spring.

12. Valuable jewels were left on the table.

13. Prominent scientists attended the conference.

14. The passengers waited patiently for the train.

15. The traffic on the boulevard is very heavy.

Caution: Check your answers to each assignment with the answer key at the end of this unit before proceeding with the next assignment.

SELF-GRADING ASSIGNMENT 2

Directions: Determine whether the subject or the predicate is compound. Draw one line under each part of a *compound subject.* Draw two lines under each part of a *compound predicate.* Some sentences have a compound subject and a compound predicate.

Example: James and Fred have formed a partnership.

1. The president and the new manager talked to the employees.

2. Ned returned to his country and joined the army.

3. Jim and Jerry worked during the summer and saved their money.

4. Marion and Ellen planned and directed the pageant.

5. The waiter took my hat and checked it.

6. The doctor came into the room and examined the patient.

7. Hope and courage should travel together.

8. Jim stopped our car and offered us refreshments.

9. The old man shut the door and locked it securely.

10. Janson and Bryant are noted newspaper correspondents.

11. The artist was born in Italy and was educated in France.

12. The scenery and the climate attracted many visitors.

13. The manager and the workman organized and arranged the exhibit.

14. June and Lorraine boxed and mailed the candy.

15. Articles and short stories are in great demand.

SELF-GRADING ASSIGNMENT 3

Directions: Diagram the following sentences to show *simple subject, simple predicate, compound subject,* and *compound predicate.*

1. Baseball and football teams entered the contest.

2. The porter checked the baggage and placed it on the truck.

3. The bill was introduced in the Senate and was sent to the House.

4. The audience and the speaker cheered and waved their flags.

5. The doctors on the case held a consultation.

PROGRESS TEST THREE

This progress test should not be taken until a day or two after you have completed the assignments. The score you make on the test will then more clearly reflect your understanding of the material in the unit.

A.

Directions: Draw a line under the *simple subject* and two lines under the *simple predicate* (verb or verb phrase). Write **s.s.** under the simple subject and **s.p.** under the simple predicate.   *(30 points)*

1. Harold handed the telegram to his father.

2. The company has purchased a new site for a factory.

3. A number of new books have been added to the library.

4. Our gardener planted two oaks in front of the house.

5. A long narrow bridge spans the turbulent river.

6. Those stunning suits were purchased in London.

7. A magnificent new building has been erected.

8. The children in the hospital have been listening to the radio.

9. A terrible fire swept through the forest.

10. The portrait revealed an interesting face.

11. The guests in the hotel played cards after dinner.

12. The bookkeeper found several errors in the account.

13. A shining new Chrysler was parked in the driveway.

14. We met many of our friends at the convention.

15. Customs have changed greatly.

PROGRESS TEST THREE (continued)

B.

Directions: Underline the parts of the *compound subjects* and the *compound predicates*. Draw a connecting line between the parts. Below this line write **c.s.** or **c.p.** to indicate whether the subject or the predicate is compound. *(10 points)*

Examples: The general and the colonel talked to the soldiers.
c.s.

The women prepared the food and served it.
c.p.

1. The moon and the stars could be seen clearly.

2. The author and the producer met and discussed the play.

3. The boat capsized and sank in the storm.

4. Pears and peaches were packed and were shipped to England.

5. Martha picked some flowers and arranged them in vases.

6. You and I understand each other.

7. The campers found some wood and built a fire.

8. The professors on our staff write and produce plays.

ANSWER KEY

for

EXERCISES, ASSIGNMENTS AND PROGRESS TEST

Grammar Unit Three

CORRECT ANSWERS TO EXERCISE 1

1. Many of the tickets | were sold at the gate.
2. The secretary of our club | read the minutes.
3. A number of planes | flew over the lake.
4. Several men | were working on the project.
5. Bob | met Ruth in the library.
6. The rugs in her living room | were sold at auction.
7. The management | gave all the men a holiday.
8. Your pronunciation of those words | is incorrect.
9. The women in the factory | received a bonus.
10. Women's fashions | change rapidly.
11. The auditor | will have his report ready by noon.
12. Everyone in our club | enjoyed the last meeting.
13. The penalty for speeding | is very severe.
14. Both trains | were delayed by the storm.
15. I | sold my grand piano to a friend.

CORRECT ANSWERS TO EXERCISE 2

1. The guard | shouted at the prowler.
2. The work on the house | began yesterday.
3. Someone in the building | heard the crash.
4. I | shall take the six o'clock plane.

5. The factory | was completed in record time.

6. The stormy weather | kept us indoors.

7. Tall trees | shaded the winding road.

8. A notorious bandit | was captured last week.

9. We | shall order our supplies from New York.

10. The automobile | skidded on the icy road.

11. Bob | drives a delivery truck.

12. The price of wool | has advanced in the last week.

13. John | swims every day.

14. One of the lost tickets | was found.

15. You | will receive your instructions tomorrow.

CORRECT ANSWERS TO EXERCISE 3

1. The secretary and the treasurer were present.   1. *subject*

2. We heard the noise and hid behind the tree.   2. *predicate*

3. Mother and I attended the concert.   3. *subject*

4. The men huddled under the tent and shivered in the cold.   4. *predicate*

5. German and French were spoken by the delegates.   5. *subject*

6. Sue made a scarf and sent it to Jean.   6. *predicate*

7. The trucks and the cars are for sale.   7. *subject*

8. The speaker presented and discussed two plans.   8. *predicate*

9. Meat and potatoes were served every day.   9. *subject*

10. The company appreciates and values your business.   10. *predicate*

11. We opened the door and entered the room.   11. *predicate*

12. The speaker and his secretary arrived late.   12. *subject*

CORRECT ANSWERS TO EXERCISE 4

1. *subject*	6. *predicate*	11. *subject*
2. *complete*	7. *predicate*	12. *complete*
3. *complete*	8. *complete*	13. *subject*
4. *subject*	9. *subject*	14. *predicate*
5. *complete*	10. *predicate*	15. *complete*

CORRECT ANSWERS TO EXERCISE 5

1. Sentence: Soldiers in uniform were walking down the avenue.

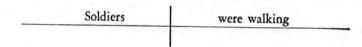

2. Sentence: My aunt and my uncle are traveling in Spain.

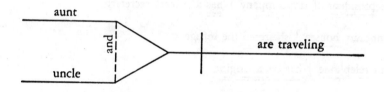

3. Sentence: The author and the producer met and discussed the play

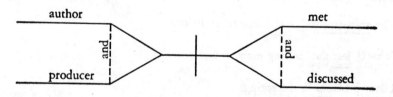

4. Sentence: The farmer and his son planted the seeds.

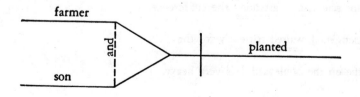

5. Sentence: The doctor examined the patient and ordered a complete rest.

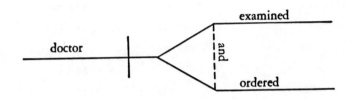

CORRECT ANSWERS TO ASSIGNMENT 1

1. Magazines | were sent to the veterans.

2. Skiing in the mountains | is a popular sport.

3. The Indians | distrusted the white men.

4. The president of the company | has a private secretary.

5. Temporary houses | sheltered the refugees.

6. Your telephone | has been ringing.

7. Beautiful trees | have been planted along the road.

8. Mike | took his sleeping bag with him to camp.

9. The ambassador | was educated in France.

10. Some | left the meeting early.

11. Lilacs | bloom in the spring.

12. Valuable jewels | were left on the table.

13. Prominent scientists | attended the conference.

14. The passengers | waited patiently for the train.

15. The traffic on the boulevard | is very heavy.

CORRECT ANSWERS TO ASSIGNMENT 2

1. The president and the new manager talked to the employees.

2. Ned returned to his country and joined the army.

3. Jim and Jerry worked during the summer and saved their money.

4. Marion and Ellen planned and directed the pageant.

5. The waiter took my hat and checked it.

6. The doctor came into the room and examined the patient.

7. Hope and courage should travel together.

8. Jim stopped our car and offered us refreshments.

9. The old man shut the door and locked it securely.

10. Janson and Bryant are noted newspaper correspondents.

11. The artist was born in Italy and was educated in France.

12. The scenery and the climate attracted many visitors.

13. The manager and the workman organized and arranged the exhibit.

14. June and Lorraine boxed and mailed the candy.

15. Articles and short stories are in great demand.

CORRECT ANSWERS TO ASSIGNMENT 3

1. Sentence: Baseball and football teams entered the contest.

2. Sentence: The porter checked the baggage and placed it on the truck.

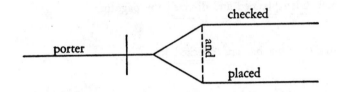

3. Sentence: The bill was introduced in the Senate and was sent to the House.

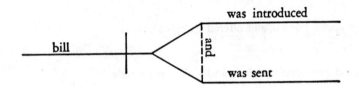

4. Sentence: The audience and the speaker cheered and waved their flags.

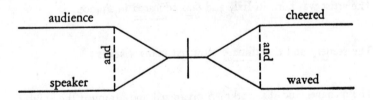

5. Sentence: The doctors on the case held a consultation.

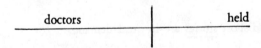

CORRECT ANSWERS TO PROGRESS TEST THREE

A. *(30 points)*

1. Harold handed the telegram to his father.
   s.s.   s.p.

2. The company has purchased a new site for a factory.
       s.s.   s.p.

3. A number of new books have been added to the library.
       s.s.   s.p.

4. Our gardener planted two oaks in front of the house.
       s.s.   s.p.

5. A long narrow bridge spans the turbulent river.
              s.s.   s.p.

6. Those stunning suits were purchased in London.
                 s.s.   s.p.

7. A magnificent new building has been erected.
                      s.s.   s.p.

8. The children in the hospital have been listening to the radio.
       s.s.   s.p.

9. A terrible fire swept through the forest.
            s.s.   s.p.

10. The portrait revealed an interesting face.
        s.s.   s.p.

11. The guests in the hotel played cards after dinner.
        s.s.   s.p.

12. The bookkeeper found several errors in the account.
        s.s.   s.p.

13. A shining new Chrysler was parked in the driveway.
                  s.s.   s.p.

14. We met many of our friends at the convention.
    s.s. s.p.

15. Customs have changed recently.
        s.s.   s.p.

B. (10 points)

1. The moon and the stars could be seen clearly.
   c.s.

2. The author and the producer met and discussed the play.
   c.s.   c.p.

3. The boat capsized and sank in the storm.
   c.p.

4. Pears and peaches were packed and were shipped to England.
   c.s.   c.p.

5. Martha picked some flowers and arranged them in vases.
   c.p.

6. You and I understand each other.
   c.s.

7. The campers found some wood and built a fire.
   c.p.

8. The professors on our staff write and produce plays.
   c.p.

HOW TO OBTAIN YOUR SCORE

The test totals 40 points. To obtain your score, divide the number of your correct answers by 40. The answer will be your score on this test. For example, if you have 35 points correct, your score is 35 divided by 40 which is 87½ per cent. In other words, your score on this test is 87½. You can obtain your score on any of the exercises or assignments by following the same procedure.

Practical English Grammar

OUTLINE OF UNIT FOUR

SENTENCE PATTERNS

SENTENCE PATTERNS

IN GRAMMAR UNIT THREE you learned that a sentence must express a complete thought. It must also have both a subject and a predicate. In this unit you will learn that it is possible to express a complete thought in a variety of ways. You should become familiar with the different ways of arranging words in sentences and the different sentence patterns that are the result of these arrangements.

KINDS OF SENTENCES

Sentences fall into four groups according to the purpose the sentence serves and the manner in which the thought is expressed. Some sentences simply *make statements*. Some sentences *ask questions*. Another type of sentence *gives a command* or *makes a request*. The last group is the kind of sentence that *expresses strong feeling* or *sudden emotion*.

In grammar, the sentence that makes a statement is called a **declarative sentence.** The sentence that asks a question is called an **interrogative sentence.** The sentence that gives a command or makes a request is called an **imperative sentence,** and the sentence that expresses strong feeling is called an **exclamatory sentence.** The following are examples of the four types of sentences:

My friend is a business executive. (*declarative sentence*)

Have you entered the contest? (*interrogative sentence*)

Clear the road at once! (*imperative sentence*—command)

Please shut the door. (*imperative sentence*—request)

What a tragedy this is! (*exclamatory sentence*)

If you examine the preceding illustrations carefully, you will notice that the *declarative sentence* ends with a *period.* The *interrogative sen-*

tence ends with a *question mark* (?). Sometimes the *imperative sentence* ends with an *exclamation mark* (!) and sometimes it ends with a *period*. If the command is given in a very emphatic or decisive manner, an exclamation mark is placed at the end. A mild request always ends with a period. An *exclamatory sentence* usually ends with an *exclamation mark*.

If you have any difficulty in determining the types of sentences in Exercise 1, refer to this brief summary:

A **declarative** sentence *makes a statement.*

An **interrogative** sentence *asks a question.*

An **imperative** sentence gives a *command* or makes a *request.*

An **exclamatory** sentence expresses *strong feeling* or *sudden emotion.*

EXERCISE 1

Supply the end punctuation for the following sentences. On the line to the right indicate whether the sentence is *declarative, interrogative, imperative,* or *exclamatory.*

1. Please let me have your ticket   1. ....

2. Does Jane live in your block   2. ....

3. How cold the wind is tonight   3. ....

4. When do you expect your father   4. ....

5. Turn left at the next corner   5. ....

6. Watch your step   6. ....

7. His farm is very productive   7. ....

8. Is it necessary to tell everything   8. ....

9. Dick is waiting for a message   9. ....

10. How many errors did you make   10. ....

11. My father has a new Cadillac   11. ....

12. Put down that gun   12. ....

13. What a gorgeous view this is   13. ....

14. Have you a copy of his speech   14. ....

15. Load the truck with those pipes   15. ....

Note: The correct answers to exercises will be found at the end of this unit. Correct your mistakes and, if necessary, reread the text material before going on to the next section.

INVERTED ORDER

You have probably observed that these four types of sentences follow certain patterns of word arrangement. These patterns will now be discussed in more detail.

Every sentence has a basic structure or framework. This is true of all four types of sentences—*declarative, interrogative, imperative,* and *exclamatory.* This framework, as you already know, consists of the subject noun or pronoun and the predicate verb.

There are a number of ways of introducing the subject in a declarative sentence. The **normal order,** or the grammatical order, is *subject first,* followed by the predicate. If you always followed this pattern, your sentences would soon become monotonous and uninteresting. The following illustration will make this clear. The sentences in this paragraph sound very much like the sentences in a primer or in a first reader.

I like this book. It is a book about Mexico. My friend sent this book to me. My friend lives in New York. She speaks Spanish.

In this short paragraph, all the sentences follow the same pattern—subject first, followed by the predicate. You can give more variety to your sentence patterns by placing words in unusual positions.

You can put the subject after the verb or throw it to the very end of the sentence. Varying the position of the subject gives you an opportunity to place other words at the beginning of the sentence to give them more emphasis. This also makes our sentences more interesting.

On my desk I found an interesting book about Mexico.

In this sentence, the subject is placed after the group of words, or the phrase, *on my desk*. This arrangement throws the phrase to the front of the sentence and gives it more emphasis.

When the subject of the sentence does not appear in its normal position, we say that the order of the sentence is inverted, or turned around. Always remember that *normal* or grammatical order *means subject first, followed by the predicate.* Examine the following sentences carefully. Note the position of the subject in the two sentences.

The *band* marched down the street.

Down the street marched the *band*.

The first sentence is in normal, or grammatical order. The subject noun *band* appears at the beginning of the sentence. The verb *marched* follows the subject.

The second sentence is the same sentence in **inverted order.** The subject noun *band* now appears at the end of the sentence. The verb *marched* comes before the subject. A phrase, *Down the street,* appears at the beginning of the sentence.

An adverb often introduces a sentence. The following sentence begins with an adverb, and not with the subject.

Suddenly the train stopped. (*inverted order*)

The train stopped *suddenly*. (*normal order*)

Some students find it difficult to determine the true subject when a sentence is not in grammatical order. This difficulty can be avoided by *transposing* the sentence and putting it back in normal order.

When you put a sentence back in grammatical order by transposing it, you will often find that the transposed sentence is not so smooth as the original sentence. The only purpose in transposing a sentence is to see the grammatical relations more clearly. The following sentence is just as effective in either order. When we start with the phrase, *Along the road,* we give more emphasis to it.

Along the road we passed a number of army trucks.

We passed a number of army trucks *along the road.*

Whenever you are dealing with a sentence in inverted order, you should transpose it before you attempt to analyze the sentence from the grammatical point of view.

EXERCISE 2

The following sentences are in inverted order. *Transpose* the sentences, placing them in grammatical, or normal order. Underline the *simple subject* once, and the *predicate verb* twice, in the transposed sentence.

Example: Yesterday the strike ended. (*inverted order*)

The strike ended yesterday. (*normal order*)

1. In a corner of the room sat a small boy.

2. For weeks the rescuing party searched for the missing crew.

3. Away ran the startled deer.

4. Under his arm he carried a large portfolio.

5. Down crashed the gigantic plane.

6. By means of a test, the candidate is given a rating.

7. At the lower end of the river the water is muddy.

8. In a recent statement, the company promised lower prices.

9. For a few cents a person can buy a good magazine.

10. A few minutes later she collapsed.

11. Against the fence we planted a row of hollyhocks.

12. That afternoon Jack washed the car.

13. Tomorrow I shall read the manuscript.

14. Suddenly the captain jumped off the boat.

15. In the shelter of the eaves Alvin discovered a bird's nest.

INTERROGATIVE SENTENCE PATTERNS

In asking a question, you seldom start with the subject first, as you do in a declarative sentence. For that reason, *the interrogative sentence is generally in inverted order.* Sometimes the interrogative sentence starts with the *verb.* Often it begins with an *adverb,* which is used to ask the question.

Did you bring your camera? (introduced by the *verb*)

Where did you buy your watch? (introduced by an *adverb*)

In order to see the grammatical constructions in an interrogative sentence that is inverted, you must transpose the sentence and put it in normal order. Sometimes the interrogative sentence becomes a statement when it is transposed.

You did bring your camera.

You did buy your watch where?

IMPERATIVE AND EXCLAMATORY SENTENCE PATTERNS

The imperative sentence presents a different problem. The *subject* of the sentence that gives a command or makes a request *is seldom expressed.* If the subject is not expressed, it is the word *you* understood.

Sound the alarm at once! (Subject is not expressed.)

(You) Sound the alarm at once! (Subject *you* is understood.)

Please read the announcement. (Subject is not expressed.)

(You) Please read the announcement. (Subject *you* is understood.)

Sometimes an imperative sentence begins with a noun that indicates the name of the person to whom the command or the request is given.

An interrogative sentence may also begin in this way. The point to keep in mind is that such a noun *is not the subject* of the sentence. In fact, it has no grammatical connection with the rest of the sentence. It is an independent element. For that reason, it is separated from the rest of the sentence by a comma. Study the following illustrations carefully:

Imperative Sentence

Fred, please close the door. (*Fred* is the person addressed.)

Fred, (you) please close the door. (Subject is *you* understood.)

Interrogative Sentence

Alice, did you lock the door? (*Alice* is a noun in direct address.)

Alice, you did lock the door. (Subject is *you* expressed.)

In the first sentence, the word *Fred* is a noun in **direct address** because it names the person spoken to directly. It is not the subject of the sentence. The subject of an imperative sentence is *you* understood. The word *Fred* is set off from the rest of the sentence by a comma to show that it is used *independently*.

In the second sentence, the word *Alice* is a noun in direct address because it names the person spoken to directly. Since this is an interrogative sentence, the subject is expressed. When the sentence is placed in normal order, you can easily see that the subject is *you*, and not Alice.

A noun in *direct address* may appear at the beginning or at the end of the sentence. It may even appear within the sentence.

Fred, please close the door. (beginning of the sentence)

Please close the door, *Fred.* (end of the sentence)

Come here, *Fred,* and look at this book. (within the sentence)

The exclamatory sentence is often expressed in inverted order. In the sentence, *What a feast she spread!*, the subject and the verb appear at the end of the sentence. When the sentence is transposed, the subject appears at the beginning of the sentence and is followed by the verb.

What a feast she spread! (*inverted order*)

She spread what a feast! (*normal order*)
s.s.   s.p.

How beautiful the sunset is tonight! (*inverted order*)

The sunset is how beautiful tonight! (*normal order*)
s.s.   s.p.

What a tragedy that would be! (*inverted order*)

That would be what a tragedy! (*normal order*)
s.s.   s.p.

EXERCISE 3

Rewrite the following sentences in grammatical order. Underline the *simple subject* once, and the *simple predicate* twice, in the transposed sentence. Write **s.s.** under the simple subject and **s.p.** under the simple predicate.

Example: Have you spoken to the clerk?

You have spoken to the clerk.
s.s.   s.p.

1. What is your hobby now?

2. Mary, put these letters in the mail box.

3. How wonderful these apples are!

4. Have the dogs been barking all night?

5. What did Sue wear to the dance?

6. Jane, did you mail those letters?

7. What a game that was!

8. Junior, stop that noise at once!

9. Did you count the money in the cash box?

10. Halt! Show your passports!

SENTENCES THAT BEGIN WITH "THERE"

Another sentence pattern that we use frequently is the sentence that begins with the word *there*. We have a very good reason for beginning some of our sentences in this way.

When the word *there* is used to introduce the sentence, it is possible to place the subject after the verb. In many cases this results in a much smoother sentence, as you will see from the following illustration:

A heavy frost was last night.

There was a heavy frost last night.

Although the first sentence is in grammatical order, it is a very awkward sentence. The second arrangement results in a much smoother style, but it presents a grammatical problem. In dealing with a sentence that begins with *there,* you must always remember that the word *there* is neither the subject of the sentence, nor an adverbial modifier. It is merely an introductory word which has a special function, that of introducing the sentence.

When the word *there* functions in this way, it is called an **expletive.** The word **expletive** comes from the Latin and means *"added merely to fill up."* This is a very suitable term because it explains exactly what takes place.

The word *there* merely "fills up" the place normally occupied by the subject. It has no other function in the sentence. Like the noun in direct address, it is an independent construction. When the sentence is transposed, and placed in grammatical order, you should enclose the word *there* in parentheses to show that it is used independently.

There are twelve candidates for the position.

(There) twelve candidates are for the position.

It is important to transpose the sentence beginning with *there* in order to determine the true subject of the sentence. It is also important to determine whether the word *there* is used as an introductory word or whether it is used as an adverb.

There they are. (*There* is an adverb of place.)

They are *there*. (*There* is an adverb of place.)

There were ten men in the band. (*there*—expletive)

(*There*) ten men were in the band. (*there*—expletive)

The coach stood *there* watching the game. (*there*—adverb of place)

There is a telephone directory on the table. (*there*—expletive)

We met *there* last year. (*there*—adverb of place)

There will be some objection to the plan. (*there*—expletive)

The word *it* is also used as an expletive in certain sentence patterns. The use of *it* as an expletive will be discussed in later units.

EXERCISE 4

Rewrite the following sentences in *normal order*. After the sentence is transposed, underline the *simple subject* once, and the *simple predicate* twice. Write **s.s.** under the simple subject, and **s.p.** under the simple predicate.

Example: There are several trunks in the attic.

(There) several <u>trunks</u> <u>are</u> in the attic.
                      s.s.   **s.p.**

1. There will be an election on Saturday.

2. There is an interesting article in *Life* magazine.

3. There must have been an earthquake in Japan.

4. There were only six members at the meeting.

5. There must be some fresh fruit in the market.

6. There were thousands of people at the exposition.

7. There should be no argument between us.

8. There is no milk in the pitcher.

9. There are many reckless motorists.

10. There have been many famous names in motion pictures.

DIAGRAMMING THE SUBJECT AND THE PREDICATE

1. Diagramming the Understood Subject

When you diagram the imperative sentence to show the subject and the predicate, you must indicate in the diagram that the subject is not expressed, but is always the word *you* understood. Do this by placing the word *you* in the position of the subject, and enclosing it in parentheses. This is done to show that the word *you* does not appear in the sentence, although it is the subject.

Sentence: Stop that noise immediately!

(You) Stop that noise immediately!

Diagram

(You) | Stop

2. Diagramming the Introductory "There"

The introductory expletive "there" is an independent construction which has no grammatical relation to any other word in the sentence. For that reason, you should place the word *there* on a separate line as shown in the following diagram:

Sentence: *There* must be a solution to that problem.

(There) a solution to that problem must be.
(*normal order*)

Diagram

There

solution | must be

3. Diagramming the Noun in Direct Address

A noun in direct address is also an independent construction. You should diagram it on a separate line to show this fact.

Sentence: Walter, bring me the telephone directory.

Walter, (you) bring me the telephone directory.

Diagram

```
Walter

        (you) | bring
              |
```

In this sentence, *Walter* is a noun in direct address. It appears on a separate line to show that it is independent. This is an imperative sentence. The subject is the word *you* understood. Since the word *you* does not appear in the sentence, enclose it in parentheses and place it in the position of the subject. The predicate verb is *bring*.

EXERCISE 5

Diagram the following sentences. Follow the methods of diagramming shown on previous pages.

1. There are two markets in our block.

2. John, where did you park the car?

3. Answer the telephone at once!

4. James, drive the truck to the garage.

5. There are several doctors in the building.

SUMMARY OF GRAMMAR UNIT FOUR

In this unit we have considered the various types of sentence patterns that are commonly used in speaking and writing. You should keep in mind that the word arrangement is not the same for the various sentence patterns.

1. A **declarative sentence** makes a statement and may be written in several different ways. The *normal order* is for the subject to appear at the beginning of the sentence. However, for variety, emphasis, or clearness, the subject may appear at other places in the sentence. The declarative sentence ends with a period.

2. An **interrogative sentence** asks a question and is usually in inverted order. To determine the subject and the predicate, the interrogative sentence should be transposed or placed in normal order. The interrogative sentence ends with a question mark.

3. An **imperative sentence** gives a command or makes a request, and its subject is seldom expressed. When the subject is not expressed, it is always the word *you* understood. An imperative sentence sometimes ends with a period and sometimes with an exclamation mark.

4. An **exclamatory sentence** expresses strong feeling or sudden emotion, and is often not in normal order. When it is not in normal order the sentence should be transposed to determine the subject and predicate. Exclamatory sentences usually end with an exclamation mark, but may end with a period.

5. The word *there* is often used as an **expletive** to introduce a sentence. When *there* performs this function, it is not used as an adverb. It is used independently merely to "fill up" the place normally occupied by the subject. The subject appears later in the sentence.

6. Imperative or interrogative sentences are often introduced by a noun in **direct address.** A noun in direct address is not the subject of the sentence but is used independently.

7. When you want to determine the subject and predicate of a sentence that is not in normal order, you should transpose the sentence. You are then able to see grammatical relations more clearly.

SELF-GRADING ASSIGNMENT 1

Directions: Supply the end punctuation for the following sentences. On the line to the right indicate whether the sentence is *declarative, interrogative, exclamatory,* or *imperative.* Give the reason for your choice.

	Kind of Sentence	Reason
Example: What is Harry doing **?**	interrogative	asks question

1. We saw a ship near the shore   1. ....

2. Did the dentist send a bill   2. ....

3. Report to the commander at once   3. ....

4. What an exciting game this is   4. ....

5. The woman gave the keys to the driver   5. ....

6. What color is your new Buick   6. ....

7. Did you see him throw that ball   7. ....

8. What glorious weather we are having   8. ....

9. Please enunciate more clearly   9. ....

10. Where did you buy that hat   10. ....

11. Back up to the curb   11. ....

12. An outburst of cheers greeted the fliers   12. ....

13. Have you tickets for the concert   13. ....

14. Please observe the rules   14. ....

15. Sound the alarm   15. ....

Note: Do all of the assignments before checking your answers with the correct answers given at the end of this unit.

SELF-GRADING ASSIGNMENT 2

Directions: Rewrite the following sentences in grammatical order. Underline the *simple subject* once, and the *predicate verb* twice, in the transposed sentence.

Example: When did Alec join the army?

Alec did join the army when?

1. Sometimes we play golf on weekdays.

2. Once a week reference books may be taken home.

3. Raise your right hand.

4. What an attractive garden you have!

5. From the audience came shouts of approval.

6. Have you decided to sell your home?

7. How wonderful your dancing is!

SELF-GRADING ASSIGNMENT 2 (continued)

8. In what way is Tim responsible?

9. For three months we traveled across the desert.

10. Did they call the fire department?

11. A few minutes later the doctor arrived.

12. On our trip we shall see many mountain lakes.

13. On Monday you will receive your last order.

14. What color of ink does Ned prefer?

15. Empty the tank immediately!

SELF-GRADING ASSIGNMENT 3

By this time, you should be able to transpose a sentence that is in inverted order without rewriting it. If you are not able to do this, continue the practice of rewriting the sentence in grammatical order.

Directions: On the line to the right, indicate the *simple subject* and the *simple predicate* (verb or verb phrase) of each of the following sentences:

	Simple Subject	Simple Predicate
Example: Where are you going?	you	are going
1. Stop that car, James.	1.	
2. Has something happened to you?	2.	
3. There was complete harmony among the three sisters.	3.	
4. Bob, bring me the dictionary.	4.	
5. There were five men in the car.	5.	
6. Did you answer the telephone, Alice?	6.	
7. There was a majority present.	7.	
8. Go immediately!	8.	
9. Out of the bag fell the stolen articles.	9.	
10. What excuse did Marvin give?	10.	
11. Suggest a good title for the article, Stephen.	11.	
12. Through the trees whistled the wind.	12.	
13. There should be some reward for faithful service.	13.	
14. What are you reading, Jane?	14.	
15. There was a radio in every room.	15.	

SELF-GRADING ASSIGNMENT 4

Directions: Diagram the following sentences. Follow the methods of diagramming that were given in this unit.

1. There were several people in the doctor's office.

2. Mr. Chairman, did anyone second that motion?

3. There should be more interest in our meetings.

4. Shut that door at once, Harold.

5. There might be some mistake in your account.

PROGRESS TEST FOUR

This progress test should not be taken until a day or two after you have completed the assignments. The score you make on the test will then more clearly reflect your understanding of the material in the unit. The problem in this test is to find the subject and the predicate in various types of sentence patterns.

Directions: Indicate the *simple subject* and the *simple predicate* on the line to the right. If the subject or the predicate is compound, indicate the *parts* of the *compound subject* or the *compound predicate*. (*50 points*)

	Subject	Verb or Verbs
Example: Doris and Sue left early.	Doris—Sue	left

1. Tell your story to the judge.   1. ....

2. There might have been another reason for his failure.   2. ....

3. What were Vincent and Albert discussing at the meeting?   3. ....

4. John, look behind you!   4. ....

5. Where will the campers eat and sleep?   5. ....

6. There is an abundance of food in the freezer.   6. ....

7. Have you and David joined the tennis club?   7. ....

8. How did you break your arm, Fred?   8. ....

9. Take the children for a walk, May.   9. ....

PROGRESS TEST FOUR (continued)

10. We read and discussed books
    on China.   10. ....

11. When did you lose your
    watch?   11. ....

12. Several members of the com-
    mittee met the following day.   12. ....

13. What is the trouble now, Ted?   13. ....

14. Behind the desk there was an
    opening in the wall.   14. ....

15. Did you receive the message?   15. ....

16. There is a good road to
    the falls.   16. ....

17. Recently a new star has been
    discovered.   17. ....

18. Leave now and come back
    later.   18. ....

19. Forward, march!   19. ....

20. The fugitive opened the door
    and looked about cautiously.   20. ....

21. At one end of the couch there
    was a magazine rack.   21. ....

22. On Wednesday a new director
    will be appointed.   22. ....

23. What were Jean and Marge
    making last night?   23. ....

24. Have you finished the dress,
    Mother?   24. ....

25. Have you cancelled the order?   25. ....

ANSWER KEY

for

EXERCISES, ASSIGNMENTS, AND PROGRESS TEST

Grammar Unit Four

CORRECT ANSWERS TO EXERCISE 1

Punctuation	Kind of Sentence
1. period	imperative
2. question mark	interrogative
3. exclamation mark	exclamatory
4. question mark	interrogative
5. period	imperative
6. exclamation mark	imperative
7. period	declarative
8. question mark	interrogative
9. period	declarative
10. question mark	interrogative
11. period	declarative
12. exclamation mark	imperative
13. exclamation mark	exclamatory
14. question mark	interrogative
15. period	imperative

CORRECT ANSWERS TO EXERCISE 2

1. A small boy sat in a corner of the room.

2. The rescuing party searched for the missing crew for weeks.

3. The startled deer ran away.

4. He carried a large portfolio under his arm.

5. The gigantic plane crashed down.

6. The candidate is given a rating by means of a test.

7. The water is muddy at the lower end of the river.

8. The company promised lower prices in a recent statement.

9. A person can buy a good magazine for a few cents.

10. She collapsed a few minutes later.

11. We planted a row of hollyhocks against the fence.

12. Jack washed the car that afternoon.

13. I shall read the manuscript tomorrow.

14. The captain jumped off the boat suddenly.

15. Alvin discovered a bird's nest in the shelter of the eaves.

CORRECT ANSWERS TO EXERCISE 3

1. Your hobby is what now?
   s.s.   s.p.

2. Mary, (you) put these letters in the mail box. (*Mary* is direct address.)

s.s.   s.p.

3. These apples are how wonderful!

s.s.   s.p.

4. The dogs have been barking all night.

s.s.   s.p.

5. Sue did wear what to the dance?

s.s.   s.p.

6. Jane, you did mail those letters. (*Jane* is direct address.)

s.s.   s.p.

7. That was what a game!

s.s.   s.p.

8. Junior, (you) stop that noise at once! (*Junior* is direct address.)

s.s.   s.p.

9. You did count the money in the cash box.

s.s.   s.p.

10. (You) Halt! (You) Show your passports!

s.s.   s.p.   s.s.   s.p.

CORRECT ANSWERS TO EXERCISE 4

1. (There) an election will be on Saturday.

s.s.   s.p.

2. (There) an interesting article is in *Life* magazine.

s.s.   s.p.

3. (There) an earthquake must have been in Japan.

s.s.   s.p.

4. (There) only six members were at the meeting.

s.s.   s.p.

5. (There) some fresh fruit must be in the market.

s.s.   s.p.

6. (There) <u>thousands</u> of people <u>were</u> at the exposition.
         s.s.   s.p.

7. (There) no <u>argument</u> <u>should be</u> between us.
           s.s.   s.p.

8. (There) no <u>milk</u> <u>is</u> in the pitcher.
           s.s. s.p.

9. (There) many reckless <u>motorists</u> <u>are</u>.
                   s.s.   s.p.

10. (There) many famous <u>names</u> <u>have been</u> in motion pictures.
                    s.s.   s.p.

CORRECT ANSWERS TO EXERCISE 5

1. *Sentence:* There are two markets in our block.

2. *Sentence:* John, where did you park the car?

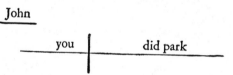

3. *Sentence:* Answer the telephone at once!

4. *Sentence:* James, drive the truck to the garage.

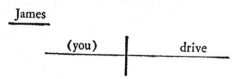

5. *Sentence:* There are several doctors in the building.

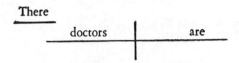

CORRECT ANSWERS TO ASSIGNMENT 1

End Punctuation	Kind of Sentence	Reason
1. period	declarative	makes statement
2. question mark	interrogative	asks question
3. exclamation mark	imperative	gives command
4. exclamation mark	exclamatory	expresses strong feeling
5. period	declarative	makes statement
6. question mark	interrogative	asks question
7. question mark	interrogative	asks question
8. exclamation mark	exclamatory	expresses strong feeling
9. period	imperative	makes request
10. question mark	interrogative	asks question
11. exclamation mark	imperative	gives command
12. period	declarative	makes statement
13. question mark	interrogative	asks question
14. period	imperative	makes request
15. exclamation mark	imperative	gives command

CORRECT ANSWERS TO ASSIGNMENT 2

1. We play golf on weekdays sometimes.

2. Reference books may be taken home once a week.

3. (You) Raise your right hand.

4. You have what an attractive garden!

5. Shouts of approval came from the audience.

6. You have decided to sell your home.

7. Your dancing is how wonderful!

8. Tim is responsible in what way?

9. We traveled across the desert for three months.

10. They did call the fire department.

11. The doctor arrived a few minutes later.

12. We shall see many mountain lakes on our trip.

13. You will receive your last order on Monday.

14. Ned does prefer what color of ink?

15. (You) Empty the tank immediately!

CORRECT ANSWERS TO ASSIGNMENT 3

	Simple Subject	Simple Predicate
1. Stop that car, James.	1. (You)	Stop
2. Has something happened to you?	2. something	has happened
3. There was complete harmony among the three sisters.	3. harmony	was
4. Bob, bring me the dictionary.	4. (you)	bring
5. There were five men in the car.	5. men	were
6. Did you answer the telephone, Alice?	6. you	did answer
7. There was a majority present.	7. majority	was
8. Go immediately!	8. (You)	Go
9. Out of the bag fell the stolen articles.	9. articles	fell
10. What excuse did Marvin give?	10. Marvin	did give
11. Suggest a good title for the article, Stephen.	11. (You)	Suggest
12. Through the trees whistled the wind.	12. wind	whistled
13. There should be some reward for faithful service.	13. reward	should be
14. What are you reading, Jane?	14. you	are reading
15. There was a radio in every room.	15. radio	was

CORRECT ANSWERS TO ASSIGNMENT 4

1. *Sentence:* There were several people in the doctor's office.

There
_____
people | were

2. *Sentence:* Mr. Chairman, did anyone second that motion?

Mr. Chairman
_____
anyone | did second

3. *Sentence:* There should be more interest in our meetings.

There
_____
interest | should be

4. *Sentence:* Shut that door at once, Harold.

Harold
_____
(you) | Shut

5. *Sentence:* There might be some mistake in your account.

There
_____
mistake | might be

CORRECT ANSWERS TO PROGRESS TEST FOUR

	Subject	Verb or Verbs
1. Tell your story to the judge.	1. (You)	Tell
2. There might have been another reason for his failure.	2. reason	might have been
3. What were Vincent and Albert discussing at the meeting?	3. Vincent—Albert	were discussing
4. John, look behind you!	4. (you)	look
5. Where will the campers eat and sleep?	5. campers	will eat—(will) sleep
6. There is an abundance of food in the freezer.	6. abundance	is
7. Have you and David joined the tennis club?	7. you—David	have joined
8. How did you break your arm, Fred?	8. you	did break
9. Take the children for a walk, May.	9. (You)	Take
10. We read and discussed books on China.	10. we	read—discussed
11. When did you lose your watch?	11. you	did lose
12. Several members of the committee met the following day.	12. members	met
13. What is the trouble now, Ted?	13. trouble	is

14. Behind the desk there was
    an opening in the wall.   14. opening   was

15. Did you receive the
    message?   15. you   did receive

16. There is a good road to
    the falls.   16. road   is

17. Recently a new star has
    been discovered.   17. star   has been discovered

18. Leave now and come back
    later.   18. (You)   Leave—come

19. Forward, march!   19. (You)   march

20. The fugitive opened the
    door and looked about
    cautiously.   20. fugitive   opened—looked

21. At one end of the couch
    there was a magazine rack.   21. rack   was

22. On Wednesday a new
    director will be appointed. 22. director   will be appointed

23. What were Jean and
    Marge making last night?   23. Jean—Marge   were making

24. Have you finished the
    dress, Mother?   24. you   have finished

25. Have you cancelled the
    order?   25. you   have cancelled

HOW TO OBTAIN YOUR SCORE

The test totals 50 points. To obtain your score, divide the number of your correct answers by 50. The answer will be your score on this test. For example, if you have 38 points correct, your score is 38 divided by 50 or 76 per cent. In other words, your score on this test is 76. You can obtain your score on any of the exercises or assignments by following the same procedure.

Practical English Grammar

OUTLINE OF UNIT FIVE

NOUNS

Kinds — Capitalization — Plurals

NOUNS

KINDS OF NOUNS

IN GRAMMAR UNIT ONE you learned that a noun is a word used as a name. You also learned that some nouns begin with capital letters, and others begin with small letters. The subject of *capitalization* is very important because it is closely concerned with the division of nouns into groups or classes.

In English, nouns are divided into two main classes called **common nouns** and **proper nouns.** A *common noun* names any one of a class of persons, places, or things. We have a name for all the chairs in the world when we use the common noun *chair.* We have a name for all the lakes in the world when we use the common noun *lake.*

But when we want to name a particular lake, we must give it a special name. The name of a particular lake might be *Lake Louise, Lake George,* or *Lake Michigan.* These particular names are called proper nouns. *A proper noun always begins with a capital letter.*

We have particular names for persons, such as *John Adams, General Eisenhower, Queen Elizabeth,* and *Governor Stevenson.* We also have particular names for certain objects, such as buildings, hotels, theaters, and clubs: *Conway Building, Congress Hotel, Harris Theater,* and *Union League Club.*

Sometimes a common noun names a collection of objects or a group of persons. When we use the word *band* in music, we include under one name all the musicians who play the different instruments. When we use the word *jury,* we include all the members who make up the jury. Nouns that name a group of persons or a collection of objects are called *collective nouns.*

A **common noun** is the name of *any one* of a class of *persons, places,* or *things.*

aviator	ocean	tiger	meat
city	book	lily	desk

A **proper noun** is the name of a *particular person, place,* or *thing.*

Pacific Ocean	Thomas Edison
Chicago	Amazon River
England	Wrigley Building
State Street	Bay of Fundy

A **collective noun** is a common noun whose singular form names a *group* of persons, objects, or acts.

herd	company	team	crowd
army	corps	audience	faculty

Some nouns are *common nouns* in one sentence and *proper nouns* in another sentence.

Common Nouns	Proper Nouns
Roy is studying to be a doctor.	The family called in Dr. Allen.
John's uncle is an engineer.	Uncle John is a colonel in the army.
I went to the theater with May.	The play was given at the Grand Theater.
We spent the summer at the lake.	Did you ever cross Lake Erie?

EXERCISE 1

Classify the following nouns as *common nouns, proper nouns,* or *collective nouns.* Write your answers on the lines opposite the words.

1. vase	....	21. magazine	....
2. Stevens Hotel	....	22. parent	....
3. troop	....	23. Hudson Bay	....
4. foreigner	....	24. Fort Hamilton	....
5. Admiral Byrd	....	25. Cape Hatteras	....
6. flock	....	26. automobile	....
7. Ditto Inc.	....	27. Ellen	....
8. State Street	....	28. canoe	....
9. army	....	29. Illinois	....
10. physician	....	30. author	....
11. blue	....	31. Art Institute	....
12. lion	....	32. manager	....
13. letter	....	33. Robert Jones	....
14. Miss Carlson	....	34. teacher	....
15. stenographer	....	35. Cadillac	....
16. United States	....	36. Yale Club	....
17. Niagara Falls	....	37. fleet	....
18. team	....	38. faculty	....
19. Sherman Hotel	....	39. Egypt	....
20. typewriter	....	40. Davis Strait	....

CAPITALIZATION OF PROPER NOUNS

A student of language should be familiar with the accepted rules regarding the capitalization of *proper nouns* and *proper adjectives.* **Proper adjectives** *are adjectives derived from proper nouns.*

Proper Nouns	Proper Adjectives
America	an *American* soldier
Spain	a *Spanish* house
a Baptist	a *Baptist* minister
China	a *Chinese* vase

The following list of rules for the capitalization of proper nouns follows accepted, present-day usage:

1. Capitalize names of *particular persons* and *places.*

Mr. Smith	Yankee Stadium
Eleanor Roosevelt	Radio City
Helen Hayes	Cuba
Senator Clark	Ellis Island
Miss Hamilton	Soldier Field

2. Capitalize *geographic names:* continents, countries, states, cities, rivers, mountains, lakes, falls, harbors, valleys, bays, etc.

Africa	Pikes Peak	Cape Horn
Brazil	Rocky Mountains	Gulf of Mexico
Montana	Victoria Falls	New York Harbor
Cleveland	Hudson Bay	Long Island

3. Capitalize names of *definite regions, localities,* and *political divisions.*

the Orient	Third Precinct
the Wheat Belt	First Ward (of a city)
the Bad Lands	Wheeling Township
the Arctic Circle	French Republic
the North Pole	the Badger State

4. Capitalize names of *bridges, buildings, monuments, parks, ships, automobiles, hotels, forts, dams, railroads, streets,* etc.

Brooklyn Bridge	Plymouth Court
Fine Arts Building	Michigan Avenue
Statue of Liberty	New York Central (railroad)
Central Park	Plaza Hotel
Dodge (car)	Eiffel Tower
Queen Mary (ship)	Missouri (battleship)
Fort Knox	Alton Railroad
Rush Street	Boulder Dam

5. Capitalize names of *historical events, historical periods,* and *historical documents.*

the Middle Ages	Battle of Gettysburg
World War II	Louisiana Purchase
the Crusades	Treaty of Paris
Atlantic Charter	Fourteenth Amendment
Magna Charta	the Civil War (American)

6. Capitalize names of *governmental bodies* and *departments.*

Bureau of Mines	Civil Service Commission
the Federal Government	Federal Trade Commission
United States Senate	Eighty-ninth Congress
Federal Courts	the President's Cabinet
Bureau of the Census	Supreme Court of the United States

7. Capitalize names of *political parties, business* and *fraternal organizations, clubs* and *societies, companies,* and *institutions.*

Republicans	County Hospital
Democratic Party (or party)	John Crerar Library
Gold Star Mothers	Chapman Chemical Company
Odd Fellows	Career Institute
a Shriner	Chicago Athletic Club
the Elks	Ford Motor Company
Volunteers of America	Northwestern University

8. Capitalize *titles of rank* when they are joined to a person's name.

Lord Beaverbrook	Professor Thomas
President Johnson	Doctor Hayden
Senator Lodge	Judge Harmon
Bishop Dudley Stark	Dean Mary Allison
Dr. Allen Reed	Pope Paul VI
Chancellor Hutchins	Cardinal Wolsey
Prime Minister Wilson	Queen Elizabeth II
Secretary U Thant	His Honor the Mayor

9. Capitalize *days* of the *week, months* of the *year, holidays,* and *days* of *special observance,* such as feast and fast days.

Monday	Feast of the Passover
September	Saint Valentine's Day
Labor Day	Mother's Day
Easter Sunday	Good Friday
Armistice Day	Memorial Day

10. You should not capitalize names of the seasons unless they are personified. When something is personified it is represented or considered as if it were a person. Personification is frequently used in poetry.

spring	winter
Spring's warm touch	Winter's icy breath

11. The words *north, east, south,* and *west* are capitalized when they refer to *sections* of the country. They are not capitalized when they refer to *directions.*

Sections of Countries	**Directions**
the Midwest	I travel north on my way home.
the Far West	The sun rises in the east.
the Near East	The southern part of Idaho is beautiful.
the Middle West	The colonists moved west to obtain more land.

12. The *special names* given to planets and stars are capitalized. The words *sun, moon, star,* and *planet* are not capitalized.

Jupiter	The *sun* rose at six that morning.
Venus	Scientists have discovered a new *star.*
Mars	The *moon* is a heavenly body.
Milky Way	A *planet* shines by reflected light.
Big Dipper	A *constellation* is a group of stars.

EXERCISE 2

Cross out small letters and insert capitals when necessary. Cross out capitals that are used incorrectly and substitute small letters.

1. the marine corps

2. spanish

3. a presbyterian

4. july

5. the Moon

6. in the Winter

7. holy week

8. senator Lodge

9. Atlantic ocean

10. fifth avenue

11. a republican

12. professor Ames

13. a Planet

14. Chicago river

15. Statler hotel

16. civil service commission

17. Passavant hospital

18. United States senate

19. victoria falls

20. the white house (Washington)

21. Lincoln park

22. milky way

23. British empire

24. Kimball building

25. Santa fe railroad

26. jupiter (a planet)

27. coronia (ship)

28. university club

29. canal zone

30. bishop anderson

SPECIAL USES OF CAPITAL LETTERS

1. Words derived from proper nouns are usually capitalized. If the word has acquired a special meaning, it is not capitalized.

Capitalized	Not Capitalized
a Pullman car	navy blue
Mongolian race	china cabinet
Venetian blinds	morocco leather
Swiss cheese	chinaware
Manila hemp	paris green
English tweeds	panama hat or Panama hat
Turkish bath	turkish towel or Turkish towel

2. The principal words in *titles of books, magazines, pictures, songs, articles,* etc., are capitalized. Prepositions, conjunctions, and the articles *a, an,* and *the* are not capitalized unless the title begins with one of these words.

The Last of the Mohicans (book)

The Saturday Evening Post (magazine)

"Outside Our World" (article)

Battle Hymn of the Republic (song)

The Angelus (picture)

"The Northerners" (radio program)

"Forum of the Air" (television program)

3. The definite article *the* is not capitalized unless it is the first word of a title. Many titles do not begin with *the.* If the word *the* is within the title, it is written with a small letter. The only way to be sure about

the correct form of a title is to check the official form, or the form adopted by the company, publication, etc.

Chicago Daily News

The Christian Science Monitor

Book Review Digest

The John C. Winston Company

National Geographic Magazine

Pinnacle Oil Company

4. All words referring to the Deity, the Bible, books of the Bible, and other *sacred books* are capitalized.

God, the Father	the Koran
Saviour	Genesis
the Trinity	Supreme Being
Talmud	Bible
Book of Job	New Testament

5. The pronoun *I* and the interjection *O* are capitalized. The word *oh* is not capitalized unless it is the first word of a sentence.

"O say! can you see, by the dawn's early light, . . ."

" 'Tis the Star Spangled Banner, oh, long may it wave . . ."

6. Names of school subjects are not capitalized unless they are names of the languages. Subjects listed in school catalogs as names of special courses are capitalized.

mathematics	History 101 (title of course)
French	Advanced Chemistry II (title of course)
economics	Economics 345 (title of course)
English	Physics II (title of course)

7. Capitalize words which show family relationships when they are used with a person's name. The words *father* and *mother* are not capitalized when they are preceded by a pronoun. When used without a pronoun, they are usually capitalized.

Aunt Martha	her cousin
Cousin John	their uncle
Sister Sue	his grandmother
Uncle Jack	my father

8. Capitalize the first word in a *compound word that is used as a proper noun*. If the second word in the compound word is a proper noun, it should also be capitalized. Capitalize both parts of *compound titles of distinction.*

Eighty-ninth Congress	un-American activities
Forty-third Street	ex-President Eisenhower
Army-Navy game	Rear Admiral Simpson
The Honorable John Willis	Vice-President Humphrey
Chief Justice Warren	or
	Vice President Humphrey

9. The names of special departments of business firms may be written with small or with capital letters. In business writing, it is considered good practice to capitalize titles such as *president, secretary, office manager, general superintendent,* etc. They may also be written with small letters.

claim department *or* Claim Department

advertising department *or* Advertising Department

The Company will reimburse you for your loss. (or company)

Our President will grant you an interview. (or president)

The Court will grant you a hearing. (or court)

EXERCISE 3

Cross out small letters and place capital letters wherever needed. Cross out capital letters that are used incorrectly, and write small letters above.

1. My Mother has some beautiful italian pottery.

2. We read the report of ex-president Eisenhower.

3. The Game was won by the cardinals.

4. Our Family spent the Summer in Jasper park.

5. The Skiers went to sun valley for the Winter sports.

6. That passage is found in the psalms which is one of the Books of the old testament.

7. The engineer applied for a position in the bureau of mines.

8. I went to europe with uncle Charles.

9. The speaker recited a poem entitled "the Wreck of the hesperus."

10. The concert was held in Carnegie hall, new York.

11. The american legion is holding a meeting in Los angeles.

12. Did the republicans or the democrats hold their Convention in San francisco?

13. On wednesdays, I have classes in spanish, Physics, and Sociology.

14. My Brother works at the first national bank in Sioux city, iowa.

15. I saw a cadillac on display in the windows of the Johnson motor company.

PLURAL FORMS OF NOUNS

When a noun refers to one person or thing, it is singular in number. When a noun refers to more than one person or thing, it is plural in number. Nouns have special forms to show these distinctions, as you will see from the following illustrations:

Singular	Plural
boy	boys
box	boxes
leaf	leaves
tomato	tomatoes

The plurals of nouns are formed in a number of different ways. Since there are exceptions to almost every one of these methods, you should consult a reliable dictionary whenever you are in doubt regarding a correct plural form. You should also be familiar with the following methods of forming the plurals of nouns:

1. Most nouns add the letter *s* to the singular to form the plural.

kite	kites	college	colleges
lamp	lamps	chimney	chimneys
dance	dances	manager	managers
zebra	zebras	dynamo	dynamos
chief	chiefs	orange	oranges
radio	radios	island	islands

2. Nouns ending in *s, sh, ch, x,* or *z* form the plural by adding *es.* The plural adds another syllable in the pronunciation.

dress	dresses	ax	axes	couch	couches
match	matches	tax	taxes	waltz	waltzes
bush	bushes	loss	losses	marsh	marshes

3. Nouns ending in *o* preceded by a vowel add *s*. Musical terms ending in *o* add *s*.

Vowel Preceding "o"		Musical Terms	
cameo	cameos	piano	pianos
patio	patios	alto	altos
rodeo	rodeos	cello	cellos

Some nouns ending in *o* preceded by a consonant add *s*. Others add *es*. Some form the plural either way.

Add "s"		Add "es"		Add "s" or "es"		
kimono	kimonos	Negro	Negroes	cargo	cargos	cargoes
zero	zeros	hero	heroes	motto	mottos	mottoes
dynamo	dynamos	potato	potatoes	tornado	tornados	tornadoes

4. Nouns ending in *y* preceded by a consonant, change the *y* to *i* and add *es*.

party	parties	country	countries
city	cities	foundry	foundries
fly	flies	enemy	enemies
lady	ladies	berry	berries

5. Nouns ending in *y* preceded by a vowel, usually add *s*. In many cases the vowel before the final *y* is *e*.

alley	alleys	journey	journeys
boy	boys	valley	valleys
key	keys	day	days

6. Some nouns ending in *f* or *fe* change the *f* or the *fe* to *v* and add *es*. Some nouns ending in *f* have two plurals, one in *s* and one in *ves*. Some simply add *s*.

Changes to "ves"		Add "s" or Change to "ves"		
wife	wives	scarf	scarfs	scarves
shelf	shelves	wharf	wharfs	wharves
thief	thieves	beef	beefs	beeves
wolf	wolves	hoof	hoofs	hooves
half	halves	chief	chiefs	(no second plural)

7. Some nouns form the plural by a change in the vowel.

man	men	mouse	mice
foot	feet	goose	geese
tooth	teeth	louse	lice

8. Some nouns have the same form for both singular and plural.

Singular and Plural		Singular and Plural	
fish	fish	species	species
sheep	sheep	series	series
gross	gross	salmon	salmon
Chinese	Chinese	deer	deer

9. The plurals of compound nouns are generally formed by adding *s* to the *principal word* in the compound.

mother-in-law	*mothers*-in-law
board of education	*boards* of education
attorney general	*attorneys* general or attorney *generals*
brigadier general	brigadier *generals*
court-martial	*courts*-martial
man-of-war	*men*-of-war

Sometimes *both parts* of the compound are made plural.

manservant	menservants
woman doctor	women doctors
Knight Templar	Knights Templars or Knights Templar

Sometimes an *s* is added to the end of the compound. In that case, there is no important word in the compound.

Jack-in-the-pulpit	Jack-in-the-pulpits
forget-me-not	forget-me-nots
toothbrush	toothbrushes

Compounds ending in *ful* are made plural by adding *s* to the end of the compound. This rule applies when the same container is filled a number of times.

spoonful	spoonfuls	handful	handfuls
bucketful	bucketfuls	cupful	cupfuls

Six cups full of flour means that there are six separate cups, and that each one is filled with flour.

10. The plurals of proper names are formed by adding *s* or *es*.

There are three *Ruths* in this class.

The two *Burnses* left the hall.

The *Joneses* and the *Smiths* attended the banquet.

The two *Marys* are friends.

The spelling of proper names must not be changed. If we followed the rule for words ending in *y* in the case of *Mary*, we would change the *y* to *i* and add *es*. The name would then be changed to *Marie*, for the plural would be *Maries*. The correct plural of *Mary* is *Marys*.

Titles are made plural in several ways. The plural of *Miss* is *Misses;* the plural of *Mr.* is *Messrs. Mrs.* has no plural. The plural of *Madam* is *Mesdames,* which is sometimes used for the plural of *Mrs. Misses* should not be followed by a period. It is not an abbreviation. In the first column of the following examples, the title is made plural. In the second column the name is made plural. Either form is correct.

the *Misses* Thomas   *or*   the Miss *Thomases*

the *Messrs.* Churchill   *or*   the Mr. *Churchills*

Mesdames Greene   *or*   the Mrs. *Greenes*

Foreign Plurals

Words taken from foreign languages usually retain their foreign plurals. Some of these words are used so commonly that they have acquired an English plural which is formed in the regular way; that is, by adding *s* or *es* to the singular.

The following list gives the foreign and English plurals for some commonly used foreign words. If no English plural is given, the foreign plural is used.

Foreign Word	Foreign Plural	English Plural
alumna *(feminine)*	alumnae	————
alumnus *(masculine)*	alumni	————
analysis	analyses	————
appendix	appendices	appendixes
axis	axes	————
bacterium	bacteria	————
basis	bases	————
cactus	cacti	cactuses
candelabrum	candelabra	candelabrums
crisis	crises	————
criterion	criteria	criterions
curriculum	curricula	curriculums
datum	data	————
focus	foci	focuses
formula	formulae	formulas
genus *(kind, class)*	genera	genuses
gymnasium	gymnasia	gymnasiums
hippopotamus	hippopotami	hippopotamuses
hypothesis	hypotheses	————
index	indices	indexes
madam	mesdames	————
medium	media	mediums
memorandum	memoranda	memorandums
parenthesis	parentheses	————
phenomenon	phenomena	————
radius	radii	radiuses
synopsis	synopses	————

12. The plural of numbers, letters, signs, and symbols is formed by adding the apostrophe and *s*.

Your *2's* look like your *3's*.

You use too many *ands* in your writing. (correct)

or

You use too many *and's* in your writing. (correct)

You must always cross your *t's*.

He received three *A's* and two *B's* last semester.

13. The following nouns are used only in the plural. You may find some of them used in the singular, but the general practice is to regard them as plural. When you are in doubt, consult the dictionary.

trousers	shears	contents
pants	pliers	riches
breeches	pincers	links (golf)
scissors	scales (weighing)	alms
tongs	forceps	remains
billiards	nuptials	suds
clothes	gallows	victuals

EXERCISE 4

Write the **plurals** of the following nouns on the lines to the right. Whenever you are in doubt about a plural form, consult the text, or refer to the dictionary.

1. dance	1.	21. monkey	21. ....
2. army	2.	22. spoonful	22. ....
3. alley	3.	23. radio	23. ....
4. lady	4.	24. Chinese	24. ....
5. bus	5.	25. wolf	25. ....
6. academy	6.	26. manservant	26. ....
7. waltz	7.	27. elf	27. ....
8. knife	8.	28. fish	28. ....
9. belief	9.	29. son-in-law	29. ....
10. sheep	10.	30. dwarf	30. ....
11. match	11.	31. Miss Smith	31. ....
12. crisis	12.	32. Henry	32. ....
13. banjo	13.	33. Roman	33. ....
14. wharf	14.	34. inquiry	34. ....
15. axis	15.	35. goose	35. ....
16. thief	16.	36. beef	36. ....
17. gas	17.	37. tomato	37. ....
18. alumnus	18.	38. family	38. ....
19. compass	19.	39. chief	39. ....
20. Jane	20.	40. louse	40. ....

SUMMARY OF GRAMMAR UNIT FIVE

A **noun** is a word used as the name of a person, place, thing, idea, or action.

A **proper noun** is the name of a particular person, place, or thing. A proper noun is written with a capital letter.

A **common noun** is the name of any one of a class of persons, places, or things. A common noun is written with a small letter unless it is the first word of a sentence.

A **collective noun** is a common noun whose singular form names a group of persons, objects, or acts.

Proper adjectives are usually written with capital letters. If the adjective has acquired a special meaning it is not capitalized.

When a noun refers to one person or thing, it is *singular* in number. When a noun refers to more than one person or thing, it is *plural* in number.

The plurals of nouns are formed in various ways. Since there are exceptions to almost every one of these ways of forming the plural, you should consult a reliable, up-to-date dictionary when you are in doubt regarding a correct plural form. You should also be familiar with the methods that are outlined in this unit.

Words taken from foreign languages usually retain their foreign plurals. A number of commonly used foreign words have acquired English plurals.

SELF-GRADING ASSIGNMENT 1

Directions: Cross out capital letters and write small letters wherever necessary. Cross out small letters and write capitals where necessary.

1. Arithmetic

2. my Aunt

3. Art institute

4. a Doctor

5. in the Winter

6. Lake shore drive

7. studying french

8. republican Platform

9. governor Dewey

10. a packard (car)

11. middle Ages (period)

12. labor day

13. mexican

14. Pro-British

15. a Star

16. boy Scouts

17. Douglas boulevard

18. university of Wisconsin

19. gulf of Mexico

20. the Planet mars

21. sixth ward (of a city)

22. the North star

23. rear admiral Nelson

24. National bank building

25. vice-president Barkley

26. indian

27. Marshall field and company

28. bureau of the Census

29. women's athletic club

30. Tom's uncle frank

31. a methodist

32. Chicago daily tribune

Caution: Check your answers to each assignment with the answer key at the end of this unit before proceeding with the next assignment.

SELF-GRADING ASSIGNMENT 2

Directions: Cross out small letters and write capital letters wherever necessary. Cross out capital letters and write small letters if necessary.

1. Several Doctors attended professor allen's lecture.

2. The president met the Senators in the United states capitol building.

3. The *declaration of independence* is an important Historical Document.

4. The President of the Company told uncle charles that he was moving to San antonio.

5. On memorial day, several Generals and Admirals attended the services at arlington cemetery.

6. We lived on wellington avenue during world War II, but after the War we moved to pratt boulevard.

7. My Cousin is studying greek, english literature, and Economics.

8. Ted's best Friend, captain Smith, is an Instructor at west Point military academy.

9. We traveled North for many miles before we returned to our home in the west.

10. The students had a discussion about the fourteenth amendment to the constitution of the United States.

11. The eighty-first congress met in Washington in november, shortly after Thanksgiving day.

12. The woolworth building is located at Forty Third street and lexington avenue in columbus, Ohio.

SELF-GRADING ASSIGNMENT 3

Directions: Write the *plural forms* of each of the following nouns on the lines to the right.

1. lasso	1.	21. cargo	21. ....
2. shelf	2.	22. deer	22. ....
3. cupful	3.	23. sheaf	23. ....
4. parenthesis	4.	24. cello	24. ....
5. a Japanese	5.	25. knife	25. ....
6. Mr. Allison	6.	26. handkerchief	26. ....
7. ally	7.	27. Negro	27. ....
8. trade-union	8.	28. Miss Jones	28. ....
9. radio	9.	29. foster parent	29. ....
10. mulatto	10.	30. forget-me-not	30. ....
11. mulberry	11.	31. maid of honor	31. ....
12. mouse	12.	32. Charles	32. ....
13. niece	13.	33. levy	33. ....
14. memorandum	14.	34. cliff	34. ....
15. country	15.	35. scarf	35. ....
16. plateau	16.	36. species	36. ....
17. valley	17.	37. formula	37. ....
18. trout	18.	38. woman doctor	38. ....
19. wolf	19.	39. father-in-law	39. ....
20. legacy	20.	40. contralto	40. ....

SELF-GRADING ASSIGNMENT 4

Directions: Fill in the blanks with the *plurals* of the words in parentheses.

1. Three (soprano)................will each sing two (solo)................

2. My uncle has fifty (sheep)................and ten (calf)................

3. The (sheriff)................caught a number of (thief)................

4. The recipe calls for six (tomato)............and five (potato)............

5. I received two (handkerchief)................and two (box)................
   of paper.

6. (Turkey)................and (goose)................are sold in the markets.

7. We have had a number of (inquiry)..........................about two
   of our (course)........................

8. Several great (hero)........................were killed in the battle.

9. The (woman)................baked twenty (loaf)................of bread.

10. We have passed through several (crisis)........................

11. The (editor-in-chief)........................met in New York last week.

12. There are three (Henry)........................on our payroll.

13. Jane will have two (maid of honor)................................

14. His (6)................look like (9)................and his (h)................
    look like (k)................

15. The (alley)................in our (city)............have not been paved.

PROGRESS TEST FIVE

This progress test should not be taken until a day or two after you have completed the assignments. The score you make on the test will then more clearly reflect your understanding of the material in the unit.

Directions: Cross out any *capital letters, small letters,* or *plural forms* of nouns that are used incorrectly in the following sentences. Write the correct form above the incorrect form.   (*100 points*)

          A   tomatoes.
Example: We sent ~~aunt~~ Mary a box of ~~tomatos.~~

1. We spent the Summer in the Country, picking and canning berrys.

2. The Astronomer made a discovery about the Planet mars.

3. Driving North on Sheridan road, we arrived at the edgewater beach hotel, where we had dinner with professor and Mrs. allerton.

4. Alice attends the fourth presbyterian church, which is located on Thirty First street near Parker avenue.

5. The boy scouts cut off the branchs with their knifes.

6. Several serieses of Lectures will be given in orchestra hall.

7. We met dr. evans, who was inspecting the new laboratorys.

8. The edison company has sold large quantitys of this Product.

9. The misses thompson gave a concert for the benefit of the red cross.

10. Both of my sister-in-laws tell storys about their travels.

11. The Entertainers were talented Musicians and Artists.

12. The alumnuses of the College are interested in a new Dormitory.

PROGRESS TEST FIVE (continued)

13. During the Elizabethan age many Explorers made long voyages to north America and the West indies.

14. queen Elizabeth and Prince charles visited the National gallery in london last Summer.

15. What datum are available in the office in regard to the financial standing of Nelson brothers company?

16. We have a Holiday on Memorial day and one on labor day, but we do not have a holiday on armistice day.

17. His office is in the empire state building in new York, and his home is on Long island. He works for the american can company.

18. Our studioes offer special opportunitys in march.

19. The chimnies of the factorys should be inspected.

20. The *Book review digest* is a digest of book reviews taken from english and american Periodicals.

21. The speakers were ex-president Eisenhower and governor Rocke-feller.

22. The notarys public signed the documents for the Employees.

23. We visited a number of spanish houses in new Mexico. Many of them were finished in italian marble.

24. The play, *Man and superman,* was written by George bernard shaw, a famous irish Dramatist and critic.

25. The "book of Job" is found in the old testament of the bible. The sacred book of the mohammedans is the koran, which was written in arabic.

ANSWER KEY

for

EXERCISES, ASSIGNMENTS, AND PROGRESS TEST

Grammar Unit Five

CORRECT ANSWERS TO EXERCISE 1

1. common	15. common	29. proper
2. proper	16. proper	30. common
3. collective	17. proper	31. proper
4. common	18. collective	32. common
5. proper	19. proper	33. proper
6. collective	20. common	34. common
7. proper	21. common	35. proper
8. proper	22. common	36. proper
9. collective	23 proper	37. collective
10. common	24. proper	38. collective
11. common	25. proper	39. proper
12. common	26. common	40. proper
13. common	27. proper	
14. proper	28. common	

CORRECT ANSWERS TO EXERCISE 2

1. the Marine Corps	16. Civil Service Commission
2. Spanish	17. Passavant Hospital
3. a Presbyterian	18. United States Senate
4. July	19. Victoria Falls
5. the moon	20. the White House
6. in the winter	21. Lincoln Park
7. Holy Week	22. Milky Way
8. Senator Lodge	23. British Empire
9. Atlantic Ocean	24. Kimball Building
10. Fifth Avenue	25. Santa Fe Railroad
11. a Republican	26. Jupiter
12. Professor Ames	27. Coronia
13. a planet	28. University Club
14. Chicago River	29. Canal Zone
15. Statler Hotel	30. Bishop Anderson

CORRECT ANSWERS TO EXERCISE 3

Capital and small letters that have been corrected are printed in **heavy type.**

1. My **m**other has some beautiful **I**talian pottery.
2. **W**e read the report of ex-**P**resident Eisenhower.
3. The **g**ame was won by the **C**ardinals.
4. Our **f**amily spent the **s**ummer in Jasper **P**ark.
5. The **s**kiers went to **S**un **V**alley for the **w**inter sports.
6. That passage is found in the "**P**salms" which is one of the **b**ooks of the **O**ld **T**estament.
7. The engineer applied for a position in the **B**ureau of **M**ines.
8. I went to **E**urope with **U**ncle Charles.
9. The speaker recited a poem entitled *The Wreck of the Hesperus.*
10. The concert was held in Carnegie **H**all, **N**ew York.
11. The **A**merican **L**egion is holding a meeting in Los **A**ngeles.
12. Did the **R**epublicans or the **D**emocrats hold their **c**onvention in San **F**rancisco?
13. On **W**ednesdays, I have classes in **S**panish, **p**hysics, and **s**ociology.
14. My **b**rother works at the **F**irst **N**ational **B**ank in Sioux **C**ity, **I**owa.
15. I saw a **C**adillac on display in the windows of the Johnson **M**otor **C**ompany.

CORRECT ANSWERS TO EXERCISE 4

1. dances
2. armies
3. alleys
4. ladies
5. busses or buses
6. academies
7. waltzes
8. knives
9. beliefs
10. sheep
11. matches
12. crises
13. banjos
14. wharfs or wharves
15. axes
16. thieves
17. gases
18. alumni
19. compasses
20. Janes
21. monkeys
22. spoonfuls
23. radios
24. Chinese
25. wolves
26. menservants
27. elves
28. fish
29. sons-in-law
30. dwarfs
31. Misses Smith or the Miss Smiths
32. Henrys
33. Romans
34. inquiries
35. geese
36. beefs or beeves
37. tomatoes
38. families
39. chiefs
40. lice

CORRECT ANSWERS TO ASSIGNMENT 1

Capital and small letters that have been corrected are printed in **heavy type.**

1. **a**rithmetic
2. my **a**unt
3. Art **I**nstitute
4. a **d**octor
5. in the **w**inter
6. Lake **S**hore **D**rive
7. studying **F**rench
8. **R**epublican **p**latform
9. **G**overnor Dewey

10. a **P**ackard
11. **M**iddle Ages
12. **L**abor **D**ay
13. **M**exican
14. **p**ro-British
15. a **s**tar
16. **B**oy Scouts

17. Douglas **B**oulevard
18. **U**niversity of **W**isconsin
19. **G**ulf of Mexico
20. the **p**lanet **M**ars
21. Sixth **W**ard
22. the North **S**tar
23. Rear **A**dmiral Nelson
24. National **B**ank Building
25. **V**ice-**P**resident Barkley *or*
     Vice **P**resident Barkley
26. **I**ndian
27. Marshall **F**ield and **C**ompany
28. **B**ureau of the Census
29. **W**omen's **A**thletic **C**lub
30. Tom's **U**ncle **F**rank
31. a **M**ethodist
32. Chicago **D**aily **T**ribune

CORRECT ANSWERS TO ASSIGNMENT 2

Capital and small letters that have been corrected are printed in **heavy type.**

1. Several **d**octors attended **P**rofessor **A**llen's lecture.
2. The **P**resident met the **s**enators in the United **S**tates **C**apitol **B**uilding.
3. The *Declaration of Independence* is an important **h**istorical **d**ocument.
4. The **p**resident of the **c**ompany told **U**ncle **C**harles that he was moving to San **A**ntonio.
5. On **M**emorial **D**ay, several **g**enerals and **a**dmirals attended the services at **A**rlington **C**emetery.
6. We lived on **W**ellington **A**venue during **W**orld War II, but after the war we moved to **P**ratt **B**oulevard.
7. My **c**ousin is studying **G**reek, **E**nglish literature, and **e**conomics.
8. Ted's best **f**riend, **C**aptain Smith, is an **i**nstructor at **W**est Point **M**ilitary **A**cademy.
9. We traveled **n**orth for many miles before we returned to our home in the **W**est.

10. The students had a discussion about the Fourteenth Amendment to the Constitution of the United States.

11. The Eighty-first Congress met in Washington in November, shortly after Thanksgiving Day.

12. The Woolworth Building is located at Forty-third Street and Lexington Avenue in Columbus, Ohio.

CORRECT ANSWERS TO ASSIGNMENT 3

1. lassos *or* lassoes
2. shelves
3. cupfuls
4. parentheses
5. Japanese
6. Messrs. Allison
   or the Mr. Allisons
7. allies
8. trade-unions
9. radios
10. mulattoes
11. mulberries
12. mice
13. nieces
14. memorandums *or* memoranda
15. countries
16. plateaus
17. valleys
18. trout
19. wolves
20. legacies

21. cargoes or cargos
22. deer
23. sheaves
24. cellos
25. knives
26. handkerchiefs
27. Negroes
28. Misses Jones
    or the Miss Joneses
29. foster parents
30. forget-me-nots
31. maids of honor
32. Charleses
33. levies
34. cliffs
35. scarfs or scarves
36. species
37. formulas *or* formulae
38. women doctors
39. fathers-in-law
40. contraltos

CORRECT ANSWERS TO ASSIGNMENT 4

Correct plurals are printed in **heavy type.**

1. Three **sopranos** will each sing two **solos.**
2. My uncle has fifty **sheep** and ten **calves.**
3. The **sheriffs** caught a number of **thieves.**
4. The recipe calls for six **tomatoes** and five **potatoes.**
5. I received two **handkerchiefs** and two **boxes** of paper.

6. **Turkeys** and **geese** are sold in the markets.

7. We have had a number of **inquiries** about two of our **courses.**

8. Several great **heroes** were killed in the battle.

9. The **women** baked twenty **loaves** of bread.

10. The country has passed through several **crises.**

11. The **editors-in-chief** met in New York last week.

12. There are three **Henrys** on our payroll.

13. Jane will have two **maids of honor.**

14. His **6's** look like **9's** and his **h's** look like **k's.**

15. The **alleys** in our **cities** have not been paved.

CORRECT ANSWERS TO PROGRESS TEST FIVE

Capitals, small letters, and plural forms of nouns that have been corrected
are printed in **heavy type.**

1. We spent the **s**ummer in the **c**ountry, picking and canning **berries.**

2. The **a**stronomer made a discovery about the **p**lanet **M**ars.

3. Driving **n**orth on Sheridan **R**oad, we arrived at the **E**dgewater Beach **H**otel, where we had dinner with **P**rofessor and Mrs. **A**llerton.

4. Alice attends the **F**ourth **P**resbyterian **C**hurch, which is located on Thirty-**f**irst **S**treet near Parker **A**venue.

5. The **B**oy **S**couts cut off the **branches** with their **knives.**

6. Several **series** of **l**ectures will be given in **O**rchestra **H**all.

7. We met **D**r. **E**vans, who was inspecting the new **laboratories.**

8. The **E**dison **C**ompany has sold large **quantities** of this product.

9. The **M**isses **T**hompson gave a concert for the benefit of the **R**ed **C**ross.

10. Both of my **sisters-in-law** tell **stories** about their travels.

11. The **e**ntertainers were talented **m**usicians and **a**rtists.

12. The **alumni** of the **c**ollege are interested in a new **d**ormitory.

13. During the Elizabethan Age, many explorers made long voyages to North America and the West Indies.

14. Queen Elizabeth and Prince Charles visited the National Gallery in London last summer.

15. What *data* are available in the office in regard to the financial standing of Nelson Brothers Company?

16. We have a holiday on Memorial Day and one on Labor Day, but we do not have a holiday on Armistice Day.

17. His office is in the Empire State Building in New York, and his home is on Long Island. He works for the American Can Company.

18. Our *studios* offer special *opportunities* in March.

19. The *chimneys* of the *factories* should be inspected.

20. The *Book Review Digest* is a digest of book reviews taken from English and American periodicals.

21. The speakers were ex-President Eisenhower and Governor Rockefeller.

22. The *notaries* public signed the documents for the *employees*.

23. We visited a number of Spanish houses in New Mexico. Many of them were finished in Italian marble.

24. The play, *Man and Superman,* was written by George Bernard Shaw, a famous Irish dramatist and critic.

25. The "Book of Job" is found in the Old Testament of the Bible. The sacred book of the Mohammedans is the Koran, which was written in Arabic.

HOW TO OBTAIN YOUR SCORE

This test totals 100 points. Your score on the test is the total of your correct answers. For example, if you had 87 correct answers, your score is 87.

Practical English Grammar

OUTLINE OF UNIT SIX

PRONOUNS

CLASSIFICATION—USE AS ADJECTIVES

6

PRONOUNS

YOU learned in Grammar Unit One that a *pronoun* is a word used in place of a noun. Because pronouns can be used in place of nouns, they avoid the monotonous repetition of nouns. The following illustration shows what happens when we repeat the same noun too often in a sentence:

> **Alice** went to **Alice's** room to dress because **Alice** was going to a reception given by **Alice's** club in **Alice's** honor.

This sentence is very awkward and monotonous because of the tiresome repetition of *Alice* and *Alice's.* When we rewrite the sentence and substitute pronouns for *Alice* and *Alice's,* we have a much better sentence.

> Alice went to **her** room to dress because **she** was going to a reception given by **her** club in **her** honor.

You should not only learn how to use pronouns effectively, but you should also learn how to use them correctly. Many of the language errors that are commonly made are errors in the use of pronouns. These mistakes occur because some of the pronouns that we use constantly have a number of different forms.

As a student of English you should know how and when to use the different forms of pronouns. In order to do this, you must be familiar with the changes in form that certain pronouns undergo. To illustrate: The pronoun *I* is used as the subject of a sentence. When this same pronoun is used as the object of a preposition, the form changes to *me.* It is incorrect to say, "between *you* and *I*." The correct form of the pronoun to use in this phrase is *me.*

Illustrations of Changes in the Forms of Pronouns

I saw the accident. (The pronoun *I* is the subject.)

Jane saw **me** at the game. (The pronoun *me* is the object of *saw.*)

He *won* the first prize. (The pronoun *he* is the subject.)

We met **him** in the lobby. (The pronoun *him* is the object of *met*.)

In the first sentence, the pronoun *I* is used as the **subject** of the sentence. When this same pronoun is used as the **object of a verb,** the form changes to *me*. In the third sentence, the pronoun *he* is the subject of the sentence. When this same pronoun is used as the object of the verb *met,* the form changes to *him*.

KINDS OF PRONOUNS

There are five groups or classes of pronouns in English: **personal** pronouns, **interrogative** pronouns, **demonstrative** pronouns, **indefinite** pronouns, and **relative** pronouns. The personal pronouns include the *compound personal* pronouns, and the relative pronouns include the *compound relative* pronouns.

PERSONAL PRONOUNS

The personal pronouns are the most important group of pronouns. They are also the pronouns that will give you the most trouble unless you are familiar with the various forms that belong to each pronoun.

A **personal pronoun** is a pronoun that shows by its form whether it refers to the *person speaking,* the *person spoken to,* or the *person or thing spoken of.* All the personal pronouns, with the exception of the pronoun *it,* refer to persons. The following sentences show the use of personal pronouns in the first, second, and third person:

I shall spend the winter in Texas. (*I* is the *person speaking.*)

You are working too hard. (*You* is the *person spoken to.*)

He bought a new Ford. (*He* is the *person spoken about*).

We built the garage. (*We* refers to the *persons speaking.*)

They operate two farms. (*They* refers to the *persons spoken about*.)

Ted has a new radio. **It** is a Zenith. (*It* refers to the *thing spoken about*.)

Jan has two fur coats. **They** are both mink coats. (*They* refers to the *things spoken about*.)

The pronoun of the **first person** is the pronoun *I* with its plural form *we*. The pronoun of the **second person** is *you*. The plural form is also *you*. The pronouns of the **third person** are *he, she,* and *it* with the common plural *they* for all three pronouns.

The personal pronouns also have different forms to indicate case. You will learn more about the case of pronouns in Unit Nine. For the present, you should be familiar with all the forms of the personal pronouns and the pronoun *who* so that you will be able to identify them.

Forms of the Personal Pronouns

1. **First person**—personal pronouns referring to the *speaker*:

I, my, mine, me (singular)
we, our, ours, us (plural)

2. **Second person**—personal pronouns referring to the *person spoken to*:

you, your, yours (same forms in both singular and plural)

3. **Third person**—personal pronouns referring to the *persons* or *things spoken about*:

he, his, him, she, her, hers, it, its (singular)
they, their, theirs, them (plural)

4. Forms of the pronoun **who**:

who, whose, whom

COMPOUND PERSONAL PRONOUNS

Sometimes the word *self* or *selves* is added to certain forms of the personal pronouns. Pronouns formed in this way are called **compound personal pronouns.**

List of Compound Personal Pronouns

myself	herself
yourself	ourselves
himself	yourselves
itself	themselves

Compound personal pronouns are used in two ways: (1) as *reflexive pronouns* and (2) as *intensive pronouns.*

A compound personal pronoun is used *reflexively* when the pronoun is the object of the verb. It tells *who* or *what* received *the* action expressed by the verb. In this case the pronoun *always refers back* to the same person or thing as the subject. The following illustration will help to make this clear.

The chef burned himself yesterday.

In this sentence the word *himself* is a compound personal pronoun used as the object of the verb *burned. Himself* refers to the same person as the subject, which is the word *chef.* In other words, *chef* and *himself* are the same person. This is called the **reflexive** use of the compound personal pronoun. It means that the pronoun *refers* or *reflects back* to the subject.

Sometimes the compound personal pronoun is used to give added emphasis to a noun or pronoun in the sentence. This is called the **emphatic** or **intensive** use of the compound personal pronoun.

When a compound personal pronoun is used in this way, it must give emphasis to some noun or pronoun that is already in the sentence. Observe the following sentences carefully. In each sentence you will find that there is a *noun* or a *pronoun* to which the compound personal pronoun refers.

I made the dress myself. (*Myself* intensifies the pronoun *I*.)

John himself built the canoe. (*Himself* intensifies the noun *John*.)

Incorrect Use of Compound Personal Pronouns

One of the mistakes commonly made in English is to use the compound personal pronoun when there is no word in the sentence to which it refers. These pronouns should never be used as a substitute for a personal pronoun. They should never be used as the subject of the sentence.

My wife and *myself* appreciate your courtesy. (incorrect)

My wife and **I** appreciate your courtesy. (correct)

The manager and *myself* checked the accounts. (incorrect)

The manager and **I** checked the accounts. (correct)

He sent the book to John and *myself*. (incorrect)

He sent the book to John and **me**. (correct)

The first sentence is incorrect because there is no noun or pronoun in the sentence which the pronoun *myself* refers to or gives emphasis to. The second sentence is correct because a *personal pronoun* is used.

Whenever you use a compound personal pronoun in a sentence, always remember that such a pronoun must have an *antecedent,* or a word in the sentence which refers to the same person or thing as the pronoun does. In other words, it must have its own antecedent in the sentence. Do not make mistakes like the following:

Alice and *yourself* were appointed on the committee. (incorrect)

Alice and **you** were appointed on the committee. (correct)

The owner gave Tom and *myself* his old lawn mower. (incorrect)

The owner gave Tom and **me** his old lawn mower. (correct)

Everyone in the club has a car as well as *myself.* (incorrect)

Everyone in the club has a car as well as **I.** (correct)

They sent an invitation to the Smiths and *ourselves.* (incorrect)

They sent an invitation to the Smiths and **us.** (correct)

EXERCISE 1

Underline the **personal pronouns** once, and the **compound personal pronouns** twice, in the following sentences. Whenever you are in doubt, refer to the lists in this unit that give the forms of these pronouns.

Example: He built the boat himself.

1. They lived with her before they lived with us.

2. It is the smallest house in the block.

3. She sat behind me at the lecture.

4. John himself delivered the message to us.

5. I am proud of you and of him.

6. The laundress injured herself last week.

7. They will be waiting for us at the pier.

8. We ourselves gave the blueprints to them.

9. It is a beautiful vase. Don't you like it?

10. They themselves are the persons to blame for the tragedy.

11. Will you mail this package for her?

12. She and I will check the accounts.

13. He did not notice where they went.

14. We deceived ourselves when we trusted him.

15. You must do this job yourself.

Note: The correct answers to exercises will be found at the end of this unit. Correct your mistakes and, if necessary, reread the text material before going on to the next section.

INTERROGATIVE PRONOUNS

Interrogative pronouns are pronouns that are used in asking questions. The interrogative pronouns are *who (whose, whom), which,* and *what.* An interrogative pronoun also has another function to perform in the sentence, just as any other pronoun has. It may be the *subject* of the sentence, or it may be the *object* of the verb or of a preposition.

Who is the director of the band?

For **whom** are you waiting?

What did they say about his speech?

Which is your car?

Whose car did you borrow?

DEMONSTRATIVE PRONOUNS

Demonstrative pronouns are pronouns that point out definite persons, places, or things. There are only two demonstrative pronouns: *this* with its plural *these,* and *that* with its plural *those.*

This is my hat. (A definite hat is pointed out.)

That is your book. (A definite book is pointed out.)

These are the theater tickets. (Definite tickets are pointed out.)

Those are John's shoes. (Definite shoes are pointed out.)

INDEFINITE PRONOUNS

A large group of pronouns are called **indefinite pronouns** because they do not point out particular places, persons, or things.

Somebody took my coat. (*Somebody* is an indefinite pronoun.)

A **few** left the hall early. (*Few* is an indefinite pronoun.)

The following list contains the commonly used indefinite pronouns. Refer to this list, and to the other lists in this unit, whenever you are not sure of the classification of a pronoun.

Commonly Used Indefinite Pronouns

all	everybody	one
any	everyone	one another
anybody	everything	ones
anyone	few	other
anything	many	others
both	neither	several
each	nobody	some
each one	none	somebody
each other	no one	someone
either	nothing	something

RELATIVE PRONOUNS

A **relative pronoun** is a pronoun that joins the clause which it introduces to its own antecedent. The *antecedent* of a pronoun is the noun or pronoun to which it refers. (Clauses will be explained in Units Eighteen, Nineteen, Twenty, and Twenty-one.)

The relative pronouns are *who, which, that,* and *what.* The pronoun *who* has two other forms, *whose* and *whom.* When the relative pronoun is combined with *ever* and *soever,* it is called a **compound relative pronoun.**

List of Compound Relative Pronouns

whoever	whosoever	whichsoever
whomever	whatsoever	whomsoever
whatever	whosesoever	whichever

The *relative pronoun* is always found in a clause which it introduces. For that reason, we shall postpone further study of relative pronouns until we take up the study of subordinate clauses.

Use of Relative Pronouns

The following distinctions are generally observed in the use of relative pronouns. A careful writer or speaker always observes these distinctions:

Who is used when the antecedent is a *person.*

That is used to refer to either *persons* or *things.*

Which is used to refer to anything *except persons.*

The book **which** (or **that**) I was reading has disappeared. (correct)

(*Which* or *that* refers to things.)

She is the girl **who** won the award. (correct)

(*Who* refers only to persons.)

This is the dog **that** (or **which**) was lost. (correct)

(*That* or *which* refers to things.)

She is the girl **that** won the award. (correct)

(*That* may refer to persons.)

Margaret is the girl **which** entered the contest. (incorrect)

(*Which* should not be used to refer to persons.)

EXERCISE 2

Underline the *interrogative, demonstrative,* and *indefinite* **pronouns** in the following sentences. On the line to the right, indicate whether the pronoun is *interrogative, demonstrative,* or *indefinite.*

Example: <u>Whose</u> car will be used?   *interrogative*
....

1. This is the man the officer wants.   1. ....

2. Everybody enjoyed the play immensely.   2. ....

3. What happened at the club meeting?   3. ....

4. That is the best television set.   4. ....

5. Several in the audience left early.   5. ....

6. Whom did you meet in Mexico?   6. ....

7. Neither of the candidates made a speech.   7. ....

8. Those are the ripe apples.   8. ....

9. Nobody saw the accident near the bridge.   9. ....

10. This is our new car.   10. ....

11. Few stayed for the program.   11. ....

12. These are the imported olives.   12. ....

13. Who sat near you at the concert?   13. ....

14. Either is the correct answer.   14. ....

15. Both are good candidates.   15. ....

Note: Check your answers before going on to the next section.

PRONOUNS USED AS ADJECTIVES

The *possessive forms* of the personal pronouns are often used with nouns in much the same way as adjectives are used to modify nouns. Although they function as adjectives when they are placed before the noun, they still retain the idea of possession. For that reason, they are sometimes called **possessive adjectives** to distinguish them from other types of adjectives.

In the sentence, *Herbert forgot his coat,* the possessive form of the pronoun *he,* which is *his,* is used as an adjective modifying the noun *coat.* It also shows that the coat belongs to Herbert. Therefore, it is called a possessive adjective. All the adjectives in the following sentences show possession. They are called possessive adjectives.

Possessive Forms of Personal Pronouns Used as Adjectives

These are **her** gloves. (modifies *gloves*)

I bought **their** home. (modifies *home*)

Did you bring **your** violin? (modifies *violin*)

The dog lost **its** collar. (modifies *collar*)

We like **our** new radio. (modifies *radio*)

Do you like **my** new coat? (modifies *coat*)

The manager has **his** report. (modifies *report*)

Demonstrative and *indefinite pronouns* are also used as adjectives. Demonstrative pronouns that function as adjectives are often called **demonstrative adjectives** because they have not lost their pointing out function. In the following sentences the demonstrative pronouns are used as adjectives:

This camera belongs to Jane. (modifies *camera*)

Those apples are delicious. (modifies *apples*)

That man is an army officer. (modifies *man*)

These cards are Easter cards. (modifies *cards*)

Indefinite pronouns used as adjectives are generally regarded as pure adjectives, although they may be called **indefinite adjectives.** They have no special function. The following examples illustrate their use as adjectives:

Each girl carried a flag. (modifies *girl*)

Both men received a promotion. (modifies *men*)

Neither answer is correct. (modifies *answer*)

Many soldiers were on that ship. (modifies *soldiers*)

Any mechanic could do that job. (modifies *mechanic*)

Several tables were ruined. (modifies *tables*)

Interrogative pronouns are also often used as adjectives. Since the adjective is the word that asks the question, these adjectives are called **interrogative adjectives.** In the sentence, *Which house did you buy?* the word *which* asks the question. It is also an adjective modifying the noun *house*. Note how the pronouns are used to ask questions in the following sentences:

What newspapers does he read? (modifies *newspapers*)

Whose name did he call? (modifies *name*)

Which play do you like best? (modifies *play*)

EXERCISE 3

Underline the **pronouns** used as *adjectives*. On the line to the right indicate the kind of adjective: *possessive, demonstrative, indefinite,* or *interrogative.*

Example: Where is <u>his</u> home?   *possessive*
....

1. This dress is very unusual.   1. ....

2. Have you seen their new car?   2. ....

3. Any artist could paint the picture.   3. ....

4. Those oranges are unusually sweet.   4. ....

5. Whose typewriter are you using?   5. ....

6. Is this my umbrella?   6. ....

7. Our summer cottage is too small.   7. ....

8. The salesman presented his credentials. 8. ....

9. Both decisions were unexpected.   9. ....

10. Few words were spoken at the meeting. 10. ....

11. Did you lose your hat?   11. ....

12. What message did they bring?   12. ....

13. Each ship had an orchestra.   13. ....

14. We took a trip with some friends.   14. ....

15. Two men lost their lives in the wreck. 15. ....

Note: Check your answers before going on to the next section.

POSSESSIVE FORMS OF PRONOUNS

The possessive forms of the *personal pronouns* and the possessive form of the pronoun *who* are never written with an apostrophe. These pronouns have a special form to show possession and do not require an apostrophe. The correct forms to use in order to show possession are the following: *my, mine, yours, his, hers, its, ours, theirs, whose.* Do not place an apostrophe either before or after the **s** in any of these words.

The word *it's* is a contraction of *it is.* It is not a form of the pronoun, and should never be used to show possession. The word *who's* is a contraction of *who is* or *who has,* and should not be confused with the possessive form *whose.*

Contractions

It's on my desk. (*It is* on my desk.)

Who's speaking tonight? (*Who is* speaking tonight?)

Who's finished the test? (*Who has* finished the test?)

Indefinite pronouns do not have special forms to show possession. Therefore, it is necessary to use the apostrophe to show the possessive forms of these pronouns. Since most of these pronouns are used only in the singular, the possessive is formed by adding the *apostrophe* and **s** (**'s**). The plural of the indefinite pronoun *other* is *others.* In the case of this plural form, the apostrophe is placed after the **s.** Study these forms carefully:

Possessive Forms of Indefinite Pronouns

everybody's job	*anyone's* opinions
somebody's hat	*someone's* car
one's relatives	*each one's* duty
another's problems	*others'* affairs (plural)

When *else* is added to an indefinite pronoun, it is regarded as part of the pronoun. In this case, the apostrophe and **s** are added to *else* to form the possessive.

I came home with *somebody else's* coat.

Someone else's book was substituted for mine.

EXERCISE 4

Cross out the incorrect forms of the **pronouns.** Write the correct form above. Make any necessary corrections in the use of **contractions.** If the sentence is correct, write the word *correct* after it.

Example: ~~Your's~~ is like ~~her's~~.

(above: Yours   hers)

1. These pictures are our's.

2. Its evident that you do not know the answer.

3. The car parked in this lot is their's.

4. Whose going to wash the windows?

5. This tree is dead. It's branches are dead.

6. The mouse made its home in the pantry.

7. Everybodys passport was examined.

8. The responsibility was theirs.

9. Who's cap is on the table?

10. We should respect others rights.

11. The speaker outlined everyones duty.

12. Someones purse was left on the aisle seat.

13. That might be anybody's guess.

14. The machine is losing it's force.

15. Whose finished reading the report?

SUMMARY OF GRAMMAR UNIT SIX

1. There are five kinds or classes of pronouns in English: *personal* pronouns, *interrogative* pronouns, *demonstrative* pronouns, *indefinite* pronouns, and *relative* pronouns.

2. **Personal pronouns** indicate by the form whether they refer to the *speaker,* the *person spoken to,* or the *person* or *thing spoken of.*

3. **Interrogative pronouns** ask questions.

4. **Demonstrative pronouns** point out definite persons, places, or things.

5. **Indefinite pronouns** do not refer to definite persons, places, or things.

6. **Relative pronouns** join subordinate clauses to their *antecedents.*

7. Pronouns often function as adjectives. When the personal pronoun functions as an adjective, it is called a **possessive adjective** because it still shows possession. When the demonstrative pronoun functions as an adjective, it is called a **demonstrative adjective** because it still retains the pointing out function.

8. When the interrogative pronoun functions as an adjective, it is still the word that asks the question. For that reason, it is called an **interrogative adjective.** When the indefinite pronoun is used as an adjective, it is generally regarded as a pure adjective, although it may be called an **indefinite adjective.**

9. The *personal pronouns* and the pronoun *who* have special forms to show possession. The following forms, which show possession, are never written with an apostrophe: *yours, theirs, ours, whose, hers, its.* The possessive forms of the indefinite pronouns are formed by adding the apostrophe and **s** (**'s**) in the singular: *anybody's, another's, each one's, everybody's, someone's,* etc.

10. **Contractions** should not be confused with the possessive forms of pronouns. *It's* is a contraction of *it is,* and *who's* is a contraction of *who is* or *who has.* These forms (contractions) should never be used as the possessive forms of pronouns.

SELF-GRADING ASSIGNMENT 1

Directions: Indicate the kind of pronoun on the line to the right: *personal, compound personal, interrogative, demonstrative,* or *indefinite.*

	Kind of Pronoun			Kind of Pronoun
1. some	1.	21. ours	21. ....
2. us	2.	22. yours	22. ....
3. any	3.	23. this	23. ....
4. mine	4.	24. none	24. ....
5. another	5.	25. her	25. ....
6. she	6.	26. his	26. ....
7. yourselves	7.	27. each one	27. ....
8. none	8.	28. anybody	28. ....
9. they	9.	29. Which is new?	29. ....
10. everybody	10.	30. themselves	30. ....
11. theirs	11.	31. him	31. ....
12. Who is here?	12.	32. we	32. ....
13. those	13.	33. many	33. ....
14. them	14.	34. others	34. ....
15. each	15.	35. these	35. ....
16. What did Ray do?	16.	36. Whom did Ted see?	36. ....
17. all	17.	37. my	37. ....
18. myself	18.	38. nobody	38. ....
19. its	19.	39. several	39. ....
20. you	20.	40. it	40. ....

Caution: Check your answers to each assignment with the answer key at the end of this unit before proceeding with the next assignment.

SELF-GRADING ASSIGNMENT 2

Directions: Underline the **pronouns** in the following sentences. On the line to the right indicate the kind of pronoun. If there is more than one pronoun in the sentence, indicate the kinds in the order in which they appear in the sentence.

Example: <u>What</u> did Nan give to <u>him</u>? interrogative—personal

1. Anyone can understand her.   1. ....

2. Who is the man with you?   2. ....

3. What were you saying to them?   3. ....

4. Betty and I help each other.   4. ....

5. Some of the work was done by him.   5. ....

6. Many admire her.   6. ....

7. Whom did they visit in Boston?   7. ....

8. The riveter injured himself.   8. ....

9. He will write it in French.   9. ....

10. None of us went to the stadium.   10. ....

11. Everybody sent a message to him.   11. ....

12. I saw the accident myself.   12. ....

13. She sent a telegram to you.   13. ....

14. Which of them is the elder brother?   14. ....

15. They themselves are responsible.   15. ....

SELF-GRADING ASSIGNMENT 3

Directions: Underline the **pronouns** *used as adjectives*. On the line to the right indicate the kind of adjective: *possessive* adjective, *demonstrative* adjective, *indefinite* adjective, or *interrogative* adjective.

Example: Did she give you her address?   *possessive*

1. John left his coat in the hall.   1. ....

2. Each job is important.   2. ....

3. I purchased those gloves in London.   3. ....

4. Which position do you prefer?   4. ....

5. Many voters expressed their opinions.   5. ....

6. A soldier ranked high in these tests.   6. ....

7. Is this your first lesson in flying?   7. ....

8. Whose plan was accepted?   8. ....

9. Our maps were found on his desk.   9. ....

10. A few answers were correct.   10. ....

11. What magazines does he recommend?   11. ....

12. Both stenographers are efficient.   12. ....

13. I picked up his traveling bag.   13. ....

14. All women should learn to cook.   14. ....

15. Whose story do you believe?   15. ....

SELF-GRADING ASSIGNMENT 4

Directions: Draw a line under the *possessive forms* of the pronouns and under the *contractions* in the following sentences. Cross out the pronouns and contractions that are used incorrectly. Write the correct form above.

               Whose
Example: ~~Who's~~ book is this?

1. Every ship has it's own officers.

2. Its very evident that they need help.

3. Ones friends are often too critical.

4. Try to put yourself in anothers place.

5. That is somebody elses hat.

6. That pin is Jan's. Did you find your's?

7. He doesn't like to pilot anyone elses plane.

8. Who's apartment was sold recently?

9. The dog has injured it's foot.

10. This is my car. That car is their's.

11. Whose going to drive to Texas with you?

12. Everybodys luggage was inspected at the pier.

13. The honor is her's.

14. Its true that he was elected president.

15. We should respect others rights.

PROGRESS TEST SIX

This progress test should not be taken until a day or two after you have completed the assignments. The score you make on the test will then more clearly reflect your understanding of the material in the unit.

Directions: Underline the *pronouns* and the *pronouns used as adjectives* in the following selection on business letters: (*50 points*)

What is the test of a good business letter? There is only one answer to that question. Does it bring about the desired results? If the letter doesn't do that, it is not a good business letter, no matter how carefully it is written, or how carefully it is set up.

How do we write letters that will bring about the results we want? In the first place, our letters must make a good impression on our readers. If the appearance of the letter is pleasing, it will make that kind of an impression from the start. But we must follow up that first impression by stating our ideas clearly and concisely.

One cannot write well about any subject unless he has a clear idea of that subject himself. The writer must think through the subject matter of his letter before he begins to write. He must plan his letter paragraph by paragraph. If he does that, he will be able to write clearly and effectively.

All writers of business letters should be critical of their own writing. They should revise the copy until they are sure the ideas are expressed simply and clearly. The one who reads the letter should have a clear understanding of its contents the first time he reads it.

The writer should always stress the *"YOU"* attitude and not the *"I"* attitude. This means he should stress his reader's point of view and keep his reader's interests in mind. The *"YOU"* attitude is also the courteous attitude —the attitude you need to develop if you want to write letters that influence your readers to action.

ANSWER KEY

for

EXERCISES, ASSIGNMENTS, AND PROGRESS TEST

Grammar Unit Six

CORRECT ANSWERS TO EXERCISE 1

Personal pronouns are printed in **heavy type.**
Compound personal pronouns are printed in *italics.*

1. **They** lived with **her** before **they** lived with **us.**

2. **It** is the smallest house in the block.

3. **She** sat behind **me** at the lecture.

4. John *himself* delivered the message to **us.**

5. **I** am proud of **you** and of **him.**

6. The laundress injured *herself* last week.

7. **They** will be waiting for **us** at the pier.

8. **We** *ourselves* gave the blueprints to **them.**

9. **It** is a beautiful vase. Don't **you** like **it**?

10. **They** *themselves* are the persons to blame for the tragedy.

11. Will **you** mail this package for **her**?

12. **She** and **I** will check the accounts.

13. **He** did not notice where **they** went.

14. **We** deceived *ourselves* when **we** trusted **him.**

15. **You** must do this job *yourself.*

CORRECT ANSWERS TO EXERCISES

EXERCISE 2

Kind of Pronoun

1. This—*demonstrative*
2. Everybody—*indefinite*
3. What—*interrogative*
4. That—*demonstrative*
5. Several—*indefinite*
6. Whom—*interrogative*
7. Neither—*indefinite*
8. Those—*demonstrative*
9. Nobody—*indefinite*
10. This—*demonstrative*
11. Few—*indefinite*
12. These—*demonstrative*
13. Who—*interrogative*
14. Either—*indefinite*
15. Both—*indefinite*

EXERCISE 3

Kind of Adjective

1. This—*demonstrative*
2. their—*possessive*
3. Any—*indefinite*
4. Those—*demonstrative*
5. Whose—*interrogative*
6. my—*possessive*
7. Our—*possessive*
8. his—*possessive*
9. Both—*indefinite*
10. Few—*indefinite*
11. your—*possessive*
12. What—*interrogative*
13. each—*indefinite*
14. some—*indefinite*
15. their—*possessive*

CORRECT ANSWERS TO EXERCISE 4

1. These pictures are **ours.**

2. **It is** (or **It's**) evident that you do not know the the answer.

3. The car parked in this lot is **theirs.**

4. **Who is** (or **Who's**) going to wash the windows?

5. This tree is dead. **Its** branches are dead.

6. The mouse made its home in the pantry. (*correct*)

7. **Everybody's** passport was examined.

8. The responsibility was theirs. (*correct*)

9. **Whose** cap is on the table?

10. We should respect **others'** rights.

11. The speaker outlined **everyone's** duty.

12. **Someone's** purse was left on the aisle seat.

13. That might be anybody's guess. (*correct*)

14. The machine is losing **its** force.

15. **Who has** (or **Who's**) finished reading the report?

CORRECT ANSWERS TO ASSIGNMENT 1

1. indefinite	21. personal
2. personal	22. personal
3. indefinite	23. demonstrative
4. personal	24. indefinite
5. indefinite	25. personal
6. personal	26. personal
7. compound personal	27. indefinite
8. indefinite	28. indefinite
9. personal	29. interrogative
10. indefinite	30. compound personal
11. personal	31. personal
12. interrogative	32. personal
13. demonstrative	33. indefinite
14. personal	34. indefinite
15. indefinite	35. demonstrative
16. interrogative	36. interrogative
17. indefinite	37. personal
18. compound personal	38. indefinite
19. personal	39. indefinite
20. personal	40. personal

CORRECT ANSWERS TO ASSIGNMENT 2

Pronouns	Kinds of Pronouns
1. Anyone—her	1. *indefinite—personal*
2. Who—you	2. *interrogative—personal*
3. What—you—them	3. *interrogative—personal—personal*
4. I—each other	4. *personal—indefinite*
5. Some—him	5. *indefinite—personal*
6. Many—her	6. *indefinite—personal*
7. Whom—they	7. *interrogative—personal*
8. himself	8. *compound personal*
9. He—it	9. *personal—personal*
10. None—us	10. *indefinite—personal*
11. Everybody—him	11. *indefinite—personal*
12. I—myself	12. *personal—compound personal*
13. She—you	13. *personal—personal*
14. Which—them	14. *interrogative—personal*
15. They—themselves	15. *personal—compound personal*

CORRECT ANSWERS TO ASSIGNMENT 3

Pronouns used as adjectives are printed in **heavy type.**

	Kind of Adjective
1. John left **his** coat in the hall.	1. *possessive*
2. **Each** job is important.	2. *indefinite*
3. I purchased **those** gloves in London.	3. *demonstrative*
4. **Which** position do you prefer?	4. *interrogative*
5. **Many** voters expressed **their** opinions.	5. *indefinite—possessive*
6. A soldier ranked high in **these** tests.	6. *demonstrative*
7. Is this **your** first lesson in flying?	7. *possessive*
8. **Whose** plan was accepted?	8. *interrogative*
9. **Our** maps were found on **his** desk.	9. *possessive—possessive*

10. A *few* answers were correct.   10. *indefinite*

11. *What* magazines does he recommend?   11. *interrogative*

12. *Both* stenographers are efficient.   12. *indefinite*

13. I picked up *his* traveling bag.   13. *possessive*

14. *All* women should learn to cook.   14. *indefinite*

15. *Whose* story do you believe?   15. *interrogative*

CORRECT ANSWERS TO ASSIGNMENT 4

Possessive pronouns and contractions are printed in **heavy type.**

1. Every ship has **its** own officers.

2. **It's** (or **It is**) very evident that they need help.

3. **One's** friends are often too critical.

4. Try to put yourself in **another's** place.

5. That is **somebody else's** hat.

6. That pin is Jan's. Did you find **yours**?

7. He doesn't like to pilot **anyone else's** plane.

8. **Whose** apartment was sold recently?

9. The dog has injured **its** foot.

10. This is **my** car. That car is **theirs**.

11. **Who's** (or **Who is**) going to drive to Texas with you?

12. **Everybody's** luggage was inspected at the pier.

13. The honor is **hers**.

14. **It's** (or **It is**) true that he was elected president.

15. We should respect **others'** rights.

CORRECT ANSWERS TO PROGRESS TEST SIX

Pronouns and pronouns used as adjectives are printed in **heavy type.**

What is the test of a good business letter? There is only **one** answer to **that** question. Does **it** bring about the desired results? If the letter doesn't do **that**, **it** is not a good business letter, no matter how carefully **it** is written, or how carefully **it** is set up.

How do **we** write letters **that** will bring about the results **we** want? In the first place, **our** letters must make a good impression on **our** readers. If the appearance of the letter is pleasing, **it** will make **that** kind of an impression from the start. But **we** must follow up **that** first impression by stating **our** ideas clearly and concisely.

One cannot write well about **any** subject unless **he** has a clear idea of **that** subject **himself**. The writer must think through the subject matter of **his** letter before **he** begins to write. **He** must plan **his** letter paragraph by paragraph. If **he** does **that**, **he** will be able to write clearly and effectively.

All writers of business letters should be critical of **their** own writing. **They** should revise the copy until **they** are sure the ideas are expressed simply and clearly. The **one who** reads the letter should have a clear understanding of **its** contents the first time **he** reads **it**.

The writer should always stress the "**YOU**" attitude and not the "**I**" attitude. **This** means **he** should stress **his** reader's point of view and keep **his** reader's interests in mind. The "**YOU**" attitude is also the courteous attitude—the attitude **you** need to develop if **you** want to write letters **that** influence **your** readers to action.

HOW TO OBTAIN YOUR SCORE

The test totals 50 points. To obtain your score, divide the number of your correct answers by 50. The answer will be your score on this test. For example, if you have 45 points correct, your score is 45 divided by 50 which is 90 per cent. In other words, your score on this test is 90. You can obtain your score on any of the exercises or assignments by following the same procedure.

Practical English Grammar

OUTLINE OF UNIT SEVEN

AGREEMENT OF PRONOUN WITH ANTECEDENT

7

AGREEMENT OF PRONOUN WITH ANTECEDENT

Y OU have already learned that a pronoun usually refers to a noun or pronoun which precedes it in the sentence. The word to which the pronoun refers is called its antecedent. The word *antecedent* comes from two Latin words which mean *"going before."* The antecedent of a pronoun is the word which *"goes before"* the pronoun. It is the word to which the pronoun refers.

In the sentence, *Robert lost his fishing tackle,* the pronoun *his* refers to *Robert.* The word *Robert* precedes the pronoun *his* or "goes before" it. *Robert* is the antecedent of *his.* It is the word to which the pronoun *his* refers.

Antecedents of Pronouns

Margaret attended her class reunion. (*Margaret* — antecedent of *her*)

Every day brings its duties. (*day*—antecedent of *its*)

The men brought their golf clubs. (*men*—antecedent of *their*)

Only a few brought their equipment. (*few*—antecedent of *their*)

The professor himself did not know the answer. (*professor*—antecedent of *himself*)

EXERCISE 1

Underline the **pronouns** in the following sentences. Draw two lines under the **antecedents** of the pronouns.

Example: Scott broke his wrist in the accident.

1. Jane left her books in the car.

2. Everyone must sign his name to this document.

3. Have all the carpenters brought their tools?

4. Not one of the men was willing to risk his money.

5. The book is famous for its humor.

6. The president said that he would preside at the meeting.

7. The manager enjoys his responsibilities.

8. You should pay more attention to your mistakes in English.

9. Both candidates gave their reasons for voting against the bill.

10. I employed an architect to plan my house.

11. The doctor injured himself.

12. All the factories show large increases in their outputs.

13. Anne does her work without much effort.

14. Anyone can overcome his prejudices.

15. The band played its fifth concert Saturday.

Note: The correct answers to exercises will be found at the end of this unit. Correct your mistakes and, if necessary, reread the text material before going on to the next section.

AGREEMENT OF PRONOUN AND ANTECEDENT IN GENDER

Since a pronoun stands for, or replaces a noun, it must agree with that noun in person, number, and gender. We have already considered the problems of number and person in Grammar Units Five and Six. In this unit we shall take up the problem of gender, and show its connection with the agreement of pronoun and antecedent.

In grammar **gender** means the classification of nouns and pronouns according to distinctions in sex. There are four genders: *masculine gender, feminine gender, common gender,* and *neuter gender.*

Masculine gender denotes the male sex. **Feminine gender** denotes the female sex. **Common gender** denotes either sex. **Neuter gender** denotes absence of sex. The following are examples of nouns and pronouns in the four genders:

Masculine gender—he, him, father, king

Feminine gender—sister, she, her, princess

Common gender—child, adult, cousin, neighbor

Neuter gender—table, book, dress, radio, it

Some nouns and a few pronouns have special forms to show gender. The following list shows the changes that occur in some words to indicate a change in the gender. Some of the distinctions formerly used to show gender are passing out of use. The words *authoress* and *poetess*, for example, are seldom used.

SPECIAL FORMS TO SHOW GENDER

Masculine	Feminine	Masculine	Feminine
uncle	aunt	god	goddess
bull	cow	aviator	aviatrix
waiter	waitress	hero	heroine

SPECIAL FORMS TO SHOW GENDER (continued)

Masculine	Feminine	Masculine	Feminine
alumnus	alumna	count (title)	countess
emperor	empress	gander	goose
host	hostess	sir	madam
peacock	peahen	ram	ewe
bridegroom	bride	lion	lioness
monk	nun	duke	duchess
actor	actress	nephew	niece
bachelor	spinster	prince	princess
executor	executrix	lord (title)	lady
baron	baroness	stallion	mare
he	she	father	mother
lad	lass	him	her
man	woman	boy	girl
rooster	hen	husband	wife
master	mistress	buck (stag)	doe
brother	sister	landlord	landlady
drake	duck	son	daughter
man-servant	maid-servant	male	female
fiancé	fiancée	salesman	saleswoman

EXERCISE 2

On the lines to the right, indicate the **gender** of each of the following nouns and pronouns:

1. baroness .... 16. manager ....

2. cup .... 17. bravery ....

3. her .... 18. employer ....

4. an American .... 19. him ....

5. bull .... 20. conductor (band) ....

6. radio .... 21. somebody ....

7. friend .... 22. typewriter ....

8. salesman .... 23. niece ....

9. madam .... 24. uncle ....

10. courage .... 25. cow ....

11. lamp .... 26. actress ....

12. bachelor .... 27. companion ....

13. executor .... 28. paper ....

14. hen .... 29. waiter ....

15. goddess .... 30. she ....

GENDER AND NUMBER OF INDEFINITE PRONOUNS

Indefinite pronouns present a problem in gender. These pronouns often refer to both sexes, masculine and feminine. When we say, *Everybody went to the game,* the indefinite pronoun *everybody* includes individuals of both genders, masculine and feminine.

The problem arises when the indefinite pronoun is the antecedent of another pronoun. In that case, the accepted practice is to *use the masculine gender for the pronoun that is used in place of the indefinite pronoun.*

In the sentence, *Everyone received his income tax form,* the indefinite pronoun *everyone* is the antecedent of the pronoun *his.* It is the word to which the pronoun *his* refers. Although *everyone* includes persons of both genders, the masculine pronoun *his* is used instead of saying *his or her* income tax form.

If the sentence shows clearly that the indefinite pronoun refers to members of only one sex, the pronoun that refers to that sex should be used.

Everyone attending the meeting of the Women's Athletic Club presented **her** membership card.

In this sentence the members are women, and the pronoun *her* is used correctly. In cases where it is not clear whether the antecedent is masculine or feminine, use the pronoun *his.*

Anyone may have **his** money refunded..

Somebody left **his** pen on my desk.

Indefinite pronouns also present a problem in number. Some of them are always singular. Some are always plural, and some may be either singular or plural.

Pronouns That Are Always Singular

The following pronouns are always singular. A pronoun that is used in place of one of these indefinite pronouns must also be singular.

anybody	everybody	neither
anyone	everyone	one
another	many a one	other
each	nobody	someone
either	no one	somebody

Study the following illustrations carefully. These sentences show the proper agreement between pronoun and antecedent when the antecedent is singular.

Neither of the men had **his** tools. (not *their*)

If **anyone** wants a pen, **he** can obtain one here. (not *they*)

One likes to do what **he** can do well. (not *they*)

Someone left **his** coat in **his** locker. (not *their*)

Pronouns That Are Always Plural

The following pronouns are always plural. A pronoun that is used in place of one of them must also be plural.

many   both   few   several   others

Notice that *many a one* is included in the list of pronouns that are always singular, whereas *many* is included in this plural list. When singular expressions, such as *a man, a one, a person,* etc. are added to *many,* the pronoun is singular, not plural.

Several found **their** cars unlocked. (*Several*—plural)

Only a **few** would sacrifice **their** savings. (*few*—plural)

Many brought **their** lunches with them. (*Many*—plural)

Others found **their** friends in the balcony. (*Others*—plural)

Pronouns That May Be Either Singular or Plural

The pronouns *all, any, some,* and *none* are singular or plural according to the meaning of the sentence. When these pronouns refer to **number,** they are generally regarded as plural. When they refer to **quantity** or to a **mass,** they are regarded as singular.

The pronoun *none* is singular when it clearly means *no one,* or *not one.* It is often difficult to determine the number of this pronoun since there are sentences in which it carries a plural idea. If you want to express the singular idea use *no one,* or *not one.*

Some found **their** children in the park. (*Some* is plural.)

Some of the candy has lost **its** flavor. (*Some* is singular.)

All were waiting for **their** salary checks. (*All* is plural.)

There is no candy in the box. **All** of **it** has been eaten. (*All* is singular.)

Did **any** of the men have **their** membership cards? (*Any* is plural.)

None have arrived. (*None*—plural in use)

None of these is a typical example. (*None*—singular in use)

EXERCISE 3

Cross out the incorrect form of the pronoun in parentheses. On the line to the right, indicate whether the *singular* or the *plural* form is required in the sentence.

Example: Both bought (his, their) hats today.   *plural*

1. Some did not present (his, their) credentials.   1. ....

2. Each one has been assigned to (his, their) job.   2. ....

3. Neither of the girls brought (her, their) sewing.   3. ....

4. Few knew the reasons for (his, their) failures.   4. ....

5. Has someone failed to do (his, their) duty?   5. ....

6. Are any of the employees going on (his, their) vacations?   6. ....

7. All were waiting for (his, their) families.   7. ....

8. Many of the girls furnished (her, their) own costumes.   8. ....

9. Has either of the women lost (her, their) suitcase?   9. ....

10. Anyone can find (his, their) place in the world.   10. ....

11. One of the guests left (his, their) hat.   11. ....

12. Not one of the men finished (his, their) work.   12. ....

13. Several seemed to like (his, their) assignments.   13. ....

14. Some were willing to give up (his, their) leisure time.   14. ....

15. All found (his, their) places at the stadium.   15. ....

AGREEMENT OF THE PRONOUN
WITH A COMPOUND ANTECEDENT

Sometimes the pronoun refers to two antecedents connected by *and*. If both of these antecedents are singular and refer to *different persons or things,* the antecedent is plural. The pronoun that refers to these antecedents must also be plural.

The president and the manager have outlined their plans.
plural   plural

If the antecedent refers to *one* person who fulfills *two* functions, the pronoun that takes the place of the antecedent is singular. In the following sentence *cook* and *housekeeper* are the same person.

The cook and housekeeper did not like her duties.
singular   singular

If the housekeeper were another individual, the word *the* would be placed before the word *housekeeper.*

The cook and the housekeeper did not like their duties.
plural   plural

When the connectives, *either—or* and *neither—nor* join singular nouns, the antecedent is singular. When they join plural nouns, the antecedent is plural. When they join nouns that differ in number, the pronoun should agree with the antecedent that is nearer to it.

Either *Jane* or *Alice* left **her** book on **her** desk.
(Both nouns are singular—pronoun is singular)

Either the *boys* or the *girls* left **their** books on the table.
(Both nouns are plural—pronoun is plural)

Neither *Harvey* nor his *cousins* wore **their** dress suits.
(Pronoun is plural—agrees with *cousins*)

Neither the *men* nor the *boy* could find **his** place in the line.
(Pronoun agrees with *boy* which is nearer to it.)

In sentences like the last one, it is better to place the plural noun nearer to the pronoun. By doing so, you make the antecedent plural, and the sentence sounds better.

AGREEMENT OF PRONOUN WITH COLLECTIVE NOUNS

Collective nouns are singular when they designate a group *acting as a unit*. They are plural when the members who make up the group are *acting independently*. The pronoun that takes the place of the collective noun must agree with it in number. If the collective noun expresses a singular idea, the pronoun is singular. If the collective noun expresses a plural idea, the pronoun is plural.

The band played its fifth concert. (*acting as a unit*)
  singular   singular

The band were tuning up their instruments. (*as individuals*)
  plural   plural

You can readily see that the second sentence could not refer to the band as a unit. That would mean that the members of the band were all working on the same instrument.

EXERCISE 4

Correct the errors in the use of **pronouns** that refer to antecedents. Cross out the incorrect form and write the correct form above it. Two of the sentences are correct.

1. Neither of the speakers could make themselves popular.

2. Neither the man nor the boy had their birth certificate.

3. The committee sent their report to the president.

4. The band is celebrating its fifth season.

5. The choir were instructed to bring its books.

6. The jury rendered their verdict.

7. Neither my mother nor my aunts will sell her stock.

8. The secretary and treasurer has presented his report.

9. Either Beth or Louise will donate their books to the library.

10. The army has made their first attack.

11. The audience left for its respective homes.

12. Neither Lowell nor Thomas has finished their work.

13. Either John or Fred will bring their television set.

14. The corporation has improved the working conditions of their employees.

15. The city should solve their transportation problem.

AGREEMENT OF PRONOUN AND ANTECEDENT IN PERSON

A pronoun must agree with its antecedent in **person.** If the antecedent of the pronoun is in the *third person,* the pronoun that refers to it must also be in the *third person.* If the antecedent is in the *second person,* the pronoun should be in the *second person.*

One of the most common mistakes in English is to start the sentence in the *third person* and then put the pronoun that refers to the antecedent in the *second person.* Study the following examples carefully:

If <u>anybody</u> wants an education, <u>you</u> can get it. (*incorrect*)
third person   second person

If <u>anybody</u> wants an education, <u>he</u> can get it. (*correct*)
third person   third person

When <u>one</u> pays attention, <u>you</u> learn better. (*incorrect*)
third person   second person

When <u>one</u> pays attention, <u>he</u> (or *one*) learns better. (*correct*)
third person   third person

VAGUE ANTECEDENTS

A pronoun should not have two possible antecedents in the same sentence. If it is not clear which of two nouns a pronoun refers to, there will be two possible interpretations of the sentence. Observe the two possible interpretations in the following illustration:

James told his friend that **he** had been elected president.

In this sentence, does the pronoun *he* refer to *James* or to *friend?* If the antecedent of the pronoun *he* is *friend,* the sentence means that *James told his friend that he (the friend) had been elected president.*

If the antecedent of the pronoun *he* is *James,* the sentence means that *James told his friend that he (James) had been elected president.*

The sentence might be rewritten in either of the two following ways, since we do not know which meaning the author intended:

James said to his friend, "You have been elected president."

James said to his friend, "I have been elected president."

Many of the errors that are made in the use of pronouns are caused by a lack of agreement between pronoun and antecedent. The pronoun should refer definitely to the noun which it represents. In the following sentence, to what does the pronoun *it* refer?

Your letter and your check arrived promptly, but we cannot ship *it* at present.

There is no antecedent for the pronoun *it* in the sentence. Neither the word *letter* nor the word *check* could be the antecedent. *It* probably refers to an order for goods which was included in the letter. If the word *it* refers to an order for goods, the sentence might be written as follows:

Your letter and your check arrived promptly, but at present we cannot ship the goods ordered.

EXERCISE 5

Correct the errors in the use of **pronouns** and **antecedents** in the following sentences. Rewrite the sentences correctly. If there are two possible interpretations, write both.

1. If one is nervous, you should try to relax.

2. When Father called the policeman, he was very angry.

3. Henry took the money from his wallet and put it in his pocket.

4. Susan asked Jane if she had been promoted.

5. When you receive a legal document, one should read it carefully.

6. Harvey's brother was married when he was six years old.

7. If one wants to become a good tennis player, you should practice constantly.

8. The teacher expects every girl to make your own dresses.

9. Has everyone handed in your paper?

10. Someone will win the prize if you can solve the puzzle.

11. Every worker must furnish their own equipment.

12. Has anyone forgotten their membership card?

ADJECTIVE—PRONOUN AGREEMENT

Demonstrative adjectives should agree in *number* with the nouns they modify. The adjectives *this, that, these,* and *those* sometimes cause agreement trouble when they modify such nouns as *kind, sort, type,* and *variety.*

Keep in mind that the demonstrative adjectives *this* and *that* are singular and should be used only with singular nouns. *These* and *those* are plural and should be used only with the plural nouns.

Incorrect	Correct
these kind of apples plural singular	**this kind** of apples (or apple) or **these kinds** of apples (plural)
those sort of roses plural singular	**that sort** of roses (or rose) or **those sorts** of roses (plural)
these variety of fruits plural singular	**this variety** of fruits (or fruit) or **these varieties** of fruits (plural)

The forms on the left are incorrect because the adjective does not agree with the noun in number. In the first illustration, the adjective *these* is plural and the noun *kind* is singular. In the second illustration, the adjective *those* is plural and the noun *sort* is singular.

The forms on the right are correct because the adjective agrees with the noun in number. In the first illustration, *this* is singular and *kind* is singular; *these* is plural and *kinds* is plural. The other illustrations on the right are correct for the same reasons.

EXERCISE 6

Cross out the incorrect form of the **demonstrative adjective** in parentheses.

1. Have you any of (these, this) kinds of oranges?

2. We have only (that, those) kinds.

3. I selected (this, these) kind of hat.

4. Do you want (this, these) or (that, those) type of eraser?

5. We recommend (this, these) kinds.

6. I prefer (this, these) kind of writing paper.

7. This shop carries only (that, those) varieties of flowers.

8. (That, Those) sort of rose is very beautiful.

9. Every woman will bring (that, those) kind of cake.

10. Martha prefers (that, those) kinds of cookies.

11. He did not order (those, that) kind of nails.

12. (That, Those) sort of gossip should be ignored.

13. (These, This) kind of music will always be popular.

14. We should disregard (those, that) kinds of rumors.

15. (These, This) types of errors in speech should be corrected.

SUMMARY OF GRAMMAR UNIT SEVEN

1. The **antecedent** of a pronoun is the noun or the pronoun to which it refers.

2. A pronoun must agree with its antecedent in **gender, person,** and **number.**

3. If the antecedent of a pronoun is **masculine gender,** the pronoun that refers to it must be masculine gender. If the antecedent is the **feminine gender,** the pronoun must be the feminine gender.

4. **Indefinite pronouns** usually refer to individuals of both genders, masculine and feminine. In such cases, the general practice is to use the *masculine form* of the pronoun that refers to the antecedent.

5. Some *indefinite pronouns* are always singular in number, others are always plural, and some are either singular or plural according to the meaning of the sentence. The pronoun that is used to refer to the antecedent must agree with it in **number.** If the indefinite pronoun is singular, the pronoun that refers to it must be singular. If the indefinite pronoun is plural, the pronoun that refers to it must be plural.

6. The pronoun must agree with its antecedent in **person.** If the antecedent is in the *third person,* the pronoun that refers to it must also be in the *third person.* If the antecedent is in the *second person,* the pronoun that refers to it must be in the *second person.*

7. A pronoun should not have two possible antecedents in the same sentence. If it is not clear which of the two antecedents the pronoun refers to, the sentence should be recast.

8. **Demonstrative adjectives** should agree in number with the nouns they modify. *This* and *that* are singular and should be used only with singular nouns. *These* and *those* are plural and should be used with plural nouns.

SELF-GRADING ASSIGNMENT 1

Directions: On the line to the right, indicate which of the forms in parentheses is the correct form to use in the sentence.

Example: Somebody has lost (his, their) house keys. **his**
....

1. Each of the men brought (his, their) tools. 1. ....
2. The town built a memorial to (its, their) war veterans. 2. ....
3. Every one of the clerks has done (her, their) work well. 3. ....
4. If either is guilty, (he, they) must pay a fine. 4. ....
5. If anyone comes, tell (him, them) to wait for me. 5. ....
6. A person shouldn't talk about (himself, themselves). 6. ....
7. If any girl wants the position, (she, they) should see Miss Smith. 7. ....
8. Every landlord paid (his, their) taxes. 8. ....
9. Neither presented (his, their) arguments clearly. 9. ....
10. Both brought (their, his) application blanks. 10. ....
11. All were in (their, his) proper places. 11. ....
12. Every girl will be given a blank form which (they, she) must fill out. 12. ....
13. Either Susan or Alice will give (her, their) services next Saturday. 13. ....
14. The board of directors will hold (its, their) meeting next Thursday. 14. ....
15. Every dealer understands that (he, they) can get goods on credit. 15. ....

Caution: Check your answers to each assignment with the answer key at the end of this unit before proceeding with the next assignment.

SELF-GRADING ASSIGNMENT 2

Directions: Cross out the **pronoun** that is used incorrectly and write the correct form of the pronoun or the correct word above it.

Example: Don't judge a person by ~~their~~ his clothes.

1. Neither Alice nor Elizabeth finished their tasks.

2. If you cannot speak well, one should not speak in public.

3. If one prefers to pay in advance, you may send a check.

4. Harry's father received a commission when he was two years old.

5. Anyone who wants their check may have it today.

6. Neither the foreman nor the workmen furnished his own tools.

7. Each of the designs had their weak points.

8. One cannot do their best work when he is tired.

9. Her secretary and companion sent in their resignation.

10. The writer and the producer gave his criticisms of the play.

11. Everyone said that they would support the project.

12. The alumni of the college will do its part in the drive.

13. Before a boy enters college, you should know the requirements.

14. If anyone wishes to do it, they may open a charge account.

15. Each one of the saleswomen knows that they will work on a salary basis.

SELF-GRADING ASSIGNMENT 3

Directions: In the first column, indicate whether the **collective noun** is *singular* or *plural* in meaning. In the second column, give the correct form of the pronoun that refers to the collective noun. Three sentences are correct.

	Singular or Plural	Correct Form of Pronoun
1. The Marine Corps is proud of their achievements.	1.	....
2. The football team finished their third season.	2.	....
3. The choir passed to its seats.	3.	....
4. The Drama Club will hold their meeting tomorrow.	4.	....
5. The audience rose to its feet.	5.	....
6. The troop were polishing its boots.	6.	....
7. Every race has their prominent members.	7.	....
8. The jury returned to their homes.	8.	....
9. The orchestra had their final rehearsal.	9.	....
10. The choir opened its books.	10.	....
11. The committee decided what to do with their funds.	11.	....
12. This community provides playgrounds for their children.	12.	....
13. The boat crew put their oars in the lockers provided for them.	13.	....
14. The corporation voted to increase their capital stock.	14.	....
15. The company is ready to move into its new building.	15.	....

PROGRESS TEST SEVEN

This progress test should not be taken until a day or two after you have completed the assignments. The score you make on the test will then more clearly reflect your understanding of the material in the unit.

Directions: Rewrite the following sentences making any corrections that are necessary in the use of pronouns. If the sentence is correct, write the word *correct* after it.   (*35 points*)

1. That employer is always concerned about the health of their employees.

2. If anyone does not like the plan, let them say so.

3. Neither the bookkeeper nor the auditor will have their report ready.

4. If a person studies hard, they will probably succeed.

5. The team received its football uniforms today.

6. Everybody should know the number of their license plate.

7. The choir opened its books.

8. Each was sure they would be the winner.

9. When one makes a mistake, you should be willing to correct it.

10. Several saleswomen left their samples in the hotel.

11. He always wears those kind of necktie, and those kind of shoes.

12. John's uncle became an ambassador when he was six years old.

13. Some of the rubber has lost their elasticity.

PROGRESS TEST SEVEN (continued)

14. The club has already moved into their new home.

15. The Navy planned their first attack.

16. Our cook and housekeeper left her money on the kitchen table.

17. Who has not paid their monthly dues?

18. Some of the candy has lost their flavor.

19. Each tenant paid their rent promptly.

20. One should always have some money in your pocket.

21. Every bystander held their breath.

22. Both were so exhausted that he could not find his way home.

23. These variety of orchids and those variety of lilies are rare.

24. The office force have been notified about its vacation dates.

25. Nobody signed their name to the petition.

26. Many a man owes his success to hard work.

27. Both the book and the motion picture had its weak points.

28. A person never does their best when they are in a hurry.

29. The members of the audience remained in its seats.

30. One can't do their best work when you are tired.

ANSWER KEY

for

EXERCISES, ASSIGNMENTS, AND PROGRESS TEST

Grammar Unit Seven

CORRECT ANSWERS TO EXERCISE 1

1. Jane left her books in the car.

2. Everyone must sign his name to this document.

3. Have all the carpenters brought their tools?

4. Not one of the men was willing to risk his money.

5. The book is famous for its humor.

6. The president said that he would preside at the meeting.

7. The manager enjoys his responsibilities.

8. You should pay more attention to your mistakes in English.

9. Both candidates gave their reasons for voting against the bill.

10. I employed an architect to plan my house.

11. The doctor injured himself.

12. All the factories show large increases in their outputs.

13. Anne does her work without much effort.

14. Anyone can overcome his prejudices.

15. The band played its fifth concert Saturday.

CORRECT ANSWERS TO EXERCISE 2

1. feminine	16. common
2. neuter	17. neuter
3. feminine	18. common
4. common	19. masculine
5. masculine	20. common
6. neuter	21. common
7. common	22. neuter
8. masculine	23. feminine
9. feminine	24. masculine
10. neuter	25. feminine
11. neuter	26. feminine
12. masculine	27. common
13. masculine	28. neuter
14. feminine	29. masculine
15. feminine	30. feminine

CORRECT ANSWERS TO EXERCISE 3

Correct pronouns are printed in **heavy type.**

1. Some did not present **their** credentials.   1. *plural*

2. Each one has been assigned to **his** job.   2. *singular*

3. Neither of the girls brought **her** sewing.   3. *singular*

4. Few knew the reasons for **their** failures.   4. *plural*

5. Has someone failed to do **his** duty?   5. *singular*

6. Are any of the employees going on **their** vacations?   6. *plural*

7. All were waiting for **their** families.   7. *plural*

8. Many of the girls furnished **their** own costumes.   8. *plural*

9. Has either of the women lost **her** suitcase?   9. *singular*

10. Anyone can find **his** place in the world.   10. *singular*

11. One of the guests left **his** hat.	11. *singular*
12. Not one of the men finished **his** work.	12. *singular*
13. Several seemed to like **their** assignments.	13. *plural*
14. Some were willing to give up **their** leisure time.	14. *plural*
15. All found **their** places at the stadium.	15. *plural*

CORRECT ANSWERS TO EXERCISE 4

Correct pronouns are printed in **heavy type.**

1. Neither of the speakers could make **himself** popular.
2. Neither the man nor the boy had **his** birth certificate.
3. The committee sent **its** report to the president.
4. The band is celebrating **its** fifth season. (*correct*)
5. The choir were instructed to bring **their** books.
6. The jury rendered **its** verdict.
7. Neither my mother nor my aunts will sell **their** stock.
8. The secretary and treasurer has presented **his** report. (*correct*)
9. Either Beth or Louise will donate **her** books to the library.
10. The army has made **its** first attack.
11. The audience left for **their** respective homes.
12. Neither Lowell nor Thomas has finished **his** work.
13. Either John or Fred will bring **his** television set.
14. The corporation has improved the working conditions of **its** employees.
15. The city should solve **its** transportation problem.

CORRECT ANSWERS TO EXERCISE 5

1. If one is nervous, **he** (or **one**) should try to relax.
2. When Father called the policeman, the **policeman** was very angry.
   or
   When Father called the policeman, **Father** was very angry.
3. Henry took the money from his wallet and put the **wallet** in his pocket.
   or
   Henry took the money from his wallet and put the **money** in his pocket.

4. Susan said to Jane, "Have **you** been promoted?"
   or
   Susan said to Jane, "Have **I** been promoted?"

5. When you receive a legal document, **you** should read it carefully.

6. Harvey's brother was married when **Harvey** was six years old.

7. If one wants to become a good tennis player, **he** (or **one**) should practice constantly.

8. The teacher expects every girl to make **her** own dresses.

9. Has everyone handed in **his** paper?

10. Someone will win the prize if **he** can solve the puzzle.

11. Every worker must furnish **his** own equipment.

12. Has anyone forgotten **his** membership card?

CORRECT ANSWERS TO EXERCISE 6

1. Have you any of **these kinds** of oranges?

2. We have only **those kinds.**

3. I selected **this kind** of hat.

4. Do you want **this** or **that type** of eraser?

5. We recommend **these kinds.**

6. I prefer **this kind** of writing paper.

7. This shop carries only **those varieties** of flowers.

8. **That sort** of rose is very beautiful.

9. Every woman will bring **that kind** of cake.

10. Martha prefers **those kinds** of cookies.

11. He did not order **that kind** of nails.

12. **That sort** of gossip should be ignored.

13. **This kind** of music will always be popular.

14. We should disregard **those kinds** of rumors.

15. **These types** of errors in speech should be corrected.

CORRECT ANSWERS TO ASSIGNMENT 1

1. his
2. its
3. her
4. he
5. him
6. himself
7. she
8. his
9. his
10. their
11. their
12. she
13. her
14. its
15. he

CORRECT ANSWERS TO ASSIGNMENT 2

1. her
2. you
3. he or one
4. Harry
5. his
6. their
7. its
8. his
9. her
10. their
11. he
12. their (as individuals)
13. he
14. he
15. she

CORRECT ANSWERS TO ASSIGNMENT 3

Singular or Plural in Meaning	Correct Form of Pronoun
1. Marine Corps—*singular*	1. its
2. team—*singular*	2. its
3. choir—*plural*	3. their
4. Drama Club—*singular*	4. its
5. audience—*plural*	5. their
6. troop—*plural*	6. their
7. race—*singular*	7. its

8. jury—*plural* (correct)   8. their—*correct*

9. orchestra—*singular*   9. its

10. choir—*plural*   10. their

11. committee—*singular*   11. its

12. community—*singular*   12. its

13. crew—*plural* (correct)   13. their—*correct*

14. corporation—*singular*   14. its

15. company—*singular* (correct)   15. its—*correct*

CORRECT ANSWERS TO PROGRESS TEST SEVEN

1. That employer is always concerned about the health of **his** employees.

2. If anyone does not like the plan, let **him** say so.

3. Neither the bookkeeper nor the auditor will have **his** report ready.

4. If a person studies hard, **he** will probably succeed.

5. The team received **their** football uniforms today.

6. Everybody should know the number of **his** license plate.

7. The choir opened **their** books.

8. Each was sure that **he** would be the winner.

9. When one makes a mistake, **he** (or **one**) should be willing to correct it.

10. Several saleswomen left **their** samples in the hotel. (*correct*)

11. He always wears **that** kind of necktie, and **that** kind of shoes.

12. John's uncle became an ambassador when **John** was six years old.

13. Some of the rubber has lost **its** elasticity.

14. The club has already moved into **its** new home.

15. The Navy planned **its** first attack.

16. Our cook and housekeeper left **her** money on the kitchen table. (*correct*)

CORRECT ANSWERS TO PROGRESS TEST SEVEN (continued)

17. Who has not paid *his* monthly dues?

18. Some of the candy has lost *its* flavor.

19. Each tenant paid *his* rent promptly.

20. One should always have some money in *his* (or *one's*) pocket.

21. Every bystander held *his* breath.

22. Both were so exhausted that *they* could not find *their* way home.

23. *This* variety of orchids and *that* variety of lilies are rare.

24. The office force have been notified about *their* vacation dates.

25. Nobody signed *his* name to the petition.

26. Many a man owes *his* success to hard work. (*correct*)

27. Both the book and the motion picture had *their* weak points.

28. A person never does *his* best when *he* is in a hurry.

29. The members of the audience remained in *their* seats.

30. One can't do *his* best work when *he* (or *one*) is tired.

HOW TO OBTAIN YOUR SCORE

The test totals 35 points. To obtain your score, divide the number of your correct answers by 35. The answer will be your score on this test. For example, if you have 32 points correct, your score is 32 divided by 35 which is 91 per cent. In other words, your score on this test is 91. You can obtain your score on any of the exercises or assignments by following the same procedure.

Practical English Grammar

OUTLINE OF UNIT EIGHT

COMPLEMENTS OF VERBS

COMPLEMENTS OF VERBS

THE DIRECT OBJECT

YOU have learned that every sentence must have a basic structure in order to express a complete thought. This basic structure may consist of only two parts, a subject noun or pronoun and a predicate verb or verb phrase. Many sentences require a third part or an additional word in order to express a complete thought. This additional word or group of words is necessary to complete the idea expressed by the verb.

The group of words, *The men lifted,* contains a subject noun *men* and a predicate verb *lifted.* Still it does not express a complete thought. A word is needed to tell **what** the men lifted. The sentence might be completed by adding the word *beam.* The completed sentence, *The men lifted the beam,* expresses a complete thought.

The word *beam* completes the meaning expressed by the verb *lifted.* For that reason it is called a **complement** or a completing word. The three essential parts of this sentence are the **subject,** the **verb,** and the **complement.** The complement is *beam.*

A complement completes the meaning expressed by a verb. The *complement* of a verb that expresses *action* is called the **direct object** of the verb. A direct object usually answers the questions *what?* or *whom?* In the preceding sentence the verb *lifted* expresses action. The complement *beam* tells *what* the men lifted. Notice how the complements in the following sentences complete the meaning of the verb.

I saw Evelyn at the convention. (*Evelyn* tells whom I saw.)
direct object

The engineer stopped the train. (*Train* tells what he stopped.)
direct object

The sailors saluted the captain. (tells *whom* they saluted)
direct object

She refused the invitation. (tells *what* she refused)
direct object

Some verbs that express action are complete without the addition of a complement. When such verbs are used in sentences, only two parts are essential—the *subject* and the *verb*. Study the following illustrations. You will readily see that the thought is complete without the addition of a complement.

Jane is singing. (*complete thought*)

The whistles are blowing. (*complete thought*)

We have been studying. (*complete thought*)

The boys are playing. (*complete thought*)

Although the verbs in the preceding sentences do not require a complement or a completing word, a complement might be added to some of them to make the meaning more explicit.

Jane is singing a ballad. (tells *what* Jane is singing)

direct object

We have been studying Spanish. (tells *what* we have been studying)

direct object

The boys are playing games. (tells *what* the boys are playing)

direct object

A complement completes the meaning of the verb.

The **direct object** of a verb names the *receiver* of the action. It completes the meaning of the verb. A direct object is usually a noun or a pronoun. Adjectives and adverbs are never used as direct objects. Adjectives and adverbs are always used as modifiers. If you have any difficulty in deciding which word is the direct object, apply this test: Find the word that answers the question *what?* or *whom?* Apply the test in the following sentences:

The farmer planted the **seeds** in rows.

What did the farmer plant? The answer is, "He planted the *seeds.*" The word *seeds* is the direct object of the verb planted. It tells **what** he planted.

I met **Uncle Henry** in the bank.

Whom did I meet? The answer is, "I met Uncle Henry." The direct object is *Uncle Henry.* It tells **whom** I met.

A verb may take two or more direct objects. In this case, the verb or verb phrase has a compound object.

He grows <u>orchids</u> and <u>lilies</u> in his garden.
        compound object

I met <u>Jerry</u> and <u>Jane</u> at the stadium.
      compound object

EXERCISE 1

Draw a line under the **subject,** the **verb,** and the **direct object** in each of the following sentences. Write **s.** under the subject, **v.** under the verb, **v.ph.** under a verb phrase, and **d.o.** under the direct object.

Example: James won the diving contest.
            s.   v.   d.o.

1. The firm is installing a new pump.

2. Add the figures correctly.

3. The janitor washed the windows.

4. Donald plays golf every Saturday.

5. That agent sells books and magazines.

6. Harvey repaired the typewriters.

7. I know the conductor of the orchestra.

8. The company purchased several duplicating machines.

9. The officer stopped the traffic.

10. Place the reports on the manager's desk.

11. The hurricane destroyed the crops and the fruit trees.

12. Did you find your watch?

13. The gardener planted pines and elms in front of the house.

14. The guide followed the bank of the stream.

15. We shall fill your order promptly.

Note: The correct answers to exercises will be found at the end of this unit. Correct your mistakes and, if necessary, reread the text material before going on to the next section.

TRANSITIVE AND INTRANSITIVE VERBS

When an action verb takes a direct object, it is called a **transitive verb.** The word *transitive* comes from two Latin words which mean *"passing across."* When the verb is transitive, the action passes across from a **doer** (the subject) to a **receiver** of the action (the direct object). When we say that a verb is *transitive,* it is the same as saying that it has a *direct object.*

Any verb that does not take a direct object is **intransitive.** That is, the verb does *not* express action that passes over to a receiver.

A verb may be transitive in one sentence and intransitive in another sentence. The verb may express action, but the action may not pass over to a receiver. In that case the verb is intransitive. When the verb is transitive, it always takes a direct object—the receiver of the action.

The following sentences show the same verb used as a *transitive* verb and as an *intransitive* verb:

Transitive	Intransitive
The sexton rang the <u>bell.</u> direct object	The bell rang loudly. (*no object*)
The ship sailed the <u>seas.</u> direct object	The ship sails at noon. (*no object*)
I met my <u>friend</u> at the airport. direct object	The delegates met yesterday. (*no object*)
The soldier saluted the <u>colonel.</u> direct object	The soldier saluted. (*no object*)

A transitive verb is a verb that takes an object.

An intransitive verb is a verb that does not take an object.

EXERCISE 2

Write **d.o.** under the direct objects in the following sentences. On the line to the right, indicate whether the verb is *transitive* or *intransitive*. Some of the verbs do not have direct objects.

Transitive or Intransitive

1. The crowd cheered the President. 1. ....

2. The snow has been falling. 2. ....

3. Two policemen were standing on the corner. 3. ....

4. Every actor played his part well. 4. ....

5. We bought these books at a sale. 5. ....

6. The horse has been running around the track. 6. ....

7. We sent food to the famine-stricken people. 7. ....

8. The men were protesting loudly. 8. ....

9. He rolled himself in a blanket. 9. ....

10. The ball rolled slowly over the carpet. 10. ....

11. The people in the grandstand shouted. 11. ....

12. The agent negotiated a sale of the property. 12. ....

13. The detective solved the mystery. 13. ....

14. The bird flew over the treetops. 14. ....

15. A water lily floated on the pond. 15. ....

THE INDIRECT OBJECT

Some verbs that express action take two objects, a direct object and an indirect object. The **indirect object** tells *to whom* the action is directed or *for whom* the action is performed.

The indirect object is used after certain verbs: *get, give, lend, offer, read, tell, buy, send, show, make, pay,* etc.

In the sentence, *Mother bought Ellen a coat,* there are two objects, a direct object and an indirect object. The word *coat* is the direct *object.* It tells *what* Mother bought. The word *Ellen* is the indirect object. It tells *for whom* Mother bought a coat. The indirect object always precedes or comes before the direct object.

The librarian read the <u>children</u> a <u>story.</u>
                           indirect   direct

Give <u>him</u> five <u>dollars</u> for his services.
     indirect   direct

The tailor made <u>Edward</u> a brown <u>suit.</u>
              indirect   direct

There are two tests that you can apply in order to identify an indirect object. One test is to determine the position of the object. The indirect object always precedes the direct object. The other test is to determine whether the indirect object seems to be the object of the preposition *to* or *for* understood. The following sentences illustrate this point:

The librarian read (**to**) the children a story.

Give (**to**) him five dollars for his services.

The tailor made (**for**) Edward a brown suit.

The words *to* and *for* are never expressed when a word functions as an indirect object. If we change the order of the sentence and supply the preposition, our sentence would read as follows: *The librarian read a story to the children.* In this sentence the word *children* is no longer the indirect object but is the object of the preposition *to.*

EXERCISE 3

Underline the **indirect objects** with one line and the **direct objects** with two lines in the following sentences. Some of the verbs do not have indirect objects. Write **d.o.** under the direct objects and **i.o.** under the indirect objects.

Example: Martha brought us some sandwiches.
                             i.o.   d.o.

1. Uncle Ned gave me his camera.

2. The guide showed them a short cut through the woods.

3. I have lost my umbrella.

4. The motorist offered the boys a ride.

5. Show the guests the way to the garden.

6. I made myself a winter coat.

7. John sent Margaret two beautiful orchids.

8. The Indian handed Irwin a sharp knife.

9. The bird flies over the building.

10. The janitor took the key from the tenant.

11. They sent us an order for some cotton goods.

12. The speaker gave us a new picture of world conditions.

13. The firm offered Bruce an important position.

14. The magician taught them some new tricks.

15. The president granted Mr. Allen an interview.

DIAGRAMMING THE DIRECT OBJECT
AND THE INDIRECT OBJECT

In diagramming, you always should start with the base line on which you place the subject and the predicate verb. The direct object follows the verb and is placed on the base line. A vertical line is drawn to separate the verb from the direct object.

Modifiers are placed on slanted lines. Adjectives and adverbs are modifiers and are always placed on slanted lines. The slanted lines are joined to the word which the adjective or the adverb modifies.

Diagram Showing the Direct Object

Sentence: The gardener planted two trees.
direct object

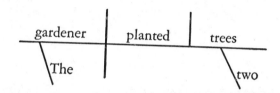

The indirect object is diagrammed on a horizontal line which is placed beneath the verb it modifies. The horizontal line is attached to the verb by means of a slanting line.

Diagram Showing the Indirect Object

Sentence: Fred wrote Father a letter. (*Letter* is the direct object.)
indirect object

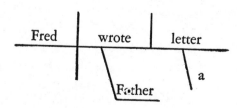

COMPOUND INDIRECT AND DIRECT OBJECTS

Diagram—Compound Indirect Object

In the following sentence, the verb *gave* takes two indirect objects—the noun *Ned* and the pronoun *me*. The verb also takes a direct object, which is the noun *tools*.

Sentence: The carpenter gave Ned and me his tools.

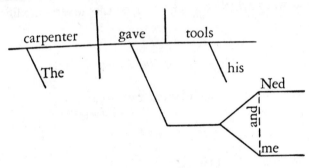

Diagram—Compound Direct Object

In the following sentence, the verb *planted* takes two direct objects—the nouns *trees* and *bushes*. The direct object is compound.

Sentence: We planted trees and bushes.

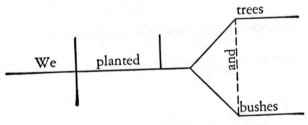

EXERCISE 4

Diagram the following sentences showing the **direct object** and the **indirect object**.

1. Father gave William a small radio.

2. We mailed you a statement.

3. The janitor will give Herbert the key.

4. Arnold painted the porch.

5. The firm gave us a large order.

LINKING VERBS

In Grammar Unit One you learned that there is a small group of verbs that do not express action. The verb **to be** is the most important verb in this group. Since it is the most irregular verb in our language, you should be familiar with its various forms. The following verbs and verb phrases are forms of the verb *to be*:

Forms of the Verb "To Be"

am	were	has been	could have been
are	will be	had been	would have been
is	shall be	shall have been	might have been
was	have been	will have been	should have been

Although the verb *to be,* as well as the other verbs belonging in this group, does not express action, it has another function in the sentence. The chief purpose of this verb is to serve as a link which joins the subject to some word in the predicate that gives the meaning to the sentence. For that reason, it is called a **linking verb.**

Linking verbs have very little meaning of their own. With the help of another word, they express various ideas in regard to the subject. In the sentence, *Mary is ill,* the verb *is* (a form of *to be*) is used with the adjective *ill* to describe the condition of the subject, *Mary.* The sentence really means *ill Mary,* but you need a verb in order to make a complete statement.

In the sentence, *The young man was an aviator,* the verb *was* is a linking verb. With the help of the noun *aviator,* it identifies or classifies the young man. The noun *aviator* means the same as the subject. In the sentence, *The actress is very beautiful,* the verb *is,* with the help of the adjective *beautiful,* describes the appearance of the actress.

Verbs like *to be* are sometimes called **copulative verbs.** This is a term that comes from the Latin and means exactly the same as **linking.**

The verbs *become* and *seem,* like the verb *to be,* are almost always used as linking verbs. The following verbs are used both as linking verbs and as action verbs. The meaning of the sentence will show to which classification they belong:

Linking and Action Verbs

grow	look	smell	remain
turn	feel	taste	keep
prove	sound	appear	stay

This group of words is important because a great many mistakes in English are made when a speaker or writer does not understand their linking function.

When these words have a linking function, they have practically the same meaning as the verb *to be* would have in the same sentence. By supplying the verb *to be* mentally after one of these verbs, you can readily tell whether the verb has a linking function or whether it is used as an action verb. Every one of the verbs in the following sentences is a linking verb. The verb *to be* has been supplied to show you how to interpret the sentence when the verbs have a linking function.

The cookies **are** wonderful. (wonderful cookies)

The cookies **look** (to be) delicious. (delicious cookies)

The cookies **smell** (to be) good. (good cookies)

The cookies **taste** (to be) sweet. (sweet cookies)

The cookies **seem** (to be) brittle. (brittle cookies)

The cookies **became** (to be) stale. (stale cookies)

The cookies **proved** (to be) sweet. (sweet cookies)

The cookies **feel** (to be) hard. (hard cookies)

The cookies **stayed** (to be) fresh. (fresh cookies)

The cookies **appear** (to be) tempting. (tempting cookies)

The cookies **remained** (to be) soft. (soft cookies)

The cookies **kept** (to be) fresh. (fresh cookies)

Some of the same verbs that were used in the preceding illustrations may also be used to express action. Note the differences in meaning when these verbs function as action verbs and not as linking verbs.

John **appeared** promptly. (made his appearance)

The horticulturist **grows** orchids. (produces by cultivation)

I **turned** the key in the lock.

We **proved** a theorem in geometry.

The doctor **felt** the broken bone.

The warden **sounded** the gong.

The chef **tasted** the sauce.

We **kept** a record of our journey.

The dog **smelled** the meat.

The judge **will stay** the trial. (postpone)

The committee **looked** at the pictures.

EXERCISE 5

Underline the **verbs** in the following sentences. On the line to the right, indicate whether the verb expresses *action,* or has a *linking function.*

1. The coffee smells good.   1. ....

2. I felt the edge of the knife.   2. ....

3. The icy wind feels bitter.   3. ....

4. The patient is becoming stronger.   4. ....

5. Skiing is a dangerous sport.   5. ....

6. Mother seemed tired after the long ride.   6. ....

7. The gong sounded shrill.   7. ....

8. He might be the winner.   8. ....

9. The northern lights appear frequently in Alaska.   9. ....

10. The lettuce looks fresh.   10. ....

11. The tailor felt the lining of the coat.   11. ....

12. That man looks suspicious.   12. ....

13. The fruit kept fresh for several days.   13. ....

14. Herbert proved a problem in algebra.   14. ....

15. The tower seems very high.   15. ....

COMPLEMENTS OF LINKING VERBS

A *linking verb* cannot make a complete predicate. It always requires a *complement.* The group of words, *My friend is,* does not make a complete statement. The verb *is* requires some additional word to complete the meaning of the sentence. That word may be a noun, a pronoun, or an adjective.

My friend is an <u>executive</u>.

noun

My friend is very <u>ambitious</u>.

adjective

That is <u>he</u>.

pronoun

The noun that completes the meaning of a linking verb is called a *predicate noun* because it is found in the predicate. A **predicate noun** completes the verb and renames or explains the subject. In the preceding illustration, *executive* is a predicate noun. It renames the subject *friend* and classifies *friend* as an *executive.* The noun *friend* and the noun *executive* refer to the same person.

A pronoun that follows a linking verb functions in the same way as the noun. It completes the verb and means the same person or thing as the subject. It is called a **predicate pronoun.**

An adjective that follows a linking verb is called a **predicate adjective** because it is found in the predicate. A predicate adjective always modifies the subject.

The following sentences illustrate the use of the predicate noun, predicate pronoun, and predicate adjective:

Our <u>manager</u> was a former army <u>colonel</u>. (*manager* and *colonel*—

subjectpredicate noun

same person)

Our <u>manager</u> is very <u>efficient</u>. (*efficient* modifies *manager*)

subjectpredicate adjective

The <u>candidate</u> for the position is <u>he</u>. (*he* and *candidate* — same

subjectpredicate pronoun

person)

In the first sentence, *colonel* is a **predicate noun.** It completes the meaning of the verb *was* and refers to the same person as the subject. In the second sentence *efficient* is a **predicate adjective.** It modifies the subject noun *manager.* In the third sentence, *he* is a **predicate pronoun.** It means the same person as the subject *candidate.*

EXERCISE 6

Underline the **complements** of the linking verbs in the following sentences. On the line to the right, indicate whether the complement is a *predicate noun,* a *predicate pronoun,* or a *predicate adjective.*

1. The old man's coat was very shabby.   1. ....

2. The speaker seemed extremely nervous.   2. ....

3. My uncle is an insurance engineer.   3. ....

4. Julia always appears happy.   4. ....

5. The butter is turning soft.   5. ....

6. It wasn't I. It was he.   6. ....

7. Philip has become a captain.   7. ....

8. Grandmother always remains calm.   8. ....

9. He has been our director for two years.   9. ....

10. That book looks too difficult.   10. ....

11. The acting was remarkable.   11. ....

12. The soldier proved a hero.   12. ....

13. Those lilacs smell very fragrant.   13. ....

14. The owner of the new dress shop is she.   14. ....

15. The weather is growing cold.   15. ....

DIAGRAMMING COMPLEMENTS OF LINKING VERBS

The complement of a linking verb is separated from the verb by a line which slants in the direction of the subject. This is to show that the complement either refers to the same person or thing as the subject, or modifies the subject. Study the following diagrams:

Sentence: My brother is an aviator. (Complement is a predicate noun.)

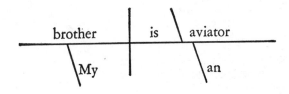

Sentence: The apple tastes sour. (Complement is a predicate adjective.)

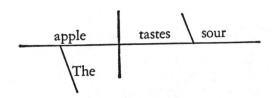

Sentence: The lucky winner is she. (Complement is a predicate pronoun.)

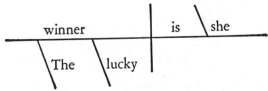

EXERCISE 7

Diagram the following sentences:

1. The patient is growing stronger.

2. Martin has become our manager.

3. The guests felt unwelcome.

4. His private secretary is Ellen.

5. The pudding tastes delicious.

SUMMARY OF GRAMMAR UNIT EIGHT

1. Every sentence must have two main parts—a subject and a verb. Some sentences require a third part, which is called the complement. A **complement** is a completing word. Some verbs require this completing word in order to express a complete predicate.

2. Verbs that express action often require a complement. The complement of a verb that expresses action is called the **direct object.** It names the *receiver* of the action.

3. Some **action verbs** do not require a complement. They express a complete predicate without the addition of a direct object.

4. A verb that takes an object is called a **transitive verb.** A verb that does not take an object is called an **intransitive verb.** An action verb may be transitive in one sentence and intransitive in another sentence.

5. Some action verbs take two complements—a *direct object* and an *indirect object.* The **indirect object** always precedes the direct object. The indirect object tells to whom the action is directed or for whom the action is performed.

6. All **linking verbs** require complements. The complement of a linking verb may be a noun, a pronoun, or an adjective.

7. A noun used as the complement of a linking verb is called a **predicate noun.** A pronoun used as the complement of a linking verb is called a **predicate pronoun.** An adjective used as the complement of a linking verb is called a **predicate adjective.**

8. A **predicate noun** or **pronoun** refers to the same person or thing as the subject. A **predicate adjective** modifies the subject.

SELF-GRADING ASSIGNMENT 1

Directions: Underline the **verbs** and the **verb phrases** in the following sentences. On the line to the right indicate whether the verb expresses *action*, or has a *linking function*.

		Action or Linking
1.	The kitchen seems warmer now.	1. ....
2.	I have been writing.	2. ....
3.	The house became unusually quiet.	3. ....
4.	Meet your payments promptly.	4. ....
5.	The plane landed safely.	5. ....
6.	You have been late too often.	6. ....
7.	We grow vegetables in our garden.	7. ....
8.	The flag was fluttering in the breeze.	8. ....
9.	Those strawberries look delicious.	9. ....
10.	The drought killed the crops.	10. ....
11.	The speaker answered several questions.	11. ....
12.	The visitor seemed very lonely.	12. ....
13.	My cousin sold his farm to an artist.	13. ....
14.	The milk kept fresh for several hours.	14. ....
15.	We found a trunk in the attic.	15. ....

Caution: Check your answers to each assignment with the answer key at the end of this unit before proceeding with the next assignment.

SELF-GRADING ASSIGNMENT 2

On the line to the right, indicate whether the underlined word is the subject noun, verb, verb phrase, direct object, predicate noun, indirect object, predicate pronoun, or predicate adjective.

1. The weary traveler <u>drank</u> the cold <u>water</u>.
   ₁   ₂

2. The <u>situation</u> was very <u>unusual</u>.
       ₃   ₄

3. Martin <u>will become</u> an <u>executive</u> in June.
          ₅   ₆

4. We <u>have mailed</u> all the <u>notices</u>.
       ₇   ₈

5. The stenographer gave the <u>manager</u> his <u>copy</u>.
                             ₉   ₁₀

6. <u>Harold</u> proved <u>eligible</u> for the position.
   ₁₁   ₁₂

7. He became her <u>adviser</u> and <u>friend</u>.
                  ₁₃   ₁₄

8. We gave our <u>director</u> a gold <u>watch</u>.
               ₁₅   ₁₆

9. The judge examined the <u>files</u> and the <u>papers</u>.
                          ₁₇   ₁₈

10. The speaker seems <u>sincere</u> and <u>fearless</u>.
                      ₁₉   ₂₀

11. Lowell <u>has been</u> our <u>lawyer</u> for years.
           ₂₁   ₂₂

12. One member <u>remained</u> <u>antagonistic</u>.
               ₂₃   ₂₄

1. ....
2. ....
3. ....
4. ....
5. ....
6. ....
7. ....
8. ....
9. ....
10. ....
11. ....
12. ....
13. ....
14. ....
15. ....
16. ....
17. ....
18. ....
19. ....
20. ....
21. ....
22. ....
23. ....
24. ....

SELF-GRADING ASSIGNMENT 3

Directions: Underline the **complements** of the verbs. On the line to the right, indicate whether the complement is a direct object, an indirect object, a predicate noun, a predicate pronoun, or a predicate adjective. Some verbs have two complements. Indicate both.

Kind of Complement

1. Disease is prevalent today.   1. ....

2. The speaker called Jane to the platform.   2. ....

3. Give her the directions slowly.   3. ....

4. The actors were amateurs.   4. ....

5. Madge designed a prize-winning costume.   5. ....

6. The attendants were nurses.   6. ....

7. The material for the book seems inadequate.   7. ....

8. Mr. Foster will become the new manager.   8. ....

9. Raymond sent Marian a box of candy.   9. ....

10. The postman delivered a message.   10. ....

11. That might have been he.   11. ....

12. The guides began the search for the child.   12. ....

13. The corn is growing ripe.   13. ....

14. Our club sent the speaker a check.   14. ....

15. The enemy bombed the supply lines.   15. ....

SELF-GRADING ASSIGNMENT 4

Directions: Diagram the following sentences:

1. The new clerk seems very capable.

2. We bought Agnes a beautiful fur coat.

3. The visitors might have been they.

4. The electrician was an excellent workman.

5. The men repaired the pipes and the faucets.

PROGRESS TEST EIGHT

This progress test should not be taken until a day or two after you have completed the assignments. The score you make on the test will then more clearly reflect your understanding of the material in the unit.

This test will show you whether you are able to identify action and linking verbs and the different types of complements that verbs take.

Directions: Classify the verbs as *action* verbs or *linking* verbs. Classify the complements as direct objects, indirect objects, predicate nouns, predicate pronouns, or predicate adjectives. Some verbs have two complements. (52 *points*)

	Kind of Verb	Kind of Complement
1. Our tasks have become endless.	1.	....
2. Mary looks attractive in that hat.	2.	....
3. The usher gave us an excellent seat.	3.	....
4. We shall meet you in the lobby.	4.	....
5. The gardenias smell too sweet.	5.	....
6. My brother became a famous actor.	6.	....
7. He plays the violin remarkably well.	7.	....
8. He proved an able statesman.	8.	....
9. It is I.	9.	....
10. We moved the furniture to Boston.	10.	....

PROGRESS TEST EIGHT (continued)

11. The fashion models might be they.   11. ....

12. The frightened woman turned pale.   12. ....

13. The governor stayed the execution.   13. ....

14. The doctor examined the broken bone.   14. ....

15. The gong sounds very shrill.   15. ....

16. The office looks very different now.   16. ....

17. She sent Marvin a copy of her book.   17. ....

18. The boy seemed hesitant.   18. ....

19. The officer wore a military cape over his uniform.   19. ....

20. Our elm trees have grown very tall.   20. ....

21. The beautiful model was she.   21. ....

22. He deceived himself.   22. ....

23. We debated the question for two hours.   23. ....

24. Father always walks rapidly.   24. ....

25. We introduced her to our friends.   25. ....

ANSWER KEY

for

EXERCISES, ASSIGNMENTS, AND PROGRESS TEST

Grammar Unit Eight

CORRECT ANSWERS TO EXERCISE 1

1. The firm is installing a new pump.
   s.   v.ph.   d.o.

2. (You) Add the figures correctly.
   s.   v.   d.o.

3. The janitor washed the windows.
   s.   v.   d.o.

4. Donald plays golf every Saturday.
   s.   v.   d.o.

5. That agent sells books and magazines.
   s.   v.   d.o.   d.o.

6. Harvey repaired the typewriters.
   s.   v.   d.o.

7. I know the conductor of the orchestra.
   s.   v.   d.o.

8. The company purchased several duplicating machines.
   s.   v.   d.o.

9. The officer stopped the traffic.
   s.   v.   d.o.

10. (You) Place the reports on the manager's desk.
    s.   v.   d.o.

11. The hurricane destroyed the crops and the fruit trees.
    s.   v.   d.o.   d.o.

12. You did find your watch. (Did you find your watch?)
    s.   v.ph.   d.o.

13. The gardener planted pines and elms in front of the house.
    s.   v.   d.o.   d.o.

14. The guide followed the bank of the stream.
    s.   v.   d.o.

15. We shall fill your order promptly.
    s.   v.ph.   d.o.

CORRECT ANSWERS TO EXERCISE 2

1. The crowd cheered the President.
   <u>d.o.</u>

2. The snow has been falling.

3. Two policemen were standing on the corner.

4. Every actor played his part well.
   <u>d.o.</u>

5. We bought these books at a sale.
   <u>d.o.</u>

6. The horse has been running around the track.

7. We sent food to the famine-stricken people.
   <u>d.o.</u>

8. The men were protesting loudly.

9. He rolled himself in a blanket.
   <u>d.o.</u>

10. The ball rolled slowly over the carpet.

11. The people in the grandstand shouted.

12. The agent negotiated a sale of the property.
    <u>d.o.</u>

13. The detective solved the mystery.
    <u>d.o.</u>

14. The bird flew over the treetops.

15. A water lily floated on the pond.

1. *transitive*
2. *intransitive*
3. *intransitive*
4. *transitive*
5. *transitive*
6. *intransitive*
7. *transitive*
8. *intransitive*
9. *transitive*
10. *intransitive*
11. *intransitive*
12. *transitive*
13. *transitive*
14. *intransitive*
15. *intransitive*

CORRECT ANSWERS TO EXERCISE 3

1. Uncle Ned gave me his camera.
   <u>i.o.</u>   <u>d.o.</u>

2. The guide showed them a short cut through the woods.
   <u>i.o.</u>   <u>d.o.</u>

3. I have lost my umbrella.
   <u>d.o.</u>

4. The motorist offered the boys a ride.
   <u>i.o.</u>   <u>d.o.</u>

5. Show the guests the way to the garden.
   <u>i.o.</u>   <u>d.o.</u>

6. I made <u>myself</u> a winter <u>coat</u>.
         i.o.   d.o.

7. John sent <u>Margaret</u> two beautiful <u>orchids</u>.
            i.o.   d.o.

8. The Indian handed <u>Irwin</u> a sharp <u>knife</u>.
           i.o.   d.o.

9. The bird flies over the building. (no objects)

10. The janitor took the <u>key</u> from the tenant.
            d.o.

11. They sent <u>us</u> an <u>order</u> for some cotton goods.
        i.o.   d.o.

12. The speaker gave <u>us</u> a new <u>picture</u> of world conditions.
           i.o.   d.o.

13. The firm offered <u>Bruce</u> an important <u>position</u>.
          i.o.   d.o.

14. The magician taught <u>them</u> some new <u>tricks</u>.
          i.o.   d.o.

15. The president granted <u>Mr. Allen</u> an <u>interview</u>.
          i.o.   d.o.

CORRECT ANSWERS TO EXERCISE 4

1. Father gave William a small radio.

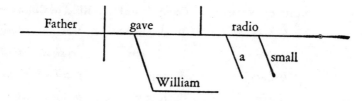

2. We mailed you a statement.

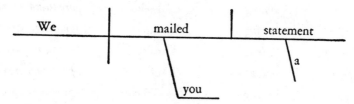

3. The janitor will give Herbert the key.

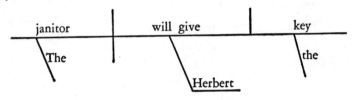

4. Arnold painted the porch.

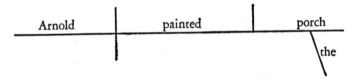

5. The firm gave us a large order.

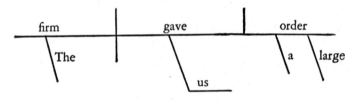

CORRECT ANSWERS TO EXERCISES

EXERCISE 5		**EXERCISE 6**	
Verbs	**Kind of Verb**	**Compliment**	**Kind of Complement**
1. smells	*linking*	1. shabby	*predicate adjective*
2. felt	*action*	2. nervous	*predicate adjective*
3. feels	*linking*	3. engineer	*predicate noun*
4. is becoming	*linking*	4. happy	*predicate adjective*
5. is	*linking*	5. soft	*predicate adjective*
6. seemed	*linking*	6. I—he	*predicate pronouns*
7. sounded	*linking*	7. captain	*predicate noun*
8. might be	*linking*	8. calm	*predicate adjective*
9. appear	*action*	9. director	*predicate noun*
10. looks	*linking*	10. difficult	*predicate adjective*

11.	felt	*action*		11.	remarkable	*predicate adjective*
12.	looks	*linking*		12.	hero	*predicate noun*
13.	kept	*linking*		13.	fragrant	*predicate adjective*
14.	proved	*action*		14.	she	*predicate pronoun*
15.	seems	*linking*		15.	cold	*predicate adjective*

CORRECT ANSWERS TO EXERCISE 7

1. The patient is growing stronger.

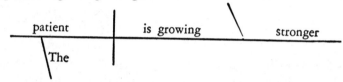

2. Martin has become our manager.

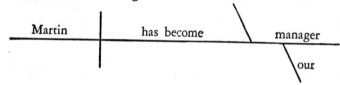

3. The guests felt unwelcome.

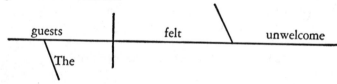

4. His private secretary is Ellen.

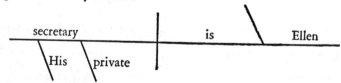

5. The pudding tastes delicious.

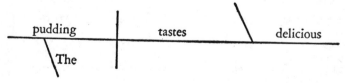

CORRECT ANSWERS TO ASSIGNMENT 1

Verbs and verb phrases are printed in **heavy type.**

Action or Linking

1. The kitchen **seems** warmer now.	1. *linking*
2. I **have been writing.**	2. *action*
3. The house **became** unusually quiet.	3. *linking*
4. **Meet** your payments promptly.	4. *action*
5. The plane **landed** safely.	5. *action*
6. You **have been** late too often.	6. *linking*
7. We **grow** vegetables in our garden.	7. *action*
8. The flag **was fluttering** in the breeze.	8. *action*
9. Those strawberries **look** delicious.	9. *linking*
10. The drought **killed** the crops.	10. *action*
11. The speaker **answered** several questions.	11. *action*
12. The visitor **seemed** very lonely.	12. *linking*
13. My cousin **sold** his farm to an artist.	13. *action*
14. The milk **kept** fresh for several hours.	14. *linking*
15. We **found** a trunk in the attic.	15. *action*

CORRECT ANSWERS TO ASSIGNMENT 2

1. drank—*verb*	10. copy—*direct object*
2. water—*direct object*	11. Harold—*subject noun*
3. situation—*subject noun*	12. eligible—*predicate adjective*
4. unusual—*predicate adjective*	13. adviser—*predicate noun*
5. will become—*verb phrase*	14. friend—*predicate noun*
6. executive—*predicate noun*	15. director—*indirect object*
7. have mailed—*verb phrase*	16. watch—*direct object*
8. notices—*direct object*	17. files—*direct object*
9. manager—*indirect object*	18. papers—*direct object*

19. sincere—*predicate adjective*   22. lawyer—*predicate noun*
20. fearless—*predicate adjective*   23. remained—*verb*
21. has been—*verb phrase*   24. antagonistic—*predicate adjective*

CORRECT ANSWERS TO ASSIGNMENT 3

Complement	Kind of Complement
1. prevalent	1. *predicate adjective*
2. Jane	2. *direct object*
3. her—directions	3. *indirect object—direct object*
4. amateurs	4. *predicate noun*
5. costume	5. *direct object*
6. nurses	6. *predicate noun*
7. inadequate	7. *predicate adjective*
8. manager	8. *predicate noun*
9. Marian—box	9. *indirect object—direct object*
10. message	10. *direct object*
11. he	11. *predicate pronoun*
12. search	12. *direct object*
13. ripe	13. *predicate adjective*
14. speaker—check	14. *indirect object—direct object*
15. lines	15. *direct object*

CORRECT ANSWERS TO ASSIGNMENT 4

1. The new clerk seems very capable.

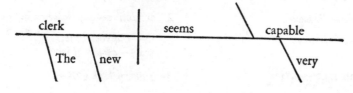

2. We bought Agnes a beautiful fur coat.

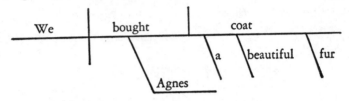

3. The visitors might have been they.

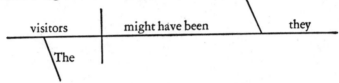

4. The electrician was an excellent workman.

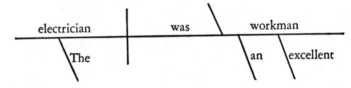

5. The men repaired the pipes and the faucets.

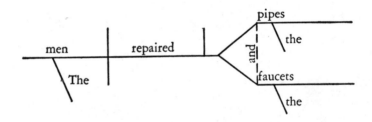

CORRECT ANSWERS TO PROGRESS TEST EIGHT

Kind of Verb	Kind of Complement
1. have become—*linking*	1. endless—*predicate adjective*
2. looks—*linking*	2. attractive—*predicate adjective*
3. gave—*action*	3. us—*indirect object* seat— *direct object*
4. shall meet—*action*	4. you—*direct object*

CORRECT ANSWERS TO PROGRESS TEST EIGHT (continued)

Kind of Verb	Kind of Complement
5. smell—*linking*	5. sweet—*predicate adjective*
6. became—*linking*	6. actor—*predicate noun*
7. plays—*action*	7. violin—*direct object*
8. proved—*linking*	8. statesman—*predicate noun*
9. is—*linking*	9. I—*predicate pronoun*
10. moved—*action*	10. furniture—*direct object*
11. might be —*linking*	11. they—*predicate pronoun*
12. turned—*linking*	12. pale—*predicate adjective*
13. stayed—*action*	13. execution—*direct object*
14. examined—*action*	14. bone—*direct object*
15. sounds—*linking*	15. shrill—*predicate adjective*
16. looks—*linking*	16. different—*predicate adjective*
17. sent—*action*	17. Marvin—*indirect object* copy—*direct object*
18. seemed—*linking*	18. hesitant—*predicate adjective*
19. wore—*action*	19. cape—*direct object*
20. have grown—*linking*	20. tall—*predicate adjective*
21. was—*linking*	21. she—*predicate pronoun*
22. deceived—*action*	22. himself—*direct object*
23. debated—*action*	23. question—*direct object*
24. walks—*action*	24. no complement
25. introduced—*action*	25. her—*direct object*

HOW TO OBTAIN YOUR SCORE

The test totals 52 points. To obtain your score, divide the number of your correct answers by 52. The answer will be your score on this test. For example, if you have 44 points correct, your score is 44 divided by 52 which is 85 per cent. In other words, your score on this test is 85. You can obtain your score on any of the exercises or assignments by following the same procedure.

Practical English Grammar

OUTLINE OF UNIT NINE

CASE OF NOUNS AND PRONOUNS

CASE OF NOUNS AND PRONOUNS

NOUNS AND PRONOUNS have certain relationships to other words in a sentence. We call attention to these relationships by indicating the case of the noun or pronoun. The word **case** is used in grammar to indicate the *relationship* a noun or a pronoun has to other words in the sentence. The case of a noun or a pronoun is determined by the particular use of that noun or pronoun in the sentence.

There are only three cases in English: the *nominative case,* the *objective case,* and the *possessive case.* The **nominative case** is the case of the *subject.* The **objective case** is the case of the *object.* The **possessive case** is the case that shows *ownership.*

CASE OF NOUNS

Nouns present very few problems in case because the same form is used for the nominative case and the objective case. The only way to determine whether a noun is in the nominative case or in the objective case is to determine its relationship to other words in the sentence. If the noun is used as the *subject* of the sentence, it is in the *nominative case.* If the noun is used as the *object* of a verb or a preposition, it is in the *objective case.*

The **door** is open. (*nominative case*—subject)

I closed the **door**. (*objective case*—direct object)

In the first sentence, the noun *door* is used as the subject of the sentence. It is in the nominative case. In the second sentence, the same form *door* is used as the direct object of the verb *closed. Door* is in the objective case in this sentence.

Like nouns, *indefinite pronouns* have the same form for the nominative case and the objective case.

Everyone contributed five dollars. (*nominative case*-subject)

I saw **everyone** at the game. (*objective case*-direct object)

NOMINATIVE CASE

The word *nominative* comes from a Latin word which means *name*. The **nominative case** names the case of the subject of the sentence. It also names the case of a predicate noun. A predicate noun is in the nominative case. For this reason, it is often called a **predicate nominative.**

A *predicate noun* must agree in case with the *subject* because it refers to the same person or thing as the subject. It also follows a verb which cannot take an object. Predicate nouns are always used after linking verbs.

My friend is a naval officer. (*nominative case*)
   subject   predicate noun
            same person

The leading lady was Mary Martin. (*nominative case*)
            same person

In the first sentence, *officer* is a predicate noun. It is used after the linking verb *is* and refers to the same person as the subject. It is in the nominative case to agree with the case of the subject *friend*.

In the second sentence, *Mary Martin* is a predicate noun. It is in the nominative case to agree with the subject *lady*. *Mary Martin* and *lady* refer to the same person.

OBJECTIVE CASE

The **objective case** is the case of the *object*. The *direct object* of a verb, the *indirect object,* and the *object* of a *preposition* are in the objective case.

Lester writes **articles** for the paper. (*articles*—direct object)

Arthur sent the **manager** a detailed report. (*manager*—indirect object)

'In the first sentence, *articles* is the direct object of the verb *writes*. It tells **what** Lester writes. *Articles* is in the objective case. In the second sentence, *manager* is the indirect object. It tells **to whom** Arthur sent his plan. *Manager* is in the objective case.

In Grammar Unit Two you learned that a preposition is always followed by some noun or pronoun which is called the *object* of the *preposition*. The object of a preposition is always in the objective case.

Edward met his lawyer at the **bank.** (object of preposition *at*)
objective case

We met Marvin in the **lobby.** (object of preposition *in*)
objective case

In the first sentence, the preposition *at* is followed by the noun *bank*. The object of the preposition is *bank*, which is in the objective case. In the second sentence, *lobby* is the object of the preposition *in*. *Lobby* is in the objective case.

It is easy to remember that direct objects of verbs, indirect objects of verbs, and objects of prepositions are in the objective case because they are all called **objects** of some type. The fact that they are objects indicates that they are in the **objective case.**

EXERCISE 1

Indicate the case of the underlined words. Write **nom.case** or **obj.case** under the word. On the line to the right, indicate whether the word is *subject, predicate noun, direct object, indirect object,* or *object of a preposition.*

Example: I read that <u>article</u> yesterday.   direct object

<small>obj. case</small>   ....

1. A <u>stranger</u> knocked on the door.   1. ....

2. Heifetz is a great <u>violinist</u>.   2. ....

3. The president read the <u>resolution</u>.   3. ....

4. The firm gave the <u>employees</u> a bonus.   4. ....

5. We sat in the tenth <u>row</u>.   5. ....

6. Michael left his <u>sister</u> a fortune.   6. ....

7. Do you know the <u>answer</u> to that question?   7. ....

8. The captain talked about the <u>recruits</u>.   8. ....

9. Did <u>Alice</u> play at the concert?   9. ....

10. Anne is our favorite <u>instructor</u>.   10. ....

11. We bought copies of his latest <u>book</u>.   11. ....

12. Have the <u>guests</u> arrived?   12. ....

13. My brother was an <u>aviator</u> in the last war.   13. ....

14. The firm offered Duncan a better <u>position</u>.   14. ....

15. We left during the <u>intermission</u>.   15. ....

Note: The correct answers to exercises will be found at the end of this unit. Correct your mistakes and, if necessary, reread the text material before going on to the next section.

CASE OF PRONOUNS

Nouns do not present any problems in case because the form of the noun is the same for the nominative case and the objective case. Pronouns do present problems in case. The *personal pronouns* and the pronoun *who* have different forms to indicate the different cases.

There are only *six pronouns* in English that have these special forms to show *case*, but the changes that occur to indicate case are very important. They are responsible for many of the errors that frequently occur in the use of pronouns. You should become familiar with the different forms of these pronouns, and you should learn how to use them correctly. The six pronouns are *I, you, he, she, it, who.*

The following table gives the nominative case forms and the objective case forms of each of the six pronouns:

Nominative Case		Objective Case	
Singular	**Plural**	**Singular**	**Plural**
I	we	me	us
you	you	you	you
he	they	him	them
she	they	her	them
it	they	it	them
who	who	whom	whom

The pronouns *he, she,* and *it* have the same form in the plural. *They* is the pronoun used in the nominative case in the plural for each of the three pronouns. *Them* is the pronoun used in the objective case in the plural for each of the three pronouns.

NOMINATIVE CASE OF PRONOUNS

Like nouns, pronouns are in the nominative case when they are used as the subjects of sentences, or as predicate pronouns after one of the linking verbs. Mistakes are seldom made in selecting the correct form of the pronoun to use as the subject of the sentence. Mistakes are frequently made, however, when a pronoun is used as a *predicate nominative*. The following sentences illustrate the correct use of the six pronouns in the nominative case:

Subject of the Sentence	Predicate Pronoun
I saw the accident.	It is **I.**
You have been elected.	It was **you.**
He attended the lecture.	It might be **he.**
She gave me her notebook.	It could be **she.**
It is my overcoat.	Could this be **it?**
We are great friends. (plural)	It is **we.** (plural)
They arrived early. (plural)	It was **they.** (plural)
Who came in?	**Who** was it? (It was **who?**)

The pronoun *you* does not present any problem in the plural, because the forms for the plural are the same as the forms for the singular. The form of the pronoun *you* is also the same for the nominative case and the objective case.

Interrogative sentences should always be transposed and put in normal order. When this is done, it is easy to determine the case of the pronoun.

OBJECTIVE CASE OF PRONOUNS

Pronouns are in the objective case when they are used as direct objects of verbs, indirect objects of verbs, or as objects of prepositions. The correct forms to use in the objective case are *me, you, him, her, it,* and *whom* in the singular, and *us, you, them, whom* in the plural. The following sentences illustrate the correct use of these pronouns in the objective case:

Object of the Verb	Indirect Object of the Verb
Mother called **me.**	Ethel gave **me** her pen.
Jack saw **him** yesterday.	I sent **him** a notice.
I met **you** in Paris.	David sent **you** a ticket.
The firm sent **her** to Texas.	Jack offered **her** a seat.
My friend invited **us** to the game.	The teacher read **them** a story.
Sue drove **them** to the station.	The tailor made **us** new uniforms.

Whom did you call? (You did call **whom?**)

Object of a Preposition

The telegram was sent to **me.** (object of the preposition *to*)

The manager created the position for **him.** (object of *for*)

The author wrote an article about **her.** (object of *about*)

The waiter placed their table near **us.** (object of *near*)

We distributed the gifts among **them.** (object of *among*)

For **whom** did you vote? (object of the preposition *for*)
(You did vote for **whom?**)

EXERCISE 2

In the first column to the right, indicate the **case** of the underlined pronouns. In the second column, give the reason for the case: *subject, predicate pronoun, object* of the *verb, indirect object,* or *object* of a *preposition.*

	Case	Reason for Case
1. Ellis gave <u>us</u> a ride in his car.	....	....
2. He was not concerned about <u>me</u>.	....	....
3. The club sent <u>them</u> food.	....	....
4. The winner is <u>she</u>.	....	....
5. Susan and <u>she</u> entertained the guests.	....	....
6. <u>Whom</u> did you see at the banquet?	....	....
7. For <u>whom</u> did you plan the dinner?	....	....
8. <u>Who</u> knocked on the door?	....	....
9. It might have been <u>they</u>.	....	....
10. Have <u>you</u> heard the news about him?	....	....
11. I bought <u>them</u> for you.	....	....
12. The firm paid <u>her</u> a dividend.	....	....
13. <u>He</u> and she will finish the job.	....	....
14. It was John and <u>he</u>.	....	....
15. <u>Whom</u> did we send to Norway?	....	....

THE POSSESSIVE CASE OF NOUNS

The **possessive case** shows *ownership* or *possession*. The use of the possessive case does not present much of a problem in speaking, but it does present a problem in writing and spelling. Although the rule for forming the possessive case of nouns is very simple, many students have considerable difficulty in spelling and writing the forms correctly.

One simple rule applies to all cases: If the singular form of the noun does not end in **s**, add the *apostrophe* and **s** (**'s**). If the singular ends in **s**, add the *apostrophe* (**'**).

The same rule applies to the plural: If the plural does not end in **s**, add the *apostrophe* and **s** (**'s**). If the plural ends in **s**, add the apostrophe ,**'**). Study the following examples carefully and try to apply the rule:

Singular	Singular Possessive	Plural	Plural Possessive
boy	boy's	boys	boys'
lady	lady's	ladies	ladies'
hero	hero's	heroes	heroes'
man	man's	men	men's
Charles	Charles'	Charleses	Charleses'
horse	horse's	horses	horses'
child	child's	children	children's
mouse	mouse's	mice	mice's

There is one fact that you must always keep in mind in order to form the possessive case correctly; that is, the sign of the possessive is something that is *added* to the word. It is not something that is inserted within the word. You must be absolutely sure of the correct form for the singular and the correct form for the plural before you add the sign of the possessive.

Take the proper name, *Dickens,* for example. This is a proper noun in the singular which ends in **s.** The sign of the possessive must be added to the complete word and not inserted within the word. The possessive form is often incorrectly written as *Dicken's.* That would be the possessive form of the name *Dicken,* and not the possessive form of the name *Dickens.* The singular possessive form of *Dickens* is *Dickens'.*

Oliver Twist is one of **Dicken's** novels. (incorrect)

Oliver Twist is one of **Dickens'** novels. (correct)

The possessive forms of proper nouns are formed according to the rule. If the singular form of the name does not end in **s,** add the *apostrophe* and **s.** If the singular ends in **s,** add the *apostrophe.* The same rule applies to the plural.

Name	Singular Possessive	Plural	Plural Possessive
Mary	Mary's	Marys	Marys'
Jones	Jones'	Joneses	Joneses'
Henry	Henry's	Henrys	Henrys'
Burns	Burns'	Burnses	Burnses'

There is one slight modification of the rule which may be followed in the case of the possessive singular of nouns that end in **s**. If you want the sound of the additional **s**, the *apostrophe* and **s** may be added:

This is **Charles'** fishing rod. (correct)

This is **Charles's** fishing rod. (correct)

I saw **Doris'** picture at the studio. (correct)

I saw **Doris's** picture at the studio. (correct)

In modern practice, the first form (*Charles' fishing rod*) is the form that is generally used. It follows the rule given, and is the simpler form to use both in writing and in pronunciation. This rule also applies to nouns ending in **x** and **z**.

I bought a jar of **Heinz'** pickles. (correct)

She has always worn **Knox'** hats. (correct)

I bought a jar of **Heinz's** pickles. (correct)

She has always worn **Knox's** hats. (correct)

EXERCISE 3

Write the *singular possessive,* the *plural,* and the *plural possessive* of each of the following nouns.

Caution: Be sure that you have the correct form for the plural.

Singular	Singular Possessive	Plural	Plural Possessive
1. girl	....	....	....
2. woman	....	....	....
3. attorney	....	....	....
4. child	....	....	....
5. sheep	....	....	....
6. goose	....	....	....
7. thief	....	....	....
8. mayor	....	....	....
9. soprano	....	....	....
10. James	....	....	....
11. artist	....	....	....
12. lady	....	....	....
13. Alice	....	....	....
14. Wells	....	....	....
15. princess	....	....	....

USE OF THE POSSESSIVE—SPECIAL FORMS

As a rule, it is better practice not to use the possessive forms for inanimate objects. Inanimate objects cannot possess anything in the sense that animate objects can. Avoid expressions such as *the table's top, the book's ending, the lake's shore,* and *the shop's window.* It is much better to use the phrase with *of* in such cases.

the top **of the table**   the shore **of the lake**

the ending **of the book**   the window **of the shop**

There are certain exceptions to this rule. Usage has established authority for using expressions such as the following:

the earth's surface   the sun's rays

the world's progress   today's edition

the law's delay   time's flight

the season's greetings   the water's edge

Certain expressions relating to *time, distance,* and *value* are also written with the sign of the possessive case. The apostrophe is generally used in expressions like the following:

a moment's delay   a stone's throw

two weeks' salary   a week's journey

a month's vacation   ten cents' worth

a few minutes' quiet   thirty days' notice

The singular possessive and the plural possessive of compound nouns are formed by adding the sign of the possessive to the end of the compound word.

Singular	**Plural**
sister-in-law's	sisters-in-law's
editor-in-chief's	editors-in-chief's
maid of honor's	maids of honor's

Joint ownership is shown by making the last word in the series possessive. Individual ownership is shown by making both parts possessive.

Baker and Johnson's factory. (joint ownership)

Baker's and Johnson's factories. (individual ownership)

Asia and China's problems. (common to both)

Asia's and China's problems. (separate problems)

Some trade names and names of organizations and institutions are written with the sign of the possessive case, and some are not. In writing letters, one should follow the form established by the organization.

When the apostrophe and **s** (**'s**) are not used, the word which would ordinarily be written as a possessive, is regarded as an adjective modifier. In the name of an institution, such as *Teachers College,* the apostrophe is not used. The word *Teachers* is regarded as an adjective modifying *College.* It tells the type of college. It does not mean that the teachers possess the college.

The following illustrations show the methods used in writing place names, institutional names, and titles of publications:

With the Apostrophe	Without the Apostrophe
Woman's Home Companion	Womens Athletic Club
Collier's	Bricklayers Union
Harper's Magazine	Executives Club
Hansen's Pharmacy	Governors Island
Queen's College (Oxford)	All Souls Church
Charles Scribner's Sons	Flanders Fields
Young Men's Christian Association	Pikes Peak
Stelter's Music House	Downers Grove
Working Girl's Club	Harris Brothers Company
Illinois Children's Home and Aid Society	Good Neighbors Service
Nowak's Optical Service	Citizens League
Ladies' Home Journal	American Bankers Association
Martha's Vineyard Island	Buzzards Bay
Christensen's Service Station	Peoples Finance Company

EXERCISE 4

On the line to the right, write the correct **possessive form** of the expression in parentheses.

1. my (sister-in-law) home   1. ....

2. the (editor-in-chief) opinion   2. ....

3. the (notary public) signature   3. ....

4. the (maidservant) room   4. ....

5. (Mrs. Estes) chauffeur   5. ....

6. (Lois) book   6. ....

7. the (vice-president) speech   7. ....

8. (James) father   8. ....

9. (Jones and Smith) factory   9. ....

10. the (commander-in-chief) report   10. ....

11. the (workmen) hours   11. ....

12. the (letter carriers) routes   12. ....

13. the (princesses) tutors   13. ....

14. her (sons-in-law) factories   14. ....

15. (H. G. Wells) literary productions 15. ....

THE POSSESSIVE CASE OF PRONOUNS

The indefinite pronouns do not have special forms to show case. The possessive case of indefinite pronouns is formed in the same way as the possessive case of nouns. Indefinite pronouns are seldom used in the plural. Two of the indefinite pronouns, *one* and *other,* have the plural forms *ones* and *others.* The following are illustrations of the possessive case form of indefinite pronouns:

everyone's opinion *one's* relatives (singular)

someone's hat *somebody's* car

anybody's guess *another's* choice

The *personal pronouns* and the pronoun *who* have special forms to show the possessive case: *my, mine, our, ours, your, yours, her, hers, his, its, their, theirs,* and *whose.* These forms are never written with an apostrophe. To add an apostrophe would be adding a possessive sign to a word that is already possessive.

Whose report did you check? (not *Who's*)

The automobile was **theirs.** (not *their's*)

I did not know that book was **yours.** (not *your's*)

The ship lost **its** anchor in the storm. (not *it's*)

That ranch type house is **ours.** (not *our's*)

Reference Table

PERSONAL PRONOUNS

First Person

Singular				Plural
Nominative	I			we
Possessive	my, mine			our, ours
Objective	me			us

Second Person

	Singular			Plural
Nominative	you			you
Possessive	your, yours			your, yours
Objective	you			you

Third Person

Nominative	he	she	it	they
Possessive	his	her, hers	its	their, theirs
Objective	him	her	it	them

RELATIVE AND INTERROGATIVE PRONOUN "WHO"

	Singular	Plural
Nominative	who	who
Possessive	whose	whose
Objective	whom	whom

EXERCISE 5

Fill in the blank space with the **possessive form** of the pronoun in parentheses.

1. The officer examined..........................baggage. (everybody)

2. That book on the table is.....................(I)

3. ....car did you buy? (Who)

4. Every ship has...........................officers. (it)

5. ....camera is here with my trunk. (You)

6. I could not listen to........................speech. (he)

7. Mary found...........................notebook in my locker. (she)

8. ....car was parked in front of our house. (Somebody)

9. ....relatives are often too inquisitive. (One)

10. Is that beautiful new hat........................? (you)

11. That is........................typewriter. (I)

12. You should share........................joys. (another)

13. ....diamonds are more beautiful than.................. (She, I)

14. The jury rendered........................verdict yesterday. (it)

15. Is this beautiful traveling bag........................? (you)

SUMMARY OF GRAMMAR UNIT NINE

Nouns and pronouns have certain relationships to other words in a sentence. We show these relationships by indicating the *case* of the noun or the pronoun. The word **case** is used to show the particular *relationship* that a noun or pronoun has to other words in the sentence.

There are three cases in English: the **nominative case**, the **objective case**, and the **possessive case**. The *nominative case* is the case of the *subject*. A **predicate noun** is also in the nominative case because it refers to the same person or thing as the subject.

The *objective case* is the case of the *object*. The *direct object* of a verb, the *indirect object* of a verb, and the *object* of a *preposition* are in the objective case.

Nouns present very few problems in case because the same form is used for the nominative case and the objective case. The only way to tell whether a noun is in the *nominative case* or the *objective case* is to study its **function** in the sentence.

Pronouns do present a problem in case. There are only *six pronouns* in the English language that have different forms for the different cases. But these changes are very important because they are responsible for many of the errors that occur in the use of pronouns. The six pronouns are *I, you, he, she, it,* and *who.* Every student of grammar should become familiar with the different forms of these pronouns.

The *possessive case* shows *ownership* or *possession.* The possessive case does not involve a change in the form of a noun, but it does require the use of certain endings to show possession. Although the rule for forming the possessive case of nouns is very simple, many students have difficulty in spelling and writing these forms correctly.

If you keep the following fact in mind, you will have little difficulty in forming the possessive case of nouns correctly: The sign of the possessive is something that is *added* to the word. It is not something that is inserted within the word. You must be sure of the correct form for the singular or the plural before you try to make either form possessive.

The *indefinite pronouns* form the possessive case in the same way that nouns do. The *personal pronouns* and the pronoun *who* have special forms to show the possessive case: *my, mine, our, ours, your, yours, her, hers, his, its, their, theirs, whose.* These forms are never written with an apostrophe.

SELF-GRADING ASSIGNMENT 1

Directions: In the first column write the **case** of the underlined nouns. In the second column, give the **reason** for the case: *subject, predicate noun, direct object, indirect object, object* of a *preposition.*

	Case	Reason for Case
1. We gave the president a <u>watch</u>.	....	....
2. He arrived in <u>Paris</u> Saturday.	....	....
3. Mr. Allerton is our <u>supervisor</u>.	....	....
4. The club sent <u>Grace</u> a book.	....	....
5. Did <u>Sue</u> publish her article?	....	....
6. They have been <u>guests</u> for a week.	....	....
7. The poems were written by <u>Burns</u>.	....	....
8. The general made the <u>decision</u>.	....	....
9. The printer gave <u>Harold</u> a copy of the speech.	....	....
10. I sent the driver my <u>address</u>.	....	....
11. The campers followed the trail through the <u>woods</u>.	....	....
12. The <u>stenographer</u> corrected the copy.	....	....
13. The old mansion is now a <u>museum</u>.	....	....
14. Is that <u>gentleman</u> our new mayor?	....	....
15. Are you a <u>typist</u>?	....	....

Caution: Check your answers to each assignment with the answer key at the back of the booklet before proceeding with the next assignment.

SELF-GRADING ASSIGNMENT 2

Directions: In the first column write the **case** of the underlined pronouns. In the second column, give the **reason** for the case: *subject, direct object, indirect object, predicate pronoun, object* of a *preposition.*

	Case	Reason for Case
1. <u>Who</u> are they?	....	....
2. Give <u>her</u> the message.	....	....
3. The book was written by <u>him.</u>	....	....
4. I know his brother and <u>him.</u>	....	....
5. The officer criticized <u>us</u> boys.	....	....
6. <u>He</u> and I sold the tickets.	....	....
7. That might have been <u>they.</u>	....	....
8. They sent the tickets to <u>them.</u>	....	....
9. <u>Who</u> called me yesterday?	....	....
10. The firm sent <u>me</u> to Boston.	....	....
11. <u>We</u> were warned by the guard and by them.	....	....
12. <u>Whom</u> did you see at the conference?	....	....
13. To <u>whom</u> did you send the announcements?	....	....
14. The tailor made <u>him</u> a suit.	....	....
15. <u>She</u> is going to Jamaica.	....	....

SELF-GRADING ASSIGNMENT 3

Directions: Write the *singular possessive*, the *plural*, and the *plural possessive* of each of the following nouns:

Singular	Singular Possessive	Plural	Plural Possessive
1. landlady			
2. woman			
3. she			
4. another			
5. deer			
6. Higgins			
7. attorney			
8. it			
9. Ruth			
10. sheriff			
11. calf			
12. countess			
13. Jones			
14. Henry			
15. ally			

SELF-GRADING ASSIGNMENT 4

Directions: Cross out the words that require *apostrophes*. Write the correct form above the incorrect form. Insert the *apostrophes*.

salesmen's
Example: The ~~salesmens~~ reports were checked.

1. Birds nests were found in the top branches.

2. The presidents secretary read Mr. Burns report.

3. Our familys estate was settled according to the judges ruling.

4. They had to abide by the umpires decision.

5. May I borrow Louis car for the evening?

6. We always buy Crosse and Blackwells jams.

7. The editor-in-chiefs comments were significant.

8. Several of Dickens novels have been dramatized.

9. He seems to be the peoples choice for governor.

10. The postmaster generals office is on the right.

11. The womens organizations planned a campaign.

12. We were granted a months vacation.

13. The committee met at Mr. Evans home.

14. Someones coat was left in Janes locker.

15. We did several days work that evening.

PROGRESS TEST NINE

A.

Directions: Cross out the incorrect forms of **pronouns.** Write the correct form above the incorrect form.   (*25 points*)

          whom
Example: To ~~who~~ did you send the check?

1. It was them. Did you think it was him?

2. Him and me are going to build a canoe.

3. The boat was their's. The canoes were our's.

4. From who did you receive the money?

5. The boys are going with James and I. With who are you going?

6. Eugene and him enlisted last week.

7. Who did you sit beside at the concert? I sat with they.

8. John, Harry, and me were appointed delegates.

9. Everybodys name was called.

10. The noise frightened her and he. It did not frighten we.

11. Her and I arrived at the same time. When did you and him arrive?

12. That television set is her's. Who's set is this?

13. No one signed the paper except he and I.

14. Someones umbrella was left in the hall. Was it your's?

15. Us boys are going to join the club.

PROGRESS TEST NINE (continued)

B.

Directions: On the line to the right, write the correct **possessive form** of the noun in parentheses.   (*15 points*)

Possessive Form

1. His (stepchildren) income was very large.   1. ....

2. The (parent) organization will meet today.   2. ....

3. He found the copy on the (editor-in-chief) desk.   3. ....

4. We shall allow him two (month) credit.   4. ....

5. The (enemy) line was broken.   5. ....

6. Her (father-in-law) business has increased in volume.   6. ....

7. They sent us the (season) greetings.   7. ....

8. (Marshall Field and Company) store is famous.   8. ....

9. We did not agree with the (attorney general) opinion.   9. ....

10. A (book reviewer) task is not easy.   10. ....

11. I like to read (Burns) poems.   11. ....

12. (Citizen) rights should be protected.   12. ....

13. (Morris) name appeared on the program.   13. ....

14. I asked for a three (week) vacation.   14. ....

15. He spoke about the (scientist) discovery.   15. ....

ANSWER KEY
for
EXERCISES, ASSIGNMENTS, AND PROGRESS TEST
Grammar Unit Nine

CORRECT ANSWERS TO EXERCISE 1

1. A <u>stranger</u> knocked on the door.
   nom. case

2. Heifetz is a great <u>violinist</u>.
   nom. case

3. The president read the <u>resolution</u>.
   obj. case

4. The firm gave the <u>employees</u> a bonus.
   obj. case

5. We sat in the tenth <u>row</u>.
   obj. case

6. Michael left his <u>sister</u> a fortune.
   obj. case

7. Do you know the <u>answer</u> to that question?
   obj. case

8. The captain talked about the <u>recruits</u>.
   obj. case

9. Did <u>Alice</u> play at the concert?
   nom. case

10. Anne is our favorite <u>instructor</u>.
    nom. case

11. We bought a copy of his latest <u>book</u>.
    obj. case

12. Have the <u>guests</u> arrived?
    nom. case

13. My brother was an <u>aviator</u> in the last war.
    nom. case

14. The firm offered Duncan a better <u>position</u>.
    obj. case

15. We left during the <u>intermission</u>.
    obj. case

1. subject

2. predicate noun

3. direct object

4. indirect object

5. object of preposition

6. indirect object

7. direct object

8. object of preposition

9. subject

10. predicate noun

11. object of preposition

12. subject

13. predicate noun

14. direct object

15. object of preposition

CORRECT ANSWERS TO EXERCISE 2

Pronoun	Case	Reason for Case
1. us	objective	indirect object
2. me	objective	object of a preposition
3. them	objective	indirect object

4. she	nominative	predicate pronoun
5. she	nominative	subject
6. Whom	objective	direct object
7. whom	objective	object of a preposition
8. Who	nominative	subject
9. they	nominative	predicate pronoun
10. you	nominative	subject
11. them	objective	direct object
12. her	objective	indirect object
13. He	nominative	subject
14. he	nominative	predicate pronoun
15. Whom	objective	direct object

CORRECT ANSWERS TO EXERCISE 3

Singular	Singular Possessive	Plural	Plural Possessive
1. girl	girl's	girls	girls'
2. woman	woman's	women	women's
3. attorney	attorney's	attorneys	attorneys'
4. child	child's	children	children's
5. sheep	sheep's	sheep	sheep's
6. goose	goose's	geese	geese's
7. thief	thief's	thieves	thieves'
8. mayor	mayor's	mayors	mayors'
9. soprano	soprano's	sopranos	sopranos'
10. James	James' or James's	Jameses	Jameses'
11. artist	artist's	artists	artists'
12. lady	lady's	ladies	ladies'
13. Alice	Alice's	Alices	Alices'
14. Wells	Wells' or Wells's	Wellses	Wellses'
15. princess	princess' or princess's	princesses	princesses'

CORRECT ANSWERS TO EXERCISE 4

1. sister-in-law's
2. editor-in-chief's
3. notary public's
4. maidservant's
5. Mrs. Estes' or Mrs. Estes's
6. Lois' or Lois's
7. vice-president's
8. James' or James's
9. Jones and Smith's
10. commander-in-chief's
11. workmen's
12. letter carriers'
13. princesses'
14. sons-in-law's
15. H. G. Wells' or H. G. Wells's

CORRECT ANSWERS TO EXERCISE 5

1. everybody's
2. mine
3. Whose
4. its
5. Your
6. his
7. her
8. Somebody's
9. One's
10. yours
11. my
12. another's
13. Her—mine
14. its
15. yours

CORRECT ANSWERS TO ASSIGNMENT 1

Noun	Case	Reason for Case
1. watch	objective	direct object of the verb *gave*
2. Paris	objective	object of preposition *in*
3. supervisor	nominative	predicate noun after the verb *is*
4. Grace	objective	indirect object
5. Sue	nominative	subject of the sentence
6. guests	nominative	predicate noun after *have been*
7. Burns	objective	object of the preposition *by*
8. decision	objective	direct object of the verb *made*
9. Harold	objective	indirect object
10. address	objective	direct object of the verb *sent*
11. woods	objective	object of the preposition *through*
12. stenographer	nominative	subject of the sentence

13. museum	nominative	predicate noun after the verb *is*
14. gentleman	nominative	subject of the sentence
15. typist	nominative	predicate noun after the verb *are*

CORRECT ANSWERS TO ASSIGNMENT 2

Pronoun	Case	Reason for the Case
1. Who	nominative	predicate pronoun after the verb *are*
2. her	objective	indirect object
3. him	objective	direct object of the preposition *by*
4. him	objective	direct object of the verb *know*
5. us	objective	direct object of the verb *criticized*
6. He	nominative	subject of the sentence
7. they	nominative	predicate pronoun after the verb *have been*
8. them	objective	direct object of the preposition *to*
9. Who	nominative	subject of the sentence
10. me	objective	direct object of the verb *sent*
11. We	nominative	subject of the sentence
12. Whom	objective	direct object of the verb *did see*
13. whom	objective	direct object of the preposition *to*
14. him	objective	indirect object
15. She	nominative	subject of the sentence

CORRECT ANSWERS TO ASSIGNMENT 3

Singular	Singular Possessive	Plural	Plural Possessive
1. landlady	landlady's	landladies	landladies'
2. woman	woman's	women	women's
3. she	her, hers	they	their, theirs
4. another	another's	(*no plural*)	(*no plural*)
5. deer	deer's	deer	deer's
6. Higgins	Higgins' or Higgins's	Higginses	Higginses'
7. attorney	attorney's	attorneys	attorneys'

8. it	its	they	their, theirs
9. Ruth	Ruth's	Ruths	Ruths'
10. sheriff	sheriff's	sheriffs	sheriffs'
11. calf	calf's	calves	calves'
12. countess	countess' or countess's	countesses	countesses'
13. Jones	Jones' or Jones's	Joneses	Joneses'
14. Henry	Henry's	Henrys	Henrys'
15. ally	ally's	allies	allies'

CORRECT ANSWERS TO ASSIGNMENT 4

1. Birds' nests were found in the top branches.

2. The president's secretary read Mr. Burns' report. (or Burns's)

3. Our family's estate was settled according to the judge's ruling.

4. They had to abide by the umpire's decision.

5. May I borrow Louis' (or Louis's) car for the evening?

6. We always buy Crosse and Blackwell's jams.

7. The editor-in-chief's comments were significant.

8. Several of Dickens' (or Dickens's) novels have been dramatized.

9. He seems to be the people's choice for governor.

10. The postmaster general's office is on the right.

11. The women's organizations planned a campaign.

12. We were granted a month's vacation.

13. The committee met at Mr. Evans' (or Mr. Evans's) home.

14. Someone's coat was left in Jane's locker.

15. We did several days' work that evening.

CORRECT ANSWERS TO PROGRESS TEST NINE

A.—(*25 points*)

1. It was **they.** Did you think it was **he?**
2. **He** and **I** are going to build a canoe.
3. The boat was **theirs.** The canoes were **ours.**
4. From **whom** did you receive the money?
5. The boys are going with James and **me.** With **whom** are you going?
6. Eugene and **he** enlisted last week.
7. **Whom** did you sit beside at the concert? I sat with **them.**
8. John, Harry, and **I** were appointed delegates.
9. **Everybody's** name was called.
10. The noise frightened her and **him.** It did not frighten **us.**
11. **She** and I arrived at the same time. When did you and **he** arrive?
12. That television set is **hers. Whose** set is this?
13. No one signed the paper except **him** and **me.**
14. **Someone's** umbrella was left in the hall. Was it **yours?**
15. **We** boys are going to join the club.

B.—(*15 points*)

1. stepchildren's income
2. parents' organization
3. editor-in-chief's desk
4. two months' credit
5. enemy's line
6. father-in-law's business
7. season's greetings
8. Marshall Field and Company's store
9. attorney general's opinion
10. book reviewer's task
11. Burns' poems (or Burns's)
12. Citizens' rights
13. Morris' name (or Morris's)
14. three weeks' vacation
15. scientist's discovery

HOW TO OBTAIN YOUR SCORE

The test totals 40 points. To obtain your score, divide the number of your correct answers by 40. The answer will be your score on this test. For example, if you have 32 points correct, your score is 32 divided by 40 which is 80 per cent. In other words, your score on this test is 80. You can obtain your score on any of the exercises or assignments by following the same procedure.

Practical English Grammar

OUTLINE OF UNIT TEN

MODIFIERS: ADJECTIVES

MODIFIERS: ADJECTIVES

IN GRAMMAR UNIT TWO you learned that adjectives and adverbs are modifiers; that is, they are words used to make the meaning of other words more definite and more vivid. In this unit you will learn more about these helpful and interesting words. You will also learn how to use them effectively in speaking and writing.

Adjectives give life and color to language. They also help us give more exact pictures of what we are telling about, if we know how to select them carefully. As you improve your skill in using these words, your language will become more interesting and more explicit.

Let us assume that you were telling someone about a man whom you had seen. You might start out with a sentence like this: "I met a man walking down the street." This sentence does not give us an interesting description or very accurate information. It tells very little about the man, his manner of walking, or the street down which he walked.

Someone who has skill in selecting words that would give a more definite and colorful description, might change the sentence into something like this:

I met a **weary** and **disheartened old** man hobbling down the **narrow, winding** street.

This sentence has been made more colorful and more accurate by the use of the adjectives *weary, disheartened,* and *old* to describe the man, and by the use of the adjectives *narrow* and *winding* to describe the street.

In order to use adjectives effectively, you must know the exact shade of meaning that you wish to convey. Then you must be able to select the adjective or adjectives that express that shade of meaning.

You might want to use an adjective to describe a certain type of individual, and you are not sure whether to use the adjective *sly* or the adjective *cunning*. Whenever you are in doubt, consult a reliable, up-to-date dictionary. In most dictionaries these differences in meaning are pointed out.

The adjective *sly* always implies that the individual is working or acting secretly, or is using underhand methods. The adjective *cunning* implies the use of intelligence, skill, or ingenuity. The two words do not mean exactly the same thing.

The following exercise will give you excellent practice in learning how to select the adjective that expresses the exact meaning you would like to convey. The adjectives listed below are divided into groups of three. Each adjective in a group of three expresses a different shade of meaning. Try to write sentences using these words. Be sure that your sentences show the differences in meaning. The dictionary will be a great help.

1. small—diminutive—little

2. funny—strange—queer

3. strong—robust—sturdy

4. beautiful—handsome—lovely

5. bright—shining—brilliant

"OVERWORKED" ADJECTIVES

There is a tendency on the part of many people to use the same adjective to apply to a number of different situations. When a person does this, the assumption is that he has a very limited vocabulary. As a result, he is not able to express his meaning precisely. For example, he may use the word *lovely* to describe many different things. In certain cases, the adjective *lovely* is appropriate. In other cases, it is not the most appropriate or the most precise word to use. Study the following illustrations carefully:

a *lovely* time	a *lovely* view
a *lovely* dress	a *lovely* voice
a *lovely* picnic	a *lovely* program
a *lovely* motion picture	a *lovely* day
a *lovely* street	a *lovely* necktie

If you wanted to describe a hat, instead of using the word *lovely,* you might use any one of the following adjectives: *becoming, stylish, fashionable, smart, colorful, modish, dashing, beautiful,* etc. The careful speaker or writer would choose the one that expressed the exact shade of meaning he wished to convey. This requires careful analysis, but it is worth the effort.

Adjectives that are applied in many different types of situations are often called "overworked" or "shopworn" adjectives. The following adjectives belong in this list:

fine	lovely	swell	cute
grand	nice	adorable	perfectly lovely
funny	terrible	keen	simply grand
awful	crazy	sweet	perfectly adorable

Some of these adjectives are called "feminine adjectives" because they are popular with women.

EXERCISE 1

The purpose of this exercise is to show you how to avoid the overworked adjective. Choose the *adjective* enclosed in parentheses that would make the meaning more precise. Place your choice on the line to the right. Other adjectives might also be used to make the meaning more precise.

1. Stephen is (a nice, an unusually good) dancer.   1. ....

2. We have a (good, competent) secretary.   2. ....

3. There is a (nice, well-kept) lawn in front of the library.   3. ....

4. That was (an awful, a difficult) job.   4. ....

5. The ice cream was (grand, delicious).   5. ....

6. What (a perfectly adorable, an attractive) child!   6. ....

7. I had (a swell, an exciting) time at the dance.   7. ....

8. Jane always wears (unbecoming, frightful) hats.   8. ....

9. That woman is a (dangerous, terrible) gossip.   9. ....

10. The speaker gave (a grand, an inspiring) talk.   10. ....

11. That was (a fine, an interesting) book you sent me.   11. ....

12. Madge is a (perfectly lovely, charming) hostess.   12. ....

13. James thinks he's (clever, cute).   13. ....

14. Father was pleased with Jane's (excellent, nice) grades.   14. ....

15. That was a (funny, peculiar) remark Dick made. (not humorous)   15. ....

Note: *The correct answers to exercises will be found at the end of this unit. Correct your mistakes and, if necessary, reread the text material before going on to the next section.*

KINDS OF ADJECTIVES

There are two kinds of adjectives: *descriptive* adjectives and *limiting* adjectives. **Descriptive adjectives,** as the name implies, give color and vividness to the persons, places, or things we talk or write about. **Limiting adjectives** indicate number or quantity.

Descriptive adjectives tell *what kind, what color, what size, what shape,* etc. Limiting adjectives tell *how many, how much, which one, whose,* etc.

three checks (limiting)	**brilliant** speaker (descriptive)
high mountain (descriptive)	**one** airplane (limiting)
a **new** car (descriptive)	a **few** children (limiting)
two branches (limiting)	a **sympathetic** listener (descriptive)

Adjectives derived from proper nouns are called **proper adjectives.** They are usually written with a capital letter. They are usually descriptive adjectives.

Siberian squirrel	**Turkish** tobacco
Canadian bacon	**Norwegian** sardines
American industries	**Danish** silver
Mexican pottery	**Swedish** crystal
United States flag	**Swiss** watches
English wool	**Brazilian** coffee
Venetian blinds	**Indian** summer
Bunsen burner	**Portland** cement

EXERCISE 2

Underline the **adjectives** in the following sentences. On the line to the right, indicate whether the adjective is *descriptive, limiting,* or a *proper adjective.* Omit the articles *a, an,* and *the.*

Example: She wore a <u>red</u> hat.   descriptive

1. The tiresome journey was now at an end.   1. ....

2. Do you like the two supervisors?   2. ....

3. We buy South American coffee.   3. ....

4. I have the latest edition of the paper.   4. ....

5. There are three magazines on the table.   5. ....

6. Which is the best seller?   6. ....

7. The doctor recommended a Turkish bath.   7. ....

8. What's wrong with that sputtering engine?   8. ....

9. We caught several fish yesterday.   9. ....

10. There are five men on the committee.   10. ....

11. Her dress was a Scotch plaid.   11. ....

12. He spoke to a very enthusiastic audience.   12. ....

13. We lived in a Swiss chalet for years.   13. ....

14. That is a very economical car to operate.   14. ....

15. Her coat was made of Alaskan seal.   15. ....

PREDICATE ADJECTIVES

Adjectives that complete the meaning of the verb and modify the subject are called **predicate adjectives.** If an adjective is found in the predicate and modifies a noun in the predicate, it is not a predicate adjective. The adjective must follow a linking verb and modify the subject in order to be classified as a predicate adjective. The predicate adjective usually *describes* the subject noun or pronoun.

The list of linking verbs which was given in Grammar Unit Eight is repeated here for reference. You should become familiar with this important list of verbs. It will help you identify the predicate adjectives that are used after linking verbs.

Linking Verbs

is	grow	look	smell	remain
become	turn	feel	taste	keep
seem	prove	sound	appear	stay

Illustrations

The cookies are <u>delicious</u>. (*delicious* cookies)
pred. adj.

Corn is <u>plentiful</u> in Illinois. (*plentiful* corn)
pred. adj.

The street has become very <u>muddy</u>. (*muddy* street)
pred. adj.

The airplane is an <u>effective</u> weapon. (*effective* weapon)
not a pred. adj.

Note that the adjective *effective* in the last sentence is not a predicate adjective, although it is found in the predicate. The adjective *effective* does not modify the subject, and it is not used to complete the verb *is*. A predicate noun *weapon* completes the verb *is*. *Effective* modifies the predicate noun (*effective* weapon).

Position of the Adjective

An adjective is usually placed directly before the noun it modifies. Sometimes the adjective follows the word it modifies. The predicate adjective is always found in the predicate after the verb it completes.

1. Adjectives placed before the noun.

   An **old, gnarled** tree lay across the stream.

2. Adjectives placed after the noun.

   A tree, **old** and **gnarled,** lay across the stream.

3. Predicate adjectives, placed after the verb.

   The tree was **old** and **gnarled.**

EXERCISE 3

Underline the **predicate adjectives** in the following sentences. On the line to the right, indicate the word the adjective *modifies*. If the sentence does not contain a predicate adjective, leave the line blank.

1. The child has become irritable.   1. ....

2. That is a tender steak.   2. ....

3. The days are growing longer.   3. ....

4. The milk tastes sour.   4. ....

5. Did you taste the sour milk?   5. ....

6. The audience seems restless.   6. ....

7. The witness turned pale.   7. ....

8. The snake proved harmless.   8. ....

9. We left on the late train.   9. ....

10. Everything was quiet on the battlefield.   10. ....

11. The prisoner remained calm.   11. ....

12. The lilacs are very fragrant.   12. ....

13. Andrew appeared very happy after the game 13. ....

14. The velvet feels smooth.   14. ....

15. My cousin is a prominent surgeon.   15. ....

NOUNS USED AS ADJECTIVES

We have already considered the use of pronouns as adjectives in Grammar Unit Six. Nouns are also frequently *used as adjectives*. The nouns in the following expressions are used as adjectives:

college credits (modifies *credits*)

dress accessories (modifies *accessories*)

window sash (modifies *sash*)

Fourth of July speech (modifies *speech*)

summer clothes (modifies *clothes*)

table lamp (modifies *lamp*)

A noun in the *possessive case* is often placed before another noun which it modifies. In such cases, the noun in the possessive case is used as an adjective although it has not lost the function of showing ownership or possession. Nouns used in this way are sometimes called **possessive adjectives**. Sometimes they are described as nouns in the possessive case used as adjectives. Observe how nouns in the possessive case are used in the following sentences:

John's car was wrecked in the crash. (*John's* modifies *car*.)

I like to shop in **Macy's** store. (*Macy's* modifies *store*.)

I am wearing my **sister's** coat. (*sister's* modifies *coat*.)

EXERCISE 4

Underline the *nouns used as adjectives*. On the line to the right, indicate the word which the noun used as an adjective modifies. Some sentences have two nouns used as adjectives. Indicate both.

Example: He wore a winter suit.

suit
....

1. The church choir sang an anthem.

1. ....

2. Did you open the morning mail?

2. ....

3. He did not meet the college requirements.

3. ....

4. The chair is a museum piece.

4. ....

5. Will you ride in Andrew's car?

5. ....

6. He has spent all of his wife's money.

6. ....

7. We spent the summer at my uncle's home.

7. ....

8. I am not responsible for the bookkeeper's mistakes.

8. ....

9. Did you ever ride on a cable car?

9. ....

10. The chef made a plum pudding.

10. ....

11. The stenographer uses a Royal typewriter.

11. ....

12. Men's clothing is on the fifth floor.

12. ....

13. A typist's error was responsible for the misunderstanding.

13. ....

14. The office force did not like the manager's attitude.

14. ....

15. Housewives' food problems have increased lately.

15. ....

COMPARISON OF ADJECTIVES

The form of an adjective is often changed to show the extent or degree to which a certain quality is present. In grammar, this change in form to show a difference in degree is called *comparison.*

There are three degrees of comparison in English: the *positive degree,* the *comparative degree,* and the *superlative degree.*

The **positive degree** is really not a degree of comparison because no comparison is indicated when the positive degree is used. The positive degree is the simple form of the adjective. It shows that the quality is present, but it does not show a comparison with anything else. The adjectives in the following sentences are all positive degree:

That is a **beautiful** rose.   Jane is **studious.**

It was a very **cold** day.   The **old** house was sold.

Peter is very **energetic.**   It was a very **warm** day.

In the preceding illustrations, the adjective simply shows that the quality is present. No comparison is made with any other person or thing.

The **comparative degree** of the adjective is used when a comparison is made between **two** persons or things. The comparative degree shows that the quality (expressed by the adjective) exists to a *greater* or to a *lesser* degree in one of the two persons or things that are being compared.

The comparative degree of almost all adjectives of *one* syllable is formed by adding **er** to the positive degree, or to the simple form of the adjective; for example, *colder, smoother, longer, greater, stronger, firmer, thicker,* etc.

John is **stronger** than Michael. (*two persons* compared)
<small>comparative degree</small>

This table is **larger** than that table. (*two objects* compared)
<small>comparative degree</small>

In the first sentence, *two persons* are compared as to strength. According to the sentence, John possesses this quality of strength to a greater degree than Michael. The comparative degree of the adjective is used because a comparison is made between *two* persons.

In the second sentence, *two tables* are being compared as to size. The comparative degree of the adjective *large* is used because a comparison is made between *two objects.*

The **superlative degree** of the adjective is used when **more than two** persons or things are compared. The superlative degree indicates that the quality (expressed by the adjective) is possessed to the *greatest* or to the *least* degree by one of the persons or things included in the comparison.

> Our house is the **largest** house in the block. (More than two are compared.)   superlative degree

> Louis is the **smallest** boy in his class. (More than two are compared.)   superlative degree

In the first sentence, *more than two* houses are being compared. The superlative degree of the adjective *large* is used to show this fact. The house that possesses the quality expressed by the adjective *large* to the greatest degree is *our* house. It is the *largest* house in a block which contains more than two houses.

In the second sentence, more than two boys are being compared as to size. Louis possesses this quality to the *least* degree. The superlative degree of the adjective *small* is used to show this fact.

DEGREES OF COMPARISON
Adjectives of One Syllable

Positive	Comparative	Superlative
neat	neater	neatest
sharp	sharper	sharpest
dark	darker	darkest
keen	keener	keenest
long	longer	longest

Adjectives of *two or more syllables* are usually compared by prefixing the words *more* and *most* to the simple form of the adjective. *More* is used to indicate the comparison between two persons or things. *Most* is used to indicate the comparison between more than two persons or things. *Less* and *least* are used in a similar way.

Positive	Comparative	Superlative
fragrant	*more* fragrant	*most* fragrant
famous	*less* famous	*least* famous
precious	*more* precious	*most* precious
difficult	*less* difficult	*least* difficult

Sometimes adjectives of *one syllable* are compared by prefixing *more* and *most*. Sometimes adjectives of *more than one syllable* are compared by adding **er** and **est**. There is no rule to follow for making these exceptions. It is usually a matter of sound. If one form of comparison sounds better than the other, that is the form of comparison to use. It sounds better to say *crisp, more crisp, most crisp,* than to say *crisp, crisper, crispest.* Therefore, the comparison with *more* and *most* is preferred.

Adjectives of more than one syllable that end in **y** are usually compared by adding **er** and **est**. Notice the change in spelling in the comparative and in the superlative degrees. The **y** changes to **i** before the addition of **er** or **est**.

Positive	Comparative	Superlative
silly	sillier	silliest
dainty	daintier	daintiest
clumsy	clumsier	clumsiest
handy	handier	handiest
noisy	noisier	noisiest

EXERCISE 5

Fill in the table by giving the **comparative** and the **superlative** degrees of the following adjectives:

Positive	Comparative	Superlative
1. clean	....	....
2. beautiful	....	....
3. abundant	....	....
4. easy	....	....
5. sweet	....	....
6. delightful	....	....
7. dangerous	....	....

8. able   ....

9. crisp   ....

10. eager   ....

11. valuable   ....

12. cautious   ....

13. calm   ....

14. industrious ....

15. round   ....

IRREGULAR COMPARISON OF ADJECTIVES

Some adjectives are compared *irregularly*. The forms for the comparative degree and for the superlative degree usually show a marked change in the form of the word; for example, *many, more, most.* You should be familiar with these changes in order to use the correct forms for the comparative and superlative degrees.

Adjectives Compared Irregularly

Positive	Comparative	Superlative
bad, evil, ill	worse	worst
far	further	furthest
far	farther	farthest
good, well	better	best
little	less	least
many	more	most
much	more	most
out	outer	outmost
		or outermost

Farther refers to *distance* or remoteness in space. **Further** refers to remoteness in *time,* to *degree, extent,* or *quantity.* It is also used to express the idea of something *more* or *additional.*

The garage is **farther** than I thought. (distance in space)

I shall give you **further** instructions tomorrow. (*additional* instructions)

The distinctions between *farther* and *further* are passing out of use. These words are now used interchangeably. There is also a tendency to use *further* to express all the meanings discussed. (See latest dictionaries.)

ADJECTIVES NOT COMPARED

There are a number of adjectives that should not be compared because the **simple** form of the adjective expresses the quality to the highest possible degree. For example, if an answer to a problem is *correct,* another answer could not possibly be *more correct.* If a circle is absolutely *round,* another circle could not be *more round.* If a bottle is *empty,* another bottle could not be *more empty.*

The following are some of the adjectives that are not compared for the reasons given:

perfect	unique	square	universal
single	supreme	fatal	empty
vertical	full	alone	dead
final	mortal	instantaneous	deadly
straight	blind	everlasting	wrong

The expression, *more nearly round,* is often used when comparing two things, one of which is *more nearly round* than the other. In this case, however, neither of the things compared is round. A line could be *more nearly straight* than another line if neither of the lines was absolutely straight.

Sometimes an adjective such as the word *honest* is used in the comparative and superlative degrees. In such cases, we have no standard of absolute honesty. What the writer or speaker means is that one person approaches the absolute state of honesty to a greater or to a lesser degree than another person. The adjective *perfect* is often used in the same way.

EXERCISE 6

Underline the **adjectives** in the following sentences. On the line to the right, indicate the degree of comparison: *positive, comparative,* or *superlative.*

1. Martha's income is smaller than Harry's.   1. ....

2. Mr. Cummings made the largest contribution.   2. ....

3. This map is exceedingly large.   3. ....

4. Paul's desk is smaller than mine.   4. ....

5. This is the most beautiful home in the suburb.   5. ....

6. Father is more lenient than Mother.   6. ....

7. The cake is better than the pie.   7. ....

8. This is the best food I have ever eaten.   8. ....

9. I have the latest edition of the paper.   9. ....

10. Irma is a very attractive model.   10. ....

11. He is the oldest employee in the bank.   11. ....

12. Our bank has more money on deposit than any other bank.   12. ....

13. The manager has more duties than the president. 13. ....

14. The kitchen is the warmest room in the house. 14. ....

15. That was the most terrible storm we have had this winter.   15. ....

DIAGRAMMING THE ADJECTIVE MODIFIER

An **adjective modifier** is placed on a slanted line which is joined to the word which the adjective modifies.

Sentence: The *beautiful old* house was demolished.

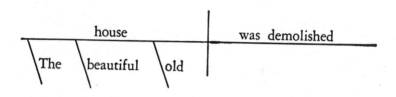

In this sentence, *the, beautiful,* and *old* are adjectives modifying the noun *house.* They are placed on slanted lines which are joined to the line on which the word *house* is placed.

The **predicate adjective** is diagrammed on the same line as the verb. It is separated from the verb by a line that slants in the direction of the subject. This is done to show that the predicate adjective completes the verb and modifies the subject.

Sentence: His novel became *famous.* (*his* — pronoun used as adjective)
<u>pred. adj.</u>

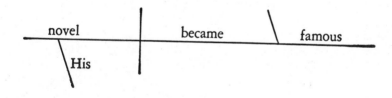

When the adjective follows the noun it modifies, it is diagrammed in exactly the same way as it would be if it were placed before the noun.

Sentence: The model, *tall* and *beautiful,* received the award.

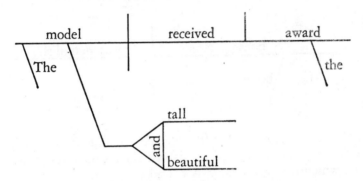

The adjectives *tall* and *beautiful* connected by *and* constitute a compound adjective modifier of the word *model.*

EXERCISE 7

Diagram the following sentences:

1. The brilliant speaker was a former journalist.

2. The factory whistle sounds shrill.

3. That is a wide, comfortable chair.

4. The road, long and winding, was hazardous.

SUMMARY OF GRAMMAR UNIT TEN

An **adjective** is a word used to modify a noun or a pronoun. A *modifier* limits or qualifies the meaning of another word. Adjectives *limit* or *describe* nouns or pronouns.

There are two main classes of adjectives — *limiting adjectives* and *descriptive adjectives*. **Descriptive adjectives** give color and vividness to the words which they modify. **Limiting adjectives** indicate number or quantity.

Adjectives derived from proper nouns are called **proper adjectives.** A proper adjective is usually written with a capital letter.

Adjectives that complete the meaning of linking verbs and modify the subject are called **predicate adjectives.**

Nouns and pronouns are frequently *used as adjectives.* A noun or a pronoun in the possessive case is often used before another noun which it modifies. Nouns and pronouns used in this way are called **possessive adjectives** because they show possession.

An adjective is usually placed before the word it modifies. It may also follow the word it modifies. An adjective is also found in the predicate following a linking verb although it modifies the subject.

The *form* of an adjective is often changed to show the degree or extent to which a certain quality is present. This change in form to show a change in degree is called *comparison*.

There are three degrees of comparison: the *positive degree,* the *comparative degree,* and the *superlative degree.*

The **positive degree** is the simple form of the adjective. No comparison is indicated when the positive degree is used. The positive degree of the adjective *small* is the word *small.*

The **comparative degree** is used when a comparison is made between **two** persons or things. The comparative degree shows that a quality exists to a *greater* or to a *lesser* degree in one of the two persons or things which are compared.

The **superlative degree** is used when **more than two** persons or things are compared. The superlative degree indicates that the quality is possessed to the *greatest* or to the *least* degree by one of the persons or things included in the comparison.

The *comparative degree* of almost all adjectives of **one** syllable is formed by adding **er** to the form of the positive degree. The comparative degree of the adjective *small* is *smaller.* The *superlative degree* of adjectives of **one** syllable is usually formed by adding **est** to the form of the positive degree. The superlative degree of the adjective *small* is *smallest.*

Adjectives of **two or more** syllables are usually compared by prefixing *more* or *most* to the simple form of the adjective (positive degree). *More* is used to indicate a comparison between **two** persons or things. *Most* is used to indicate a comparison between **more than two** persons or things.

Jane is <u>more studious</u> than her sister.
       comparative degree

Alice is the <u>most ambitious</u> girl in the class.
       superlative degree

SELF-GRADING ASSIGNMENT 1

Directions: Underline the **adjectives** in the following sentences. On the line to the right, indicate whether the adjective is *limiting*, *descriptive*, a *proper adjective*, or a *predicate adjective*. Do not list the articles.

Example: We ordered <u>Swiss</u> cheese.   *proper*

1. He is a man of firm convictions.   1. ....

2. The American consul attended the meeting.   2. ....

3. The boy became sullen.   3. ....

4. The newspaper received a thousand replies.   4. ....

5. The sky appears cloudy.   5. ....

6. That was the ninth inning.   6. ....

7. My friend collects Indian blankets.   7. ....

8. I want four pounds of candy.   8. ....

9. They refused to accept Argentine beef.   9. ....

10. She is a woman eager to serve others.   10. ....

11. Ten plans were submitted to the committee.   11. ....

12. The dress, simple and attractive, was worn by a model.   12. ....

13. We were allowed to make a second choice.   13. ....

14. Temporary windows were put in the building.   14. ....

15. That was a delicious pudding.   15. ....

Caution: Check your answers to each assignment with the answer key at the end of this unit before proceeding with the next assignment.

SELF-GRADING ASSIGNMENT 2

Directions: Underline the **nouns** and the **pronouns** that are used as *adjectives*. On the line to the right, indicate the word that the noun or pronoun (used an adjective) *modifies*.

Example: <u>Which</u> boy won the prize?   boy

1. Each employee was given a raise in salary.   1. ....

2. The manager's office is on the first floor.   2. ....

3. The officers were discussing submarine strategy.   3. ....

4. His new novel is very popular.   4. ....

5. Did you read their letters?   5. ....

6. The firm tries to satisfy its customers.   6. ....

7. Any suggestions will be welcome.   7. ....

8. We built a wood fire in the old stove.   8. ....

9. The president's plan was accepted by the trustees.   9. ....

10. Has everyone completed the grammar assignment?   10. ....

11. Everybody's luggage was checked at the airport.   11. ....

12. The salesmen asked for new sample cases.   12. ....

13. Interest rates have declined recently.   13. ....

14. Your last letter was very well written.   14. ....

15. Some changes will be made next year.   15. ....

SELF-GRADING ASSIGNMENT 3

In working out this assignment, keep this fact in mind: Use the *comparative degree* when comparing **two** persons or things, and the *superlative degree* when comparing **more than two.**

Directions: Rewrite the following sentences making any corrections that are necessary. If the sentence is correct, write the word *correct* (enclosed in parentheses) after it.

1. That is the worse letter we have ever received.

2. Of the three sisters, Jane is the more attractive.

3. Is this the stronger of the five ropes?

4. This typewriter is better than the one on your desk.

5. He has the littlest initiative of any worker in the plant.

6. Fred's article is the better of the three.

7. Your writing is bad, but mine is badder.

8. Andrew plays the violin better than his sister.

9. That was the wonderfulest place I ever visited.

10. Which of the three writers is the better?

11. That was the most happiest moment in her life.

12. Of the two bookkeepers, he is the least capable.

13. Morris works faster than any other man on the job.

14. This hat is becoming, but that hat is most becoming.

15. After the long ride, I was tireder than Mother.

PROGRESS TEST TEN

This progress test should not be taken until a day or two after you have completed the assignments. The score you make on the test will then more clearly reflect your understanding of the material in the unit.

Directions: Fill in the blanks with the correct forms of the **adjectives** enclosed in parentheses. The form you select should be the correct degree of comparison required in the sentence: *positive, comparative,* or *superlative. (25 points)*

Example: John is .... than Frank. (reliable)

John is **more reliable** than Frank.

1. The lily is the.....................................of all flowers. (beautiful)

2. This book is the.................................of the two. (instructive)

3. Anne is the...girl in the class. (studious)

4. This traffic law is........................than the previous law. (severe)

5. Which of the four boys sells the........................papers? (many)

6. He is the........................member on the committee of five. (able)

7. The yellow apple is...........................than the red apple. (sweet)

8. The last concert was the...............concert of the season. (good)

9. Shark meat is the...of all meats. (tough)

10. Today is..than yesterday. (pleasant)

11. That knife is...than this knife. (good)

12. Is this the...of the six copies? (recent)

13. Ethel is the...girl I know. (happy)

14. That is the..............................story I have ever read. (unusual)

15. Louis is the...of the two brothers. (tall)

16. Neil is the..................................boy in the Scout troop. (active)

17. Who is the....................scientist, Darwin or Einstein? (famous)

18. Who is the................................merchant in town? (progressive)

19. Yesterday was the..............day we have had in many years. (bad)

20. Mrs. Ehlers is the............................woman in the club. (talkative)

21. Marvin is a..manager than Kate. (good)

22. The supervisor's suggestion was the...................................of the two. (practical)

23. January was the................................month of the year. (cold)

24. Clare is a................................tennis player than Merton. (fast)

25. Lillian is the...girl in our circulating department. (amiable)

ANSWER KEY

for

EXERCISES, ASSIGNMENTS, AND PROGRESS TEST

Grammar Unit Ten

CORRECT ANSWERS TO EXERCISE 1

1. unusually good	6. attractive	11. interesting
2. competent	7. exciting	12. charming
3. well-kept	8. unbecoming	13. clever
4. difficult	9. dangerous	14. excellent
5. delicious	10. inspiring	15. peculiar

CORRECT ANSWERS TO EXERCISE 2

1. tiresome—*descriptive*
2. two—*limiting*
3. South American—*proper*
4. latest—*limiting or descriptive*
5. three—*limiting*
6. best—*descriptive*
7. Turkish—*proper*
8. sputtering—*descriptive*
9. several—*limiting*
10. five—*limiting*
11. Scotch—*proper*
12. enthusiastic—*descriptive*
13. Swiss—*proper*
14. economical—*descriptive*
15. Alaskan—*proper*

CORRECT ANSWERS TO EXERCISE 3

1. irritable	child	9. *no predicate adjective*	
2. *no predicate adjective*		10. quiet	everything
3. longer	days	11. calm	prisoner
4. sour	milk	12. fragrant	lilacs
5. *no predicate adjective*		13. happy	Andrew
6. restless	audience	14. smooth	velvet
7. pale	witness	15. *no predicate adjective*	
8. harmless	snake		

CORRECT ANSWERS TO EXERCISE 4

1.	church	choir	9. cable	car
2.	morning	mail	10. plum	pudding
3.	college	requirements	11. Royal	typewriter
4.	museum	piece	12. Men's	clothing
5.	Andrew's	car	13. typist's	error
6.	wife's	money	14. office	force
7.	uncle's	home	manager's	attitude
8.	bookkeeper's	mistakes	15. Housewives' food	problems problems

CORRECT ANSWERS TO EXERCISE 5

Positive	Comparative	Superlative
1. clean	cleaner	cleanest
2. beautiful	more beautiful	most beautiful
3. abundant	more abundant	most abundant
4. easy	easier	easiest
5. sweet	sweeter	sweetest
6. delightful	more delightful	most delightful
7. dangerous	more dangerous	most dangerous
8. able	abler more able	ablest most able
9. crisp	more crisp	most crisp
10. eager	more eager	most eager
11. valuable	more valuable.	most valuable
12. cautious	more cautious	most cautious
13. calm	calmer more calm	calmest most calm
14. industrious	more industrious	most industrious
15. round	(*usually not compared*)	

CORRECT ANSWERS TO EXERCISE 6

Adjective	Degree of Comparison	Adjective	Degree of Comparison
1. smaller	*comparative*	9. latest	*superlative*
2. largest	*superlative*	10. attractive	*positive*
3. large	*positive*	11. oldest	*superlative*
4. smaller	*comparative*	12. more	*comparative*
5. most beautiful	*superlative*	13. more	*comparative*
6. more lenient	*comparative*	14. warmest	*superlative*
7. better	*comparative*	15. most terrible	*superlative*
8. best	*superlative*		

CORRECT ANSWERS TO EXERCISE 7

1. The <u>brilliant</u> speaker was a <u>former</u> journalist.
    adjective   adjective

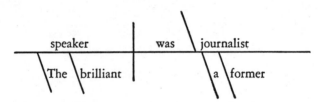

2. The <u>factory</u> whistle sounds <u>shrill</u>.
    adjective   adjective

3. That is a wide, comfortable chair.

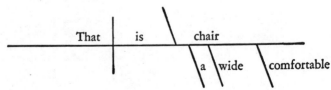

4. The road, long and winding, was hazardous.

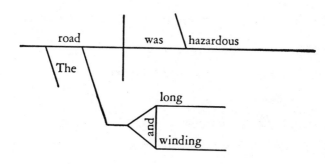

CORRECT ANSWERS TO ASSIGNMENTS

ASSIGNMENT 1

	Adjective	Kind
1.	firm	*descriptive*
2.	American	*proper*
3.	sullen	*predicate adjective descriptive*
4.	thousand	*limiting*
5.	cloudy	*predicate adjective descriptive*
6.	ninth	*limiting*
7.	Indian	*proper*
8.	four	*limiting*
9.	Argentine	*proper*
10.	eager	*descriptive*
11.	Ten	*limiting*
12.	simple attractive	*descriptive descriptive*
13.	second	*limiting*
14.	Temporary	*descriptive*
15.	delicious	*descriptive*

ASSIGNMENT 2

	Noun or Pronoun Used as Adjective	Modifies
1.	Each	employee
2.	manager's	office
3.	submarine	strategy
4.	His	novel
5.	their	letters
6.	its	customers
7.	Any	suggestions
8.	wood	fire
9.	president's	plan
10.	grammar	assignment
11.	Everybody's	luggage
12.	sample	cases
13.	Interest	rates
14.	Your	letter
15.	Some	changes

CORRECT ANSWERS TO ASSIGNMENT 3

Correct forms of adjectives are printed in **heavy type.**

1. That is the **worst** letter we ever received.

2. Of the three sisters, Jane is the **most attractive.**

3. Is this the **strongest** of the five ropes?

4. This typewriter is **better** than the one on your desk. (*correct*)

5. He has the **least** initiative of any worker in the plant.

6. Fred's article is the **best** of the three.

7. Your writing is bad, but mine is **worse.**

8. Andrew plays the violin **better** than his sister. (*correct*)

9. That was the **most wonderful** place I ever visited.

10. Which of the three writers is the **best?**

11. That was the **happiest** moment in her life.

12. Of the two bookkeepers, he is the **less** capable.

13. Morris works **faster** than any other man on the job. (*correct*)

14. This hat is becoming, but that hat is **more becoming.**

15. After the long ride, I was **more tired** than Mother.

CORRECT ANSWERS TO PROGRESS TEST TEN

Correct forms of adjectives are printed in **heavy type.**

1. The lily is the **most beautiful** of all flowers.

2. This book is the **more instructive** of the two.

3. Anne is the **most studious** girl in the class.

4. This traffic law is **more severe** than the previous law.

5. Which of the four boys sells the **most** papers?

6. He is the **ablest** (or **most able**) member on the committee of five.

7. The yellow apple is **sweeter** than the red apple.

8. The last concert was the **best** concert of the season.

9. Shark meat is the **toughest** of all meats.

10. Today is **more pleasant** than yesterday.

11. That knife is **better** than this knife.

12. Is this the **most recent** of the six copies?

13. Ethel is the **happiest** girl I know.

14. That is the **most unusual** story I have ever read.

15. Louis is the **taller** of the two brothers.

16. Neil is the **most active** boy in the Scout troop.

17. Who is the **more famous** scientist, Darwin or Einstein?

18. Who is the **most progressive** merchant in town?

19. Yesterday was the **worst** day we have had in many years.

20. Mrs. Ehlers is the **most talkative** woman in the club.

21. Marvin is a **better** manager than Kate.

22. The supervisor's suggestion was the **more practical** of the two.

23. January was the **coldest** month of the year.

24. Clare is a **faster** tennis player than Merton.

25. Lillian is the **most amiable** girl in our circulating department.

HOW TO OBTAIN YOUR SCORE

The test totals 25 points. To obtain your score, divide the number of your correct answers by 25. The answer will be your score on this test. For example, if you have 22 points correct, your score is 22 divided by 25 which is 88 per cent. In other words, your score on this test is 88. You can obtain your score on any of the exercises or assignments by following the same procedure.

Practical English Grammar

OUTLINE OF UNIT ELEVEN

MODIFIERS: ADVERBS

MODIFIERS: ADVERBS

BEFORE beginning this detailed study of adverbs, you should review the discussion of adverbs given in Grammar Unit Two. In Unit Two we considered the adverb as a modifier of the verb, telling *how, when, where,* and *to what degree* the action is performed. In this unit, we shall study other uses of the adverb, and the relation of adverbs to adjectives and to other adverbs.

FORMS OF ADVERBS

Students sometimes have the idea that all adverbs end in **ly.** There are a great many adverbs that do end in **ly,** but there are probably just as many that do not end in **ly.** Many adverbs are formed by adding **ly** to the adjective form:

Adjective	Adverb	Adjective	Adverb
strange	strangely	awkward	awkwardly
sudden	suddenly	necessary	necessarily
calm	calmly	strict	strictly
sure	surely	forcible	forcibly
usual	usually	extreme	extremely
swift	swiftly	similar	similarly
rapid	rapidly	slight	slightly

The following are some of the adverbs that do not end in **ly:**

seldom	little	why	fast
again	here	now	twice
soon	there	then	too
very	rather	since	much
almost	often	well	quite
late	when	near	yonder
hard	where	far	how

Many adjectives end in **ly**. They should not be confused with adverbs that end in **ly**. The following words ending in **ly** are commonly used as adjectives. Some of them might also be used as adverbs:

stately	lovely	saintly	manly
lonely	womanly	lively	courtly

Some adjectives have the same form as the adverb. In such cases, the only way you can tell whether the word is an *adjective* or an *adverb,* is to determine its use in a particular sentence. Study the following illustrations carefully:

That was a **hard** task. (*hard*—adjective, modifies *task*)

Our janitor works **hard**. (*hard*—adverb, modifies *works*)

We arrived at the airport **early**. (*early*—adverb, modifies *arrived*)

We had to make an **early** start. (*early*—adjective, modifies *start*)

That was a **cowardly** act. (*cowardly*—adjective, modifies *act*)

He acted **cowardly** in that situation. (*cowardly*—adverb, modifies *acted*)

Some adverbs have two forms, one ending in **ly** and one that does not end in **ly**. The form that does not end in **ly** is the shorter form and is commonly used in giving commands and directions. The form ending in **ly** is preferred in formal writing.

Drive *slow.* (or *slowly*)

Come *quick!* (or *quickly*)

Buy *cheap.* (or *cheaply*)

Hold *tight!* (or *tightly*)

Don't talk so *loud.* (or *loudly*)

Sleep *sound.* (or *soundly*)

EXERCISE 1

On the line to the right, indicate whether the words printed in heavy type are **adjectives** or **adverbs**.

Example: He writes **effectively**.   *adverb*
....

1. She is really **lovely**.   1.   ....

2. A 1950 car went **past**.   2.   ....

3. That was a very **lively** entertainment.   3.   ....

4. The arrow flew **straight**.   4.   ....

5. Why doesn't he act **friendly**?   5.   ....

6. Draw a **straight** line on your paper.   6.   ....

7. He is a very **cowardly** person.   7.   ....

8. Drive **slow**!   8.   ....

9. Those Indians are a **friendly** tribe.   9.   ....

10. Why did he behave so **cowardly**?   10. ....

11. Harry always arrives **late**.   11. ....

12. We are not interested in **past** events.   12. ....

13. They always travel at a **slow** pace.   13. ....

14. The train arrived at a **late** hour.   14. ....

15. The child was very **lonely**.   15. ....

Note: The correct answers to exercises will be found at the end of this unit. Correct your mistakes and, if necessary, reread the text material before going on to the next section.

INTERROGATIVE ADVERBS

An adverb is often used at the beginning of a sentence to ask a question. When an adverb is used in this way, it is called an **interrogative adverb**. An *interrogative adverb* also modifies some word in the sentence.

When did you arrive? (*When*—interrogative adverb)

Where did you put my hat? (*Where*—interrogative adverb)

How many books have you read? (*How*—interrogative adverb)

In the first sentence, the adverb *When* asks the question. It also modifies the verb *did arrive*. (You *did arrive* when?) In the second sentence, the adverb *Where* asks the question and modifies the verb *did put*. (You *did put* my hat where?) In the third sentence, the adverb *How* asks the question and modifies the adjective *many*. (You have read how *many* books?)

YES, NO, AND NOT

The affirmative adverb *yes* and the negative adverb *no* are used independently. They are usually set off by commas. *Not* is an adverb. It is never used as part of the verb, although it often comes between the parts of a verb phrase. The adverb *not* makes the verb express an idea which is the exact opposite of the regular meaning of the verb.

Yes, I shall take the course.

I did *not* give him the plans. (No plans were given.)

No, we are *not* going to Florida this winter.

ADVERBS OF DEGREE

Adverbs of degree tell *how large, how small, how long, how much, to what extent,* etc. They answer the questions *"How much?" "To what extent?" "In what degree?"* Adverbs of degree usually modify adjectives or other adverbs. In the following illustrations the adverbs of degree modify *adjectives*:

This apple is very sour. (*very*—modifies the adjective *sour*)
adv. of degree

The play was rather dull. (*rather*—modifies the adjective *dull*)
adv. of degree

The price is too high. (*too*—modifies the adjective *high*)
adv. of degree

In the first sentence, the adverb of degree *very* modifies the predicate adjective *sour*. It tells to what degree the apple is sour, or how sour it is. In the second sentence, the adverb *rather* modifies the predicate adjective *dull*. It tells the extent to which the play was *dull*. In the third sentence, the adverb *too* modifies the predicate adjective *high*. It tells the extent to which the price is *high*. The adverbs *very, too,* and *rather* are commonly used as adverbs of degree.

In the following sentences, the adverbs of degree modify other *adverbs*:

The old man moved too slowly. (*too*—modifies the adverb *slowly*)
adv. of degree

John swims much faster than Ned. (*much*—modifies the adverb
faster)   adv. of degree

Don't talk so loud. (*so*—modifies the adverb *loud*)
adv. of degree

In the first sentence, the adverb of degree *too* modifies the adverb *slowly*. It tells the extent to which the old man moved *slowly*. In the second sentence, the adverb of degree *much* modifies the adverb *faster*. The adverb of degree tells that John swims fast to a greater degree than Ned. In the third sentence, the adverb of degree *so* modifies the adverb *loud*. The sentence means that you should not talk loud to the extent expressed by the adverb *so*. In this sentence, the short form of the adverb (*loud*) is used instead of the longer form, *loudly*.

EXERCISE 2

Underline the **adverbs of degree** in the following sentences. On the line to the right, indicate whether the adverb modifies an *adjective* or *another adverb*.

Example: These apples are <u>very</u> sour.   *adjective*
....

1. You are entirely wrong.   1. ....

2. Jane is a very clever girl.   2. ....

3. The car stopped very suddenly.   3. ....

4. I have told you that too often.   4. ....

5. Do not drive so recklessly.   5. ....

6. He pays his bills very promptly.   6. ....

7. There was scarcely enough gas in the tank. 7. ....

8. Mary is quite ill.   8. ....

9. The kitchen of the inn was spotlessly clean. 9. ....

10. The speaker had an unusually keen sense of humor. 10. ....

11. He paints portraits rather skillfully.   11. ....

12. Those cookies are too hard.   12. ....

13. We go to the country very seldom.   13. ....

14. The men did the work quite easily.   14. ....

15. The senator spoke very forcefully.   15. ....

NOUNS USED AS ADVERBS

Nouns that express *time, size, place, measurement, degree,* or *number* are often used as adverbs. We identify these nouns by calling them *nouns used as adverbs.* Such nouns are not only used as adverbs, but they retain an important characteristic of nouns; namely, they may take an *adjective modifier.*

I am going *home.* (*home*—noun used as an adverb)

Horace will arrive *Monday.* (*Monday*—noun used as an adverb)

We worked all *day.* (*day*—noun used as an adverb)

The fish weighed five *pounds.* (*pounds*—noun used as an adverb)

In the first sentence, the noun *home* tells **where** I am going. It performs the same function as an **adverb of place.** In the second sentence, the noun *Monday* tells **when** Horace will arrive. It performs the same function as an **adverb of time.** In the third sentence, the noun *day* tells **how long** we worked, or the extent to which we worked. In the last sentence, the noun *pounds* tells the amount, or **how much** the fish weighed.

The noun *pounds* in the last sentence is modified by the adjective *five.* Although the noun *pounds* functions as an adverb, it may take an adjective modifier. It still retains that particular characteristic of a noun. It functions as two parts of speech at the same time—both as a **noun** and as an **adverb.**

Some students have difficulty in understanding the use of a noun as an adverb. A noun used as an adverb is really the equivalent of a phrase. The following illustrations will help make this clear:

I am going home. This sentence really means that I am going *to my home.* The noun *home* is the equivalent of the phrase, *to my home.*

Horace will arrive Monday. This sentence means that Horace will arrive *on Monday.* The noun *Monday* is the equivalent of the phrase, *on Monday.*

We worked all day. This sentence means that we worked for the period or to *the extent of a day.*

The fish weighed five pounds. This sentence means that the fish weighed to the extent or *to the amount of five pounds.*

EXERCISE 3

Underline the *nouns used as adverbs* in the following sentences. On the line to the right indicate the word which the noun (used as an adverb) modifies.

Example: I am going <u>home</u>.   am going
                                              ....

1. Call for the package tomorrow.   1. ....

2. We do not work Saturdays.   2. ....

3. My aunt arrived from Paris yesterday. 3. ....

4. The steak weighed three pounds.   4. ....

5. We walked five miles into the forest. 5. ....

6. The hat cost ten dollars.   6. ....

7. I went to Maine last summer.   7. ....

8. The king ruled many years.   8. ....

9. We drove all day.   9. ....

10. The water is ten feet deep.   10. ....

11. I read two books every month.   11. ....

12. The speaker hesitated a minute.   12. ....

13. My brother is six feet tall.   13. ....

14. I am going to a convention next week. 14. ....

15. We traveled in Europe last year.   15. ....

COMPARISON OF ADVERBS

Adverbs are compared in exactly the same way as adjectives are compared. They have the same three degrees of comparison: the *positive degree,* the *comparative degree,* and the *superlative degree.*

A few adverbs form the comparative degree by adding **er** to the positive degree. They form the superlative degree by adding **est** to the positive degree.

Positive	Comparative	Superlative
late	later	latest
hard	harder	hardest
soon	sooner	soonest
fast	faster	fastest
near	nearer	nearest
quick (*short form*)	quicker	quickest
slow (*short form*)	slower	slowest

Most adverbs are compared by placing *more* (for the comparative degree) and *most* (for the superlative degree) before the positive forms. *Less* and *least* are used in the same way as *more* and *most.*

Positive	Comparative	Superlative
carefully	more carefully	most carefully
discreetly	more discreetly	most discreetly
abruptly	more abruptly	most abruptly
gratefully	more gratefully	most gratefully
efficiently	more efficiently	most efficiently
awkwardly	less awkwardly	least awkwardly
favorably	less favorably	least favorably
gracefully	less gracefully	least gracefully

IRREGULAR COMPARISON OF ADVERBS

A few adverbs are compared *irregularly*. In the following list you will find some words that were also in the list of adjectives that are compared irregularly. Such words are used both as *adjectives* and as *adverbs*.

Positive	Comparative	Superlative
far	farther	farthest
far	further	furthest
badly	worse	worst
little	less	least
much	more	most
well	better	best

Some adverbs are not compared. The following adverbs can not be used in the comparative or in the superlative degrees:

before	never	now	there	very	by
ever	no	so	thus	past	back
here	not	then	too	yes	whenever

The comparative degree of adverbs is used when comparing two things. The superlative degree is used when comparing more than two.

We drove <u>more slowly</u> than our guide.
comparative degree

Of the three speakers, the senator spoke <u>most convincingly</u>.
superlative degree

EXERCISE 4

Underline the **adverbs** in the following sentences. Include the words that show the degree of comparison: *more, most, less, least.* On the line to the right, indicate whether the adverb is in the *positive degree,* the *comparative degree,* or the *superlative degree.*

Example: Jack works <u>more diligently</u> than Fred.

comparative degree
....

1. Jack drives faster than he should.   1. ....

2. She answered all the questions correctly.   2. ....

3. The senator wrote an article recently.   3. ....

4. Why didn't you go home earlier?   4. ....

5. The model walks very gracefully.   5. ....

6. He spoke more distinctly than he usually does.   6. ....

7. The old man walked more slowly than the child.   7. ....

8. Of all the speakers, the man from New York talked most eloquently.   8. ....

9. Of the five articles submitted, Jack's article was written most carefully.   9. ....

10. The fog lifted gradually.   10. ....

11. I like Saturday better than any other day of the week.   11. ....

12. My uncle visits us more frequently than my aunt.   12. ....

13. The scientist examined the specimen carefully.   13. ....

14. Of all the men I know, he drives his car least often.   14. ....

15. You have traveled farther than I.   15. ....

DIAGRAMMING ADVERBS

Adverbial modifiers are diagrammed in exactly the same way as adjective modifiers are diagrammed. The adverb is placed on a slanted line which is joined to the word the adverb modifies.

Sentence: The race horse ran swiftly.
adverb

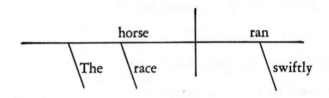

A noun used as an adverb is diagrammed in exactly the same way as a simple adverb. In the sentence, *The strike began yesterday,* the word *yesterday* is a noun used as an adverb. The sentence is diagrammed as follows:

Sentence: The strike began yesterday.

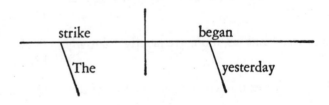

Sometimes the adverb is modified by another adverb. In the sentence, *We play tennis there very often,* the adverb *often* is modified by the adverb of degree *very.* Note the way in which the adverb *very* (a modifier of a modifier) is diagrammed.

Sentence: We play tennis there very often.
         adv.   adv.   adv.

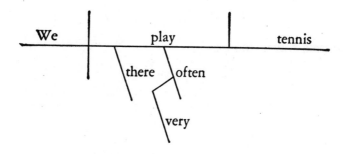

Sentence: An extremely large crowd gathered early.
            adv.   adv.

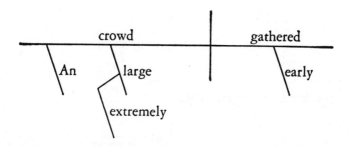

In this sentence, the adverb *extremely* modifies the adjective *large.* It is a modifier of a modifier and is diagrammed in exactly the same way as the adverb *very* in the preceding sentence. *Very* modifies the adverb *often,* and *extremely* modifies the adjective *large.* An adverb may modify an adjective or another adverb.

EXERCISE 5

Diagram the following sentences:

1. The employees worked Saturday.

2. The train travels too fast.

3. Margaret plays the harp very well.

4. The speaker is a very tall man.

CORRECT USE OF ADJECTIVES AND ADVERBS

Errors are frequently made in the use of adjectives and adverbs. The most common error is the use of an adjective for an adverb, or the use of an adverb when the meaning requires an adjective.

If you keep certain facts in mind regarding these modifiers, you will soon learn how to use them correctly. Note that adjectives never modify *verbs*. They modify *nouns* and *pronouns*. Adverbs modify *verbs, adjectives,* and other *adverbs.*

Never use an adjective after an action verb. An action verb requires an adverb as a modifier. The adverb tells the manner in which the action is performed. You may often hear a sentence like this: *Don't drive so reckless.* The adjective *reckless* is used after the action verb *drive.* The sentence requires an adverb. The correct form would be: *Don't drive so recklessly.* The adverb is *recklessly,* not *reckless. Reckless* is an adjective.

Mistakes are commonly made after linking verbs. These verbs must be watched carefully, for they should be followed by adjectives and not by adverbs. When a modifier follows a linking verb it is used to describe the subject, which is usually a noun or a pronoun. Adverbs do not modify nouns and pronouns.

The problem is also complicated by the fact that some of the linking words are often used as action verbs. In that case, they may take an adverbial modifier. Notice the change in the meaning of the verb *looked* in the following sentences:

Helen <u>looked</u> *sad.*   (not *sadly*)
linking

Helen <u>looked</u> *sadly* at the burnt cake.   (not *sad*)
action

In the first sentence, the verb *looked* is a linking verb. The sentence means that Helen looked (to be) *sad.* The predicate adjective *sad,* which follows the linking verb *looked,* modifies the subject, which is *Helen.* The verb *looked,* with the help of the predicate adjective *sad,* describes the condition of the subject, *Helen.*

In the second sentence, *looked* is an action verb. Helen is actually looking at the cake. The adverb *sadly* describes the manner in which she looked at the cake.

EXERCISE 6

In this exercise the problem is to choose between an **adjective** and an **adverb**.

Cross out the word in parentheses that would be used incorrectly in the sentence. On the line to the right indicate whether an *adjective* or an *adverb* is required.

Example: The velvet feels (smooth, ~~smoothly~~).   *adjective*

1. The problem seemed (hopeless, hopelessly.)   1. ....

2. The driver feels (bad, badly) about the crash.   2. ....

3. The piano sounds (terrible, terribly).   3. ....

4. I tasted the medicine (cautious, cautiously).   4. ....

5. The ammonia smells (strong, strongly).   5. ....

6. The child cried (bitter, bitterly).   6. ....

7. You did that very (clumsily, clumsy).   7. ....

8. The officer became very (angrily, angry).   8. ....

9. The crowd walked away very (quiet, quietly).   9. ....

10. The stranger looked around (suspiciously, suspicious).   10. ....

11. The new clerk does her work (easy, easily).   11. ....

12. The bell sounded (shrill, shrilly) (linking verb)   12. ....

13. These oranges taste (sweetly, sweet).   13. ....

14. The woman hurt her knee (bad, badly).   1 4. ....

15. The northern lights appear (frequently, frequent). (action verb)   15. ....

SPECIAL FORMS

There are several adjectives and adverbs that require special attention because they are used incorrectly so often. If you study the following distinctions in *meaning* and *use,* you should be able to use these adjectives and adverbs correctly.

1. **Good** and **well.** The word *good* is always an adjective. It should never be used as an adverb. The word *well* is used both as an adjective and as an adverb. When *well* is used as an adjective, it refers to a state of health, or to a satisfactory condition of affairs. When *well* is used as an adverb, it refers to the manner in which some action is performed.

I have a good saddle horse. (*good*—adjective, modifies *horse*)
    adj.

The child is well. (*well*—adjective, modifies *child*)
    adj.

All is well. (*well*—adjective, modifies *all*)
  adj.

Heifetz plays the violin well. (*well*—adverb, modifies *plays*)
    adv.

2. **Bad** and **badly.** The word *bad* is an adjective. The word *badly* is an adverb. The adverb *badly* should not be used after a linking verb. You would not say, *I feel illy* or *I feel sickly.* For the same reason you should not say, *I feel badly,* when you refer to your state of health.

Mother feels bad today. (*bad*—adjective, modifies *Mother*)
    adj.

Mother managed the affair badly. (*badly*—adverb, modifies *managed*)
    adv.

When you say, *Mother feels badly,* you mean that Mother performs the act of feeling something in an imperfect manner. Of course, that is not the meaning that you intend to convey. Do not use *badly* unless the verb expresses action. *Badly* indicates the manner in which the action is performed.

Some writers maintain that the sentence, *Mother feels badly today* is correct. They give two reasons for taking this position. One is that the forms *bad* and *badly* are both used as adjectives. The other reason given is that the expression *feels badly* has become an American idiom.

3. **Sure** and **surely**. *Sure* is an adjective. *Surely* is an adverb.

The hunter's aim was sure. (*sure*—adjective, modifies *aim*)
<u>adj.</u>

That is the only sure way to succeed. (*sure*—adjective, modifies *way*)
<u>adj.</u>

I am surely grateful to you. (*surely*—adverb, modifies *grateful*)
<u>adv.</u>

When you say, *I am sure grateful to you,* the adjective *sure* modifies the adjective *grateful*. Adjectives never modify adjectives. Adverbs modify adjectives. The sentence requires the adverb. The use of the adjective *sure* is incorrect. The correct modifier is *surely:* I am *surely grateful* to you.

4. **Real** and **really**. The adjective is *real*. The adverb is *really*. A common error is the use of the adjective *real* for the adverb *very*. Do not say, *The apple is real good.* In this sentence, *real* is an adjective and modifies another adjective, which is grammatically incorrect. The correct form would be, *The apple is very good.* Note the correct use of *real* and *really* in the following sentences:

This is a real emerald. (*real*—adjective, modifies *emerald*)
<u>adj.</u>

The play was really excellent. (*really*—adverb, modifies *excellent*)
<u>adv.</u>

In the last sentence, the adverb *really* modifies the adjective *excellent.* This is a correct use of the adverb *really*. Do not use the adverb *really* unless you mean *actually*. The sentence means that the play was actually excellent.

5. **Most** and **almost**. Both *most* and *almost* are adverbs. The error is one in meaning. The adverb *most* means to the greatest degree. The adverb *almost* means *nearly*. Do not say, *He is most five years old.* The correct word to use in this sentence is *almost.* (means *nearly*)

Of all the fruits, I like plums most. (*most*—adverb, modifies *like*)
<u>adv.</u>

I am almost ready. (*almost*—adverb, modifies *ready*)
<u>adv.</u>

THE DOUBLE NEGATIVE

Only *one negative word* should be used to express a *negative idea.* A common error in English is to use two negative words to express one negative idea. When you use the adverb *not* with such words as *hardly, scarcely, never, no, barely,* and *but,* you are introducing two negative ideas.

Incorrect

We *haven't barely* paid for our car.
   (*haven't* and *barely*—two negatives)

Nobody can't say that I *don't* work hard.
   (*can't* and *don't*—two negatives)

I *can't hardly* hear the speaker.
   (*can't* and *hardly*—two negatives)

There *isn't but* one woman on the committee.
   (*isn't* and *but*—two negatives)

Correct

We have *barely* paid for our car. (one negative)

Nobody can say that I *don't* work hard. (one negative)

I can *hardly* hear the speaker. (one negative)

There is *but* one woman on the committee. (one negative)

Other words used as negatives are *never, no, nobody, none, no one,* and *nothing.* These words should not be used with another negative.

I *haven't no* money. (incorrect)

I *have no* money. (correct)

No one *never* gave me a book. (incorrect)

No one *ever* gave me a book. (correct)

The word *but* requires careful analysis when it is used with a negative. When *but* means *only,* it should not be preceded by a negative such as the word *not.* This combination results in a double negative.

I haven't but one car. (double negative—incorrect)
   only

I have but one car. (correct)

When the word *but* is used as a preposition, it means *except.* When *but* means *except* it is often preceded by a negative. This does not mean that a double negative idea is suggested as you will readily see if you analyze the following sentences carefully:

It never rains but it pours. (correct)
<u>except</u>

He does nothing but complain. (correct)
<u>except</u>

Expressions like *cannot help but,* and *can't help but* are generally regarded as colloquial and should not be used in formal speaking or writing.

I *can't help but* criticize the management. (colloquial)

I *can't help* criticizing the management. (better)

EXERCISE 7

Cross out the incorrect forms in the following sentences. Write the correct form above the incorrect form. One sentence is correct.

Example: I don't want ~~no~~ cake or pie.   *[any written above "no"]*

1. He is suffering bad from a broken arm.

2. Hubert is most six feet tall.

3. How good Andrew skates!

4. Jack sure has gained weight.

5. We all felt bad about the accident.

6. I have most finished reading the book.

7. That dinner was real good.

8. We haven't scarcely time to finish the job.

9. The play was real excellent.

10. Ted hasn't done nothing all year.

11. Are you real serious about becoming a doctor?

12. Harvey is doing very good at college.

13. A fashion model always walks graceful.

14. You speak too indistinct.

15. I can't help but (blame, blaming) him for the accident.

SUMMARY OF GRAMMAR UNIT ELEVEN

An **adverb** is a word that is used to modify a verb, an adjective, or another adverb. Adverbs usually express time, place, manner, or degree.

An **interrogative adverb** asks a question and modifies some word in the sentence.

Some adjectives and adverbs have the same form. The only way to tell whether a word is an *adjective* or an *adverb* is to determine its use in the sentence. If it modifies a *noun* or a *pronoun,* it is an adjective. If it modifies a *verb,* an *adjective,* or *another adverb,* it is an adverb.

Adverbs are compared in exactly the same way as adjectives are compared. Some adverbs are compared by adding **er** or **est** to the *positive degree.* Some are compared by prefixing *more* or *most* to the positive degree. A few adverbs are compared irregularly.

Errors are frequently made in the use of adjectives and adverbs. This error is commonly made after the *linking verb,* which requires an *adjective* as a complement, and not an adverb. *Verbs* of *action* should be modified by *adverbs,* and not by adjectives.

Nouns are often used as adverbs to express *time, place, measurement, degree, size,* or *number.* A noun used as an adverb may be modified by an adjective or an adjective phrase because it retains that noun characteristic.

Some adverbs have two forms, a short form and a form that ends in **ly.** The form ending in **ly** should be used in formal writing.

SELF-GRADING ASSIGNMENT 1

Directions: Underline the **adverbs** in the following sentences. On the line to the right, indicate whether the adverb is an *adverb of degree*, an *interrogative adverb*, or a *noun used as an adverb*.

1. We remained in the Ozarks a month.   1. ....

2. She has too little patience.   2. ....

3. When will he sign the contract?   3. ....

4. Have the reports ready tomorrow.   4. ....

5. The steak was very tough.   5. ....

6. Your writing is too difficult to read.   6. ....

7. This rose is unusually fragrant.   7. ....

8. Why did you go to California?   8. ....

9. We stayed at the inn a week.   9. ....

10. Where are you going?   10. ....

11. The package weighed five pounds.   11. ....

12. It rained all day.   12. ....

13. The assignment was too long.   13. ....

14. The task seemed utterly impossible.   14. ....

15. His suit cost fifty dollars.   15. ....

Caution: Check your answers to each assignment with the answer key at the end of this unit before proceeding with the next assignment.

SELF-GRADING ASSIGNMENT 2

Directions: Fill in the blanks with the correct forms of the **adverbs** enclosed in parentheses. The form you select should be the *degree of comparison* required in the sentence.

Example: He reads .... than I. (rapidly)
He reads *more rapidly* than I.

1. The speaker arrived.................................than the singer. (late)

2. The child writes..................today than he did yesterday. (badly)

3. Of all the men, Edward works................................. (skillfully)

4. The storm broke................................than we expected. (soon)

5. Which of the four candidates talked..........................? (fluently)

6. The prima donna sang that song very.................... (artistically)

7. The manager talked.................than the supervisor. (effectively)

8. Of all the children, Susan speaks........................... (distinctly)

9. Speak.................to the men today than you did last week. (firmly)

10. The tools are very...made. (accurately)

11. The audience listened.....................................to the first speaker than to the second speaker. (intently)

12. I watched the game...................................than Lester. (closely)

13. Come...than you did yesterday. (early)

14. The boy does the work...........................than an adult. (easily)

15. Did I speak too...................................? (hastily)

SELF-GRADING ASSIGNMENT 3

Directions: Cross out the *incorrect form* in the parentheses. On the line to the right, indicate whether the sentence requires an *adjective* or an *adverb*.

Adjective or Adverb

Example: The stranger appeared (nervous, ~~nervously~~).   adjective

1. The popcorn smells (good, well).   1. ....

2. Marian looks (beautiful, beautifully) in white.   2. ....

3. Brush your teeth (good, well).   3. ....

4. A shower feels (well, good) on a hot day.   4. ....

5. Apply cosmetics (careful, carefully).   5. ....

6. She remained (calm, calmly) during the storm.   6. ....

7. Hugh writes (illegible, illegibly).   7. ....

8. Marvin (sure, surely) deserves praise.   8. ....

9. This fruit juice tastes (sour, sourly).   9. ....

10. Jessie is (most, almost) ten years old.   10. ....

11. The manager became (real, very) angry.   11. ....

12. The case is (real, really) serious.   12. ....

13. The police acted (prompt, promptly).   13. ....

14. Drive (slow, slowly) today, Eric.   14. ....

15. Katherine injured her foot (bad, badly).   15. ....

PROGRESS TEST ELEVEN

This progress test should not be taken until a day or two after you have completed the assignments. The score you make on the test will then more clearly reflect your understanding of the material in the unit.

Directions: Rewrite the following sentences, correcting any errors made in the use of *adjectives* and *adverbs*. Two sentences are correct.

(30 points)

1. Grace is the more industrious of all the girls in the sewing class.

2. All of us feel happily about the increase in salary.

3. The music sounds inharmoniously.

4. Madge is the less attractive of the three sisters.

5. Father didn't sleep good last night.

6. This circle is the most nearly perfect of the five I have drawn.

7. Have you most finished decorating your new home?

8. You should write more careful, David.

9. She hasn't done nothing all year.

10. Mabel promised that she would sure go.

11. There weren't scarcely enough sandwiches for the boys.

12. Jonathan played tennis real good today

PROGRESS TEST ELEVEN (continued)

13. Does the food taste well?

14. The detective looked suspicious about the room.

15. The oldest of the two girls sings good.

16. Jane looks badly after that attack of influenza.

17. Peas taste more sweeter to some people than sugar.

18. My uncle manages his affairs badly.

19. This apple tastes sourly.

20. Guy has worked steady for three months.

21. Of the three brothers, Robert is the younger.

22. The watchman is cleverer than he appears.

23. I can't hardly hear the speaker.

24. Which of the two magazines is most frequently read?

25. Margaret came to work real early this morning.

26. There isn't but one stenographer in our office.

27. Are you going to the skating rink? I sure am.

28. When one is working, time passes rapid.

ANSWER KEY

for

EXERCISES, ASSIGNMENTS, AND PROGRESS TEST

GRAMMAR UNIT ELEVEN

CORRECT ANSWERS TO EXERCISES

	Exercise 1		Exercise 2	
Word	**Adjective or Adverb**	**Adverb**	**Modifies**	
1. lovely	*adjective*	1. entirely	*adjective* wrong
2. past	*adverb*	2. very	*adjective* clever
3. lively	*adjective*	3. very	*adverb* suddenly
4. straight	*adverb*	4. too	*adverb* often
5. friendly	*adverb*	5. so	*adverb* recklessly
6. straight	*adjective*	6. very	*adverb* promptly
7. cowardly	*adjective*	7. scarcely	*adjective* enough
8. slow	*adverb*	8. quite	*adjective* ill
9. friendly	*adjective*	9. spotlessly	*adjective* clean
10. cowardly	*adverb*	10. unusually	*adjective* keen
11. late	*adverb*	11. rather	*adverb* skillfully
12. past	*adjective*	12. too	*adjective* hard
13. slow	*adjective*	13. very	*adverb* seldom
14. late	*adjective*	14. quite	*adverb* easily
15. lonely	*adjective*	15. very	*adverb* forcefully

CORRECT ANSWERS TO EXERCISES

Exercise 3

Exercise 4

Noun Used as Adverb	Modifies	Adverb	Degree of Comparison
1. tomorrow	call	1. faster	*comparative*
2. Saturdays	do work	2. correctly	*positive*
3. yesterday	arrived	3. recently	*positive*
4. pounds	weighed	4. earlier	*comparative*
5. miles	walked	5. gracefully	*positive*
6. dollars	cost	6. more distinctly	*comparative*
7. summer	went	7. more slowly	*comparative*
8. years	ruled	8. most eloquently	*superlative*
9. day	drove	9. most carefully	*superlative*
10. feet	deep	10. gradually	*positive*
11. month	read	11. better	*comparative*
12. minute	hesitated	12. more frequently	*comparative*
13. feet	tall	13. carefully	*positive*
14. week	am going	14. least often	*superlative*
15. year	traveled	15. farther	*comparative*

CORRECT ANSWERS TO EXERCISE 5

Sentence: The employees worked Saturday.

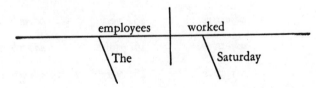

Sentence: The train travels too fast.

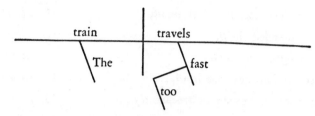

Sentence: Margaret plays the harp very well.

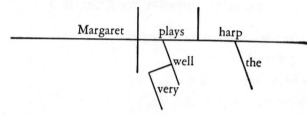

Sentence: The speaker is a very tall man.

CORRECT ANSWERS TO EXERCISE 6

1. The problem seemed **hopeless.**   1. *adjective*

2. The driver feels **bad** about the crash.   2. *adjective*

3. The piano sounds **terrible.**   3. *adjective*

4. I tasted the medicine **cautiously.**   4. *adverb*

5. The ammonia smells **strong.**   5. *adjective*

6. The child cried **bitterly.**   6. *adverb*

7. You did that very **clumsily.**   7. *adverb*

8. The officer became very **angry.**   8. *adjective*

9. The crowd walked away very **quietly.**   9. *adverb*

10. The stranger looked around **suspiciously.**	10. *adverb*
11. The new clerk does her work **easily.**	11. *adverb*
12. The bell sounded **shrill.**	12. *adjective*
13. These oranges taste **sweet.**	13. *adjective*
14. The woman hurt her knee **badly.**	14. *adverb*
15. The northern lights appear **frequently.**	15. *adverb*

CORRECT ANSWERS TO EXERCISE 7

1. He is suffering **badly** from a broken arm.
2. Hubert is **almost** six feet tall.
3. How **well** Andrew skates!
4. Jack **surely** has gained weight.
5. (This sentence is correct.)
6. I have **almost** finished reading the book.
7. That dinner was **very** good.
8. We **have** scarcely time to finish the job.
9. The play was **really** excellent. (*Really* means actually.)
10. Ted **has** done nothing all year. (Ted hasn't done anything all year.)
11. Are you **really** serious about becoming a doctor?
12. Harvey is doing very **well** at college.
13. A fashion model always walks **gracefully.**
14. You speak too **indistinctly.**
15. I can't help **blaming** him for the accident.

CORRECT ANSWERS TO ASSIGNMENTS

ASSIGNMENT 1

Adverb	Kind of Adverb
1. month	*noun used as adverb*
2. too	*adverb of degree*
3. When	*interrogative*

ASSIGNMENT 2

Correct Forms of Adverbs

1. later
2. worse
3. most skillfully

4. tomorrow	*noun used as adverb*	4. sooner	
5. very	*adverb of degree*	5. most fluently	
6. too	*adverb of degree*	6. artistically	
7. unusually	*adverb of degree*	7. more effectively	
8. Why	*interrogative*	8. most distinctly	
9. week	*noun used as adverb*	9. more firmly	
10. Where	*interrogative*	10. accurately	
11. pounds	*noun used as adverb*	11. more intently	
12. day	*noun used as adverb*	12. more closely	
13. too	*adverb of degree*	13. earlier	
14. utterly	*adverb of degree*	14. more easily	
15. dollars	*noun used as adverb*	15. hastily	

CORRECT ANSWERS TO ASSIGNMENT 3

1. The popcorn smells **good**.

    1. *adjective*

2. Marian looks **beautiful** in white.

    2. *adjective*

3. Brush your teeth **well**.

    3. *adverb*

4. A shower feels **good** on a hot day.

    4. *adjective*

5. Apply cosmetics **carefully**.

    5. *adverb*

6. She remained **calm** during the storm.

    6. *adjective*

7. Hugh writes **illegibly**.

    7. *adverb*

8. Marvin **surely** deserves praise.

    8. *adverb*

9. This fruit juice tastes **sour**.

    9. *adjective*

10. Jessie is **almost** ten years old.

    10. *adverb*

11. The manager became **very** angry.

    11. *adverb*

12. The case is **really** serious.

    12. *adverb*

13. The police acted **promptly**.

    13. *adverb*

14. Drive (**slow, slowly**) today, Eric.
    (*both forms are correct*)

    14. *adverb*

15. Katherine injured her foot **badly**.

    15. *adverb*

CORRECT ANSWERS TO PROGRESS TEST ELEVEN

1. Grace is the **most industrious** of all the girls in the sewing class.
2. All of us feel **happy** about the increase in salary.
3. The music sounds **inharmonious.**
4. Madge is the **least attractive** of the three sisters.
5. Father didn't sleep **well** last night.
6. (This sentence is correct.)
7. Have you **almost** finished decorating your new home?
8. You should write **more carefully,** David.
9. She hasn't done **anything** all year. (correct)
   She has done **nothing** all year. (correct)
10. Mabel promised that she would **surely** go.
11. There **were scarcely** enough sandwiches for the boys.
12. Jonathan played tennis **very well** today. (*2 points*)
13. Does the food taste **good**?
14. The detective looked **suspiciously** about the room.
15. The **older** of the two girls sings **well.** (*2 points*)
16. Jane looks **bad** after that attack of influenza.
17. Peas taste **sweeter** to some people than sugar.
18. (This sentence is correct.)
19. This apple tastes **sour.**
20. Guy has worked **steadily** for three months.
21. Of the three brothers, Robert is the **youngest.**
22. The watchman is **more clever** than he appears.
23. I **can hardly** hear the speaker.
24. Which of the two magazines is **more frequently** read?
25. Margaret came to work **very** early this morning.
26. There **is** but one stenographer in our office.
27. Are you going to the skating rink? I **surely** am (going).
28. When one is working, time passes **rapidly.**

HOW TO OBTAIN YOUR SCORE

The test totals 30 points. To obtain your score, divide the number of your correct answers by 30. The answer will be your score on this test. For example, if you have 27 points correct, your score is 27 divided by 30 which is 90 per cent. In other words, your score on this test is 90. You can obtain your score on any of the exercises or assignments by following the same procedure.

Practical English Grammar

OUTLINE OF UNIT TWELVE

PRINCIPAL PARTS OF VERBS

12

PRINCIPAL PARTS OF VERBS

THE BASIC FORMS OF VERBS

THE student of grammar should become familiar with the *principal parts* of a number of important verbs in English. Studies have shown that more than half of the errors made in English were errors in the use of verbs. Most of this trouble occurred because of confusion in the use of the principal parts.

Every verb has *three basic forms* which are called the *principal parts* of the verb. These three forms are the **present tense,** the **past tense,** and the **past participle.** They are called the principal parts of the verb because (with a few exceptions) the six tenses of the verb can be built from them.

Tense is a property that belongs to verbs. In grammar, *tense* means *time.* Every verb has certain forms which show the *time* of the *action* or the *time* of the *state of condition.* When we want to indicate that a certain action is going on now, or that a certain state of condition exists at the present time, we use the **present tense.**

Present Tense

I **drive.** (Action occurs at the *present time.*)

He **sings.** (Action occurs at the *present time.*)

Florence **is** ill. (The state of condition exists at the *present time.*)

When we want to indicate that the action occurred yesterday, or in some past time, we use the **past tense** of the verb. With a few exceptions, the past tense of the verb is not the same form as the present tense of the verb.

Past Tense .

I **drove.** (The action occurred in the *past.*)

He **sang** at the concert. (The action occurred in the *past.*)

Florence **was** ill yesterday. (The state of condition existed in the *past.*)

In the preceding illustrations, the forms, *drive* and *sings,* are used to show that action is going on at the present time. The forms, *drove* and *sang,* are used to show that action occurred at some time in the past. The forms *drive* and *sings* are the present tense of the verbs *drive* and *sing.* The forms *drove* and *sang* are the past tense of the verbs *drive* and *sing.*

The **past participle** of the verb is a verb form that is used with *have, has,* or *had* to form the perfect tenses. The past participle cannot function as the predicate verb. It is always combined with an auxiliary, such as *have, has,* or *had.* It is a part of the verb phrase.

Past Participles

I *have* **called** her every day this week. (*called*—past participle)
<u>verb phrase</u>

We *have* **driven** there often. (*driven*—past participle)
<u>verb phrase</u>

The three forms, the *present tense,* the *past tense,* and the *past participle,* constitute the **principal parts** of a verb. It is necessary for the student of grammar to become familiar with the principal parts of certain verbs so that he will be able to use them correctly. The verbs that cause most of our verb troubles are the verbs that form the principal parts irregularly. We shall make a special study of these verbs.

REGULAR AND IRREGULAR VERBS

Verbs are divided into two classes on the basis of the way in which the past tense and the past participle are formed. Some are called *regular* or weak verbs, and others are called *irregular* or strong verbs.

A **regular verb** is a verb that forms the past tense and the past participle by adding **ed** or **d** to the form of the present tense. Sometimes the **ed** or **d** changes to **t**: *build, built, built.*

Verb	Past Tense	Past Participle
call	called	called
bake	baked	baked
build	built	built

The past tense and the past participle of the verb *call* are formed by adding **ed** to the form of the present tense: *call**ed**.* The past tense and the past participle of the verb *bake* are formed by simply adding **d** to the form of the present tense: *bake**d**.* The past tense and the past participle of the verb *build* are formed by changing the **d** to **t**. The old form of the verb build was *builded* in the past tense. That form is no longer used. The simpler form *built* has taken its place.

An **irregular verb** is a verb that does *not* form the past tense and the past participle in the regular way; that is, by adding **d** or **ed** to the form of the present tense. The past tense and the past participle of irregular verbs are formed in various ways. The most common way is by a change in the vowel; for example, *sing, sang, sung.* In the case of a few verbs, the same form is used for the present tense, the past tense and the past participle: *hurt, hurt, hurt.*

Verb	Past Tense	Past Participle
s**i**ng	s**a**ng	s**u**ng
dr**i**ve	dr**o**ve	dr**i**ven
beg**i**n	beg**a**n	beg**u**n
go	went	gone
burst	burst	burst

The past tense and the past participle of the verb *sing* are formed by a change in vowel. The **i** in *sing* changes to **a** in the past tense (*sang*) and to **u** in the past participle (*sung*). The verb *begin* follows a similar change in the vowel. The verb *go* has a different form for the past tense and for the past participle: *go, went, gone.* The verb *burst* has the same form for the present tense, the past tense, and the past participle.

VERBS ADDED TO THE LANGUAGE

New verbs are added to the English language as the need arises. Practically all of these new verbs form the past tense and the past participle by adding **ed** or **d**; that is, they follow the pattern of the regular verbs. The following verbs have been introduced in recent years. To form the past tense or the past participle of these verbs, add **ed** or **d**.

Verb	Past Tense	Past Participle
activate	activated	activated
radio	radioed	radioed
camouflage	camouflaged	camouflaged
audition	auditioned	auditioned
laminate	laminated	laminated

THE TROUBLESOME VERBS

The *regular verbs* cause very little trouble in speaking and writing because the past tense and the past participle usually follow the rule of forming the past tense and the past participle by adding **d** or **ed.** It is the *irregular verbs* that are responsible for most of the verb errors.

Errors are frequently made in using the *past tense* and the *perfect tense* forms of irregular verbs. This is due to the fact that these verbs form the past tense and the perfect tenses irregularly. In order to use these verbs correctly, it is highly important for you to become familiar with the principal parts of the irregular verbs that are in common use. You will learn these forms by checking constantly until you are familiar with the correct forms for the past tense and the past participle.

Mistakes are commonly made in using the wrong form for the **past tense:** *done* for *did; seen* for *saw; come* for *came; swum* for *swam; dove* for *dived; run* for *ran; drunk* for *drank.* Mistakes are also made in using the wrong form for the **past participle:** *went* for *gone; did* for *done; swam* for *swum; tore* for *torn; began* for *begun; came* for *come.* The past participle is used in forming the perfect tenses.

Correct Forms for the Past Tense

I <u>did</u> the work assigned to me. (not *done*)
past tense

We <u>saw</u> the parade yesterday. (not *seen*)
past tense

He <u>came</u> from Ireland two years ago. (not *come*)
past tense

She <u>swam</u> across the English Channel last summer. (not *swum*)
past tense

The swimming teacher <u>dived</u> off the pier. (not *dove*)
past tense

The boy <u>ran</u> through the traffic. (not *run*)
past tense

We <u>drank</u> all the milk in the pitcher. (not *drunk*)
past tense

Correct Forms for the Past Participle

The delegates **have gone** home. (not *have went*)

He **has done** the work well. (not *has did*)

She **has swum** the channel several times. (not *has swam*)

The actress **has torn** her dress. (not *has tore*)

They **have begun** to check the accounts. (not *have began*)

Has the mail **come?** (not *has came*)

In the first sentence, the past participle is *gone*. It is combined with the auxiliary *have* to form the verb phrase *have gone*. The form *went* should never be used with *have, has* or *had*.

In the second sentence, the past participle is *done*. It is the correct form of the verb to combine with *has*. In the third sentence, the past participle is *swum*. It is correctly used with *has*. *Tore* should never be used with *have, has*, or *had*. The correct form is *have, has*, or *had torn*.

Began is the correct form for the past tense. It should not be used for the past participle. The correct form for the past participle is *begun*. Never use the forms *have began, had began*, or *has began*. The correct forms are *have begun, had begun*, and *has begun*.

The following table gives the principal parts of the irregular verbs that cause most of the verb errors. You should become familiar with the principal parts of these verbs. Consult this list whenever you are in doubt about the correct form to use. If the verb you want is not in this list, consult a reliable, up-to-date dictionary. The principal parts of verbs are given in most dictionaries.

PRINCIPAL PARTS OF TROUBLESOME VERBS

Present Tense (present time)	Past Tense (past time)	Past Participle (*used with have, has, had*)
awake	awaked, awoke	awaked, awoke
be (am)	was	been
beat	beat	beaten
become	became	become
begin	began	begun
bid (offer to buy)	bid	bid
bid (command)	bade	bidden, bid
blow	blew	blown
break	broke	broken
bring	brought	brought
broadcast	broadcast, broadcasted	broadcast, broadcasted
burst	burst	burst
catch	caught	caught
choose	chose	chosen
climb	climbed	climbed
come	came	come
cut	cut	cut
dive	dived	dived
do	did	done

PRINCIPAL PARTS OF TROUBLESOME VERBS (Continued)

Present Tense (present time)	Past Tense (past time)	Past Participle (*used with have, has, had*)
drag	dragged	dragged
draw	drew	drawn
drink	drank	drunk
drive	drove	driven
drown	drowned	drowned
eat	ate	eaten
fall	fell	fallen
flow	flowed	flowed
fly	flew	flown
forget	forgot	forgotten, forgot
freeze	froze	frozen
get	got	got, gotten
give	gave	given
go	went	gone
hang (a picture)	hung	hung
hang (a criminal)	hanged	hanged
know	knew	known
lay (to place, to put)	laid	laid
lead	led	led
leave	left	left
lend	lent	lent
let	let	let
lie (to recline)	lay (not laid)	lain (not laid)
lie (tell a falsehood)	lied	lied
lose	lost	lost
prove	proved	proved
ride	rode	ridden
ring	rang	rung
rise	rose	risen (not rose)
run	ran	run
say	said	said
see	saw	seen
send	sent	sent

PRINCIPAL PARTS OF TROUBLESOME VERBS (Continued)

Present Tense (present time)	Past Tense (past time)	Past Participle (*used with* have, has, had)
set	set	set
shake	shook	shaken
shine (give light)	shone	shone
shine (polish)	shined	shined
show	showed	shown, showed
shrink	shrank	shrunk
sing	sang	sung
sink	sank	sunk
sit	sat	sat
spring	sprang, sprung	sprung
steal	stole	stolen
swear	swore	sworn
swim	swam	swum
swing	swung	swung
take	took	taken
teach	taught	taught
tear	tore	torn
tell	told	told
think	thought	thought
throw	threw	thrown
try	tried	tried
understand	understood	understood
wake	waked, woke	waked
wear	wore	worn
weave	wove	woven
weep	wept	wept
wind	wound	wound
wring	wrung	wrung
write	wrote	written

EXERCISE 1

Fill in the blank spaces with the correct forms for the **past tense** and the **past participle** of each of the following verbs:

Present Tense (present time)	Past Tense (past time)	Past Participle (*used with have, has, had*)
1. fall	....	....
2. break	....	....
3. know	....	....
4. see	....	....
5. speak	....	....
6. lie (to recline)	....	....
7. eat	....	....
8. sink	....	....
9. ride	....	....
10. take	....	....
11. rise	....	....
12. cut	....	....
13. freeze	....	....
14. throw	....	....
15. ring	....	....

Note: The correct answers to exercises will be found at the end of this unit. Correct your mistakes and, if necessary, reread the text material before going on to the next section.

EXERCISE 2

Fill in the blank with the correct form of the verb enclosed in parentheses. The form required is the **past participle.**

1. Where have they .... the car? (take)

2. Have you .... all the milk? (drink)

3. I have .... this hat for several years. (wear)

4. John has never .... that far before. (swim)

5. The officers have .... to the convention. (go)

6. The child has .... too many apples. (eat)

7. Have you .... that motion picture before? (see)

8. We have .... that song every day for a week. (sing)

9. The dress has .... from washing. (shrink)

10. The income tax statements have .... (come)

11. A pipe in the basement has .... (burst)

12. The swimmer has .... into that pool six times. (dive)

13. The birds have .... toward the South. (fly)

14. The decorators have .... the pictures too low. (hang)

15. Why have you .... so morbid? (become)

EXERCISE 3

Cross out the *incorrect verb forms* in the following sentences. Write the correct form above the incorrect form. Two sentences are correct.

Example: The visitors from England have ~~went~~ gone home.

1. The vandals have broke the windows.

2. The water in the pipe has froze.

3. I seen the picture again last night.

4. He give me the book with the references in it.

5. We begun the project this morning.

6. I brung my friend a gift from Paris.

7. The lifeguard swum out to the drowning child.

8. Fred is the plumber who done the work.

9. They hanged the traitor yesterday.

10. The birds have flowed to the South.

11. The torn ligament hurted badly.

12. The lion sprang at the hunter.

13. He has became involved in illegal practices.

14. I have spoke to the manager about the mistakes Jane makes.

15. For many years he has growed orchids in his garden.

SIX CONFUSING VERBS

Six of the irregular verbs require special attention and study because they are so frequently confused. As a result, they are used incorrectly more often than any of the other irregular verbs. These verbs fall into three sets or pairs: *lie, lay; sit, set; rise, raise*. The forms of the verbs in each pair are somewhat similar, but the meanings are quite different. We shall make a special study of these verbs so that you will be able to use them correctly.

LIE AND LAY

There are two different verbs that are spelled alike (*lie*). One means to tell a falsehood. This is a regular verb and causes no difficulty, either in speaking or in writing. The verb that is confused with *lay* is the verb *lie*, which means *to recline, to rest*, or *to remain in a reclining position*. This verb is an irregular verb. The principal parts are *lie, lay,* and (*have, has, had*) *lain*. The present participle, the form that ends in *ing*, is *lying*.

There are two important facts regarding the verb *lie* (to recline) that you should always keep in mind: (1) There is no form ending in **d** that belongs to the verb *lie*, meaning *to recline*. The form *laid* should never be used when you mean *to recline, rest,* or *remain in a reclining position*. (2) The verb *lie* never takes an object.

Mother **lies** down every afternoon. (*rests, reclines*)

Mother **lay** on the couch all afternoon. (not *laid*)

Mother **is lying** on the couch. (not *laying*)

Mother **has lain** on that couch often. (not *has laid*)

The verb *lie* is also the verb to use when we speak about inanimate objects that are in a reclining or in a *lying-down* position.

The pen **lies** on my desk. (not *lays*)

The pen **lay** on my desk all day. (not *laid*)

The pen **is lying** on my desk. (not *is laying*)

The pen **has lain** on my desk all week. (not *has laid*)

The verb **lay,** that is so often confused with *lie,* means *to put something down, to place something somewhere.* The principal parts of this verb are *lay, laid,* (*have, has,* or *had*) *laid.* The present participle is *laying.* The verb *lay* always takes an object.

John **lays** carpets for Macey's store. (*carpets*—object of *lays*)

John **laid** carpets all week. (*carpets*—object of *laid*)

John **has laid** carpets for many years. (*carpets*—object of *has laid*)

In the first sentence, the verb *lays* is the present tense of the verb *lay,* which means to put something down. The word *carpets* is the direct object of the verb *lays.* It tells what John put down. In the second sentence, the verb *laid* is the past tense of the verb *lay.*

When we use the form *laid,* we must supply an object telling what we *laid,* or *what we put down. Carpets* is the direct object of the verb *laid.* It tells what John *laid.* In the last sentence, *laid* is the correct form of the verb *lay* to combine with *has.* It helps form the verb phrase *has laid.*

EXERCISE 4

Cross out the incorrect verb form enclosed in parentheses. On the line to the right, indicate whether the sentence requires the verb *lie* (to recline) or *lay* (to place, to put down).

1. The injured man has (laid, lain) unconscious all day.

    1. ....

2. We (lay, laid) our wraps on the bench.

    2. ....

3. Have you been (laying, lying) down?

    3. ....

4. As I (lie, lay) here, I can see the hilltops.

    4. ....

5. Broken glass (laid, lay) on the floor.

    5. ....

6. They found the man (lying, laying) on the road.

    6. ....

7. Martha (lay, laid) her packages on the table.

    7. ....

8. She could not have (laid, lain) on that broken cot.

    8. ....

9. I (lie, lay) down every afternoon.

    9. ....

10. We (laid, lay) quite still, hidden by the trees.

    10. ....

11. The lawyer (lay, laid) the case before the jury.

    11. ....

12. James often (lies, lays) down on the porch.

    12. ....

13. The pen is (lying, laying) where I (lay, laid) it last week.

    13. ....

14. Did you (lie, lay) down when you came home?

    14. ....

15. We (lay, laid) the cards on the table.

    15. ....

SIT AND SET

The verb *sit* means *to assume a sitting position* or *to occupy a seat*. The principal parts of the verb *sit* are *sit, sat, (have, has, had) sat*. The present participle is *sitting*. The verb *sit* never takes an object. The form *set* does not belong to this verb.

Joe **sat** very still, watching the game.

The children **were sitting** on the floor.

I always **sit** near the fireplace when I read.

My aunt likes **to sit** in a rocking chair.

She **has sat** in the same chair for many years.

The verb *set* means *to place, to put something in position, to make rigid, solid*, or *stiff*. The principal parts of the verb *set* are *set, set, (have, has, had) set*. The present participle is *setting*. The verb *set* usually takes an object. There are a few idiomatic uses of the verb in which it does *not* take an object. The verb *set* takes an object in the following sentences:

Esther **set** the basket on the table. (*basket*—direct object)

We **set** the clock back yesterday. (*clock*—direct object)

The operator **set** her hair beautifully. (*hair*—direct object)

The buyer **has set** the price too low. (*price*—direct object)

Idiomatic Uses

The verb *set* is used *without an object* in the following sentences. Study the types of situations in which the verb *set* is used without an object. These are idiomatic uses of the verb *set*.

The sun **was setting** when we left the lodge.

The cement **will set** in two hours.

We **set** out on a long journey.

The men **set** to work at once.

Jelly **sets** as it cools.

EXERCISE 5

Cross out the incorrect verb form enclosed in parentheses. On the line to the right, indicate whether the verb *sit* or *set* should be used in the sentence.

1. (Sit, Set) the groceries on the table.   1. ....

2. The porter (set, sat) our baggage in the lobby.   2. ....

3. Please (set, sit) the stage for the next scene.   3. ....

4. The coat (sits, sets) well on his shoulders.   4. ....

5. I (set, sat) in the front row during the meeting.   5. ....

6. The gardener has been (setting, sitting) out the bulbs.   6. ....

7. The plaster will (set, sit) in a few hours.   7. ....

8. Janice (sat, set) the table for dinner.   8. ....

9. The sun will (set, sit) at seven o'clock today.   9. ....

10. I have often (set, sat) in that room.   10. ....

11. The president has (set, sat) the time for the meeting.   11. ....

12. (Sit, Set) in that chair. It is more comfortable than this one.   12. ....

13. I (set, sat) my traveling bags down beside me.   13. ....

14. This is a wonderful place to (sit, set).   14. ....

15. Let us (sit, set) here and discuss the matter.   15. ....

RISE AND RAISE

The verb *rise* means *to ascend, to go up, to extend upward, to swell up,* as bread dough in fermentation, *to increase in value, force* or *intensity.* The principal parts of the verb *rise* are *rise, rose,* and (*have, has, had*) *risen.* The present participle is *rising.* The verb *rise* expresses action, but it does not take an object.

The building **rises** to a height of eighty feet.

This river **rises** in the north.

The tide **was rising.**

Dan **has risen** in his profession.

The plane **rose** steadily.

The sun **will rise** at six o'clock tomorrow.

The cliffs **rise** far above the sea.

The verb *raise* means *to lift up something* or cause it *to go up, to increase the amount or price, to collect a number of things,* etc. The verb *raise* always takes an object. You can't raise without raising something. The verb *raise* is a regular verb. The principal parts are *raise, raised, raised.* The present participle is *raising.*

I **raised** my arm. (to lift up)

Don't **raise** so much dust! (to cause to rise)

The leader **raised** an army. (collected)

We **shall raise** the flag at sunrise. (to cause to go up)

The farmer **raises** wheat. (to cause to grow)

The landlord **raised** the rent. (increased)

Do not **raise** your voice. (to make louder)

EXERCISE 6

Supply the appropriate forms of **rise** or **raise** in the blank spaces.

1. She .... the window as soon as she .... from the chair.

2. Do you .... flowers in your garden?

3. The audience .... to honor the speaker at the lecture yesterday.

4. You'll need a jack to .... the car.

5. We .... a question during the meeting.

6. The company intends to .... the salaries of the employees.

7. The tower .... to a height of sixty feet.

8. Prices of food have .... during the last two months.

9. I .... early in the morning when I stay at the lodge.

10. Mr. Allen has .... in his profession.

11. The river .... steadily for several days.

12. The committee .... the necessary funds.

13. The sun .... at six that morning.

14. We .... several objections to his plan during the conference last week.

15. Put the dough in a warm place so that it will ....

SUMMARY OF GRAMMAR UNIT TWELVE

Every verb has three basic forms which are called the **principal parts.** These three forms are the *present tense,* the *past tense,* and the *past participle.*

Tense in grammar means *time.* Every verb has certain forms which show the time of the action or the state of condition (linking verbs). The **present tense** denotes *present time.* The **past tense** denotes *past time.*

The **past participle** of a verb is the form that is combined with the auxiliaries *have, has,* or *had* to form a verb phrase. The past participle cannot function as the predicate verb.

Verbs are divided into two classes on the basis of the way in which the past tense and the past participle are formed. Some are called *regular verbs* and others are called *irregular verbs.*

A **regular verb** is a verb which forms the past tense and the past participle by adding **d** or **ed** to the form used in the present tense. Sometimes the **d** changes to **t**: *build, built, built.*

An **irregular verb** is a verb which does *not* form the past tense and the past participle in the regular way; that is, by adding **d** or **ed** to the present tense. The most common way of forming the past tense and the past participle of irregular verbs is by a change of vowel: *sing, sang, sung; drink, drank, drunk; ring, rang, rung.*

The *irregular verbs* are responsible for most of our verb errors. Six of these verbs require special study because they are so frequently confused. These verbs fall into three sets or pairs: *lie, lay; sit, set; rise, raise.*

SELF-GRADING ASSIGNMENT 1

Directions: Fill in the blanks with the correct forms for the **past tense** and the **past participle** of the following verbs.

Present Tense (*now*)	Past Tense (*yesterday*)	Past Participle (*have, has had*)
1. spring	....	....
2. bid (command)	....	....
3. shrink	....	....
4. hang (a picture)	....	....
5. leave	....	....
6. prove	....	....
7. bid (offer to buy)	....	....
8. drown	....	....
9. shine (reflect light)	....	....
10. fly	....	....
11. wring	....	....
12. broadcast	....	....
13. beat	....	....
14. let	....	....
15. teach	....	....

Caution: Check your answers to each assignment with the answer key at the end of this unit before proceeding with the next assignment.

SELF-GRADING ASSIGNMENT 2

Directions: Fill in the blank with the *correct form* of the **verb** enclosed in parentheses.

1. I have often .... at an auction sale. (bid)

2. How many times has he .... that speech? (broadcast)

3. The ship had .... before help arrived. (sink)

4. He has .... my faith in him. (shake)

5. The laundress .... out the clothes by hand. (wring)

6. The Indians have .... a beautiful rug. (weave)

7. They have .... the project too late. (begin)

8. The sailors had .... before the plane sighted the sinking ship. (drown)

9. Grandfather has .... that old watch for many years. (wind)

10. I have .... several courses in English. (take)

11. The judge .... me tell everything. (bid)

12. The specialist .... the broken arm. (X-ray)

13. He should have .... the ball to me. (throw)

14. Mason has .... that machine for several years. (run)

15. We had .... a hundred miles before sunset. (ride)

SELF-GRADING ASSIGNMENT 3

This assignment will show whether you are able to distinguish between the forms and uses of the six troublesome verbs: *lie, lay; sit, set; rise, raise.*

Directions: Cross out the *incorrect verb form.* Write the correct form above it. Two sentences are correct.

risen

Example: The sun had ~~rose~~ before we started out.

1. The old man has set in that chair all day.

2. I laid your coat on the table in the hall.

3. You lay here while I call the doctor.

4. The builders used the stones which were laying about.

5. Mother likes to set in the front row of the theater.

6. By noon the temperature had rose twenty degrees.

7. Lay down and try to get some rest.

8. The river has already raised two feet.

9. We lay the books where he could see them.

10. I often sit the table for twelve guests.

11. Prices are raising every day.

12. Sit the dough where it will raise quickly.

13. The farmer has been sitting out the bulbs.

14. How long have I laid on the beach?

15. The nurse set the lamp on the table near his bed.

PROGRESS TEST TWELVE

This progress test should not be taken until a day or two after you have completed the assignments. The score you make on the test will then more clearly reflect your understanding of the material in the unit.

Directions: Rewrite the following sentences making any corrections that are necessary in the use of *verb forms*. Three sentences are correct. (*30 points*)

1. Alice has lain on the couch all day.

2. The sun has shined for several days.

3. The vessel laid at anchor in the harbor.

4. The janitor has throwed out some valuable papers.

5. The manager give us our instructions.

6. The soldiers begun the attack at dawn.

7. The boys drunk all the milk in the container.

8. The big seal swum toward the fishermen.

9. I seen her yesterday at the Art Institute.

10. Why has she hurted my pride so often?

11. Frances has wrote several letters to the employment agency.

12. The girls in the office come home with me for dinner last night.

13. They have broke off relations with the firm.

14. Has anyone spoken to you about the election of officers?

15. I think I have set here for an hour.

PROGRESS TEST TWELVE (continued)

16. The fish have not bit yet.

17. The loud noise drownded the music.

18. We sung that song at the last concert.

19. The water flowed over the bank for several feet.

20. The committee hanged the pictures in the south gallery.

21. The milk in the pitcher has froze solid.

22. The gate swang open.

23. My father has drove his car ten thousand miles.

24. He has already gave her many beautiful presents.

25. The birds have flowed to the South.

26. Has the church bell rang?

27. If he had been well, he might have broke the record.

28. The manager done the job thoroughly and efficiently.

29. The robber run fast, but the officer ran faster.

30. The wind blowed hard last night.

ANSWER KEY

for

EXERCISES, ASSIGNMENTS, AND PROGRESS TEST

Grammar Unit Twelve

CORRECT ANSWERS TO EXERCISE 1

Present Tense	Past Tense	Past Participle
1. fall	fell	fallen
2. break	broke	broken
3. know	knew	known
4. see	saw	seen
5. speak	spoke	spoken
6. lie (to recline)	lay	lain
7. eat	ate	eaten
8. sink	sank	sunk
9. ride	rode	ridden
10. take	took	taken
11. rise	rose	risen
12. cut	cut	cut
13. freeze	froze	frozen
14. throw	threw	thrown
15. ring	rang	rung

CORRECT ANSWERS TO EXERCISE 2

1. Where **have** they **taken** the car?
2. **Have** you **drunk** all the milk?
3. I **have worn** this hat for several years.

4. John **has** never **swum** that far before.

5. The officers **have gone** to the convention.

6. The child **has eaten** too many apples.

7. **Have** you **seen** that motion picture before?

8. We **have sung** that song every day for a week.

9. The dress **has shrunk** from washing.

10. The income tax statements **have come.**

11. A pipe in the basement **has burst.**

12. The swimmer **has dived** into that pool six times.

13. The birds **have flown** toward the South.

14. The decorators **have hung** the pictures too low.

15. Why **have** you **become** so morbid?

CORRECT ANSWERS TO EXERCISE 3

1. The vandals have **broken** the windows.

2. The water in the pipe has **frozen.**

3. I **saw** the picture again last night.

4. He **gave** me the book with the references in it.

5. We **began** the project this morning.

6. I **brought** my friend a gift from Paris.

7. The lifeguard **swam** out to the drowning child.

8. Fred is the plumber who **did** the work.

9. They **hanged** the traitor yesterday. (*correct*)

10. The birds have **flown** to the South.

11. The torn ligament **hurt** badly.

12. The lion **sprang** at the hunter. (*correct*)

13. He has **become** involved in illegal practices.

14. I have **spoken** to the manager about the mistakes Jane makes.

15. For many years he has **grown** orchids in his garden.

CORRECT ANSWERS TO EXERCISE 4

1. The injured man has **lain** unconscious all day.

2. We **laid** our wraps on the bench.

3. Have you been **lying** down?

4. As I **lie** here, I can see the hilltops.

5. Broken glass **lay** on the floor.

6. They found the man **lying** on the road.

7. Martha **laid** her packages on the table.

8. She could not have **lain** on that broken cot.

9. I **lie** down every afternoon.

10. We **lay** quite still, hidden by the trees.

11. The lawyer **laid** the case before the jury.

12. James often **lies** down on the porch.

13. The pen is **lying** where I **laid** it last week.

14. Did you **lie** down when you came home?

15. We **laid** the cards on the table.

1. *lie,* to recline

2. *lay,* to place, to put

3. *lie,* to recline

4. *lie,* to recline

5. *lie,* to be in a flat position

6. *lie,* to be in a flat position

7. *lay,* to place, to put

8. *lie,* to recline

9. *lie,* to recline

10. *lie,* to recline

11. *lay,* to place, to put

12. *lie,* to recline

13. *lie,* to be in a flat position
    lay, to place

14. *lie,* to recline

15. *lay,* to place, to put

CORRECT ANSWERS TO EXERCISE 5

1. **Set** the groceries on the table.

2. The porter **set** our baggage in the lobby.

3. Please **set** the stage for the next scene.

4. The coat **sets** well on his shoulders.

5. I **sat** in the front row during the meeting.

1. *set*

2. *set*

3. *set*

4. *set*

5. *sit*

6. The gardener has been **setting** out the bulbs.	6. *set*
7. The plaster will **set** in a few hours.	7. *set*
8. Janice **set** the table for dinner.	8. *set*
9. The sun will **set** at seven o'clock today.	9. *set*
10. I have often **sat** in that room.	10. *sit*
11. The president has **set** the time for the meeting.	11. *set*
12. **Sit** in that chair. It is more comfortable than this one.	12. *sit*
13. I **set** my traveling bags down beside me.	13. *set*
14. This is a wonderful place to **sit**.	14. *sit*
15. Let us **sit** here and discuss the matter.	15. *sit*

CORRECT ANSWERS TO EXERCISE 6

1. She **raised** the window as soon as she **rose** from the chair.

2. Do you **raise** flowers in your garden?

3. The audience **rose** to honor the speaker at the lecture yesterday.

4. You'll need a jack **to raise** the car.

5. We **raised** a question during the meeting.

6. The company intends **to raise** the salaries of the employees.

7. The tower **rises** to a height of sixty feet. (or **rose**)

8. Prices of food **have risen** during the last two months.

9. I **rise** early in the morning when I stay at the lodge.

10. Mr. Allen **has risen** in his profession.

11. The river **rose** steadily for several days.

12. The committee **raised** the necessary funds.

13. The sun **rose** at six that morning.

14. We **raised** several objections to his plan during the conference last week.

15. Put the dough in a warm place so that it **will rise**.

CORRECT ANSWERS TO ASSIGNMENT 1

Present Tense	Past Tense	Past Participle
1. spring	sprang (sprung)	sprung
2. bid (command)	bade	bidden, bid
3. shrink	shrank	shrunk
4. hang (a picture)	hung	hung
5. leave	left	left
6. prove	proved	proved
7. bid (offer to buy)	bid	bid
8. drown	drowned	drowned
9. shine (reflect light)	shone	shone
10. fly	flew	flown
11. wring	wrung	wrung
12. broadcast	broadcast **or** broadcasted	broadcast **or** broadcasted
13. beat	beat	beaten
14. let	let	let
15. teach	taught	taught

CORRECT ANSWERS TO ASSIGNMENT 2

1. I **have** often **bid** at an auction sale.

2. How many times **has** he **broadcast** (broadcasted) that speech?

3. The ship **had sunk** before help arrived.

4. He **has shaken** my faith in him.

5. The laundress **wrung** out the clothes by hand.

6. The Indians **have woven** a beautiful rug.

7. They **have begun** the project too late.

8. The sailors **had drowned** before the plane sighted the sinking ship.

9. Grandfather **has wound** that old watch for many years.

10. I **have taken** several courses in English.

11. The judge **bade** me tell everything.

12. The specialist **X-rayed** the broken arm.

13. He **should have thrown** the ball to me.

14. Mason **has run** that machine for several years.

15. We **had ridden** a hundred miles before sunset.

CORRECT ANSWERS TO ASSIGNMENT 3

1. The old man has **sat** in that chair all day.

2. I **laid** your coat on the table in the hall. (*correct*)

3. You **lie** here while I call the doctor.

4. The builders used the stones which were **lying** about.

5. Mother likes to **sit** in the front row of the theater.

6. By noon the temperature had **risen** twenty degrees.

7. **Lie** down and try to get some rest.

8. The river has already **risen** two feet.

9. We **laid** the books where he could see them.

10. I often **set** the table for twelve guests.

11. Prices are **rising** every day.

12. **Set** the dough where it will **rise** quickly.

13. The farmer has been **setting** out the bulbs.

14. How long have I **lain** on the beach?

15. The nurse **set** the lamp on the table near his bed. (*correct*)

CORRECT ANSWERS TO PROGRESS TEST TWELVE

1. Alice **has lain** on the couch all day. (*correct*)

2. The sun **has shone** for several days.

3. The vessel **lay** at anchor in the harbor.

4. The janitor **has thrown** out some valuable papers.

5. The manager **gave** us our instructions.

6. The soldiers **began** the attack at dawn.

7. The boys **drank** all the milk in the container.

8. The big seal **swam** toward the fishermen.

9. I **saw** her yesterday at the Art Institute.

10. Why **has** she **hurt** my pride so often?

11. Frances **has written** several letters to the employment agency.

12. The girls in the office **came** home with me for dinner last night.

13. They **have broken** off relations with the firm.

14. **Has** anyone **spoken** to you about the election of officers? (*correct*)

15. I think I **have sat** here for an hour.

16. The fish **have** not **bitten** yet.

17. The loud noise **drowned** the music.

18. We **sang** that song at the last concert.

19. The water **flowed** over the bank for several feet. (*correct*)

20. The committee **hung** the pictures in the south gallery.

21. The milk in the pitcher **has frozen** solid.

22. The gate **swung** open.

23. My father **has driven** his car ten thousand miles.

24. He **has** already **given** her many beautiful presents.

25. The birds **have flown** to the South.

26. Has the church bell **rung**?

27. If he had been well, he **might have broken** the record.

28. The manager **did** the job thoroughly and efficiently.

29. The robber **ran** fast, but the officer **ran** faster.

30. The wind **blew** hard last night.

HOW TO OBTAIN YOUR SCORE

The test totals 30 points. To obtain your score, divide the number of your correct answers by 30. The answer will be your score on this test. For example, if you have 24 points correct, your score is 24 divided by 30 which is 80 per cent. In other words, your score on this test is 80. You can obtain your score on any of the exercises or assignments by following the same procedure.

Practical English Grammar

OUTLINE OF UNIT THIRTEEN

COMPREHENSIVE REVIEW

13

MEASURING YOUR PROGRESS

G ROWTH in the study of language should be continuous. In order to insure this growth, it is necessary to test your progress at certain intervals. Grammar Unit Thirteen has been designed to measure the extent to which you have mastered the grammatical principles developed in the first twelve units of the course.

A thorough understanding of these principles is essential before you take up the study of more complicated problems presented in later units. You will find it difficult to understand the different functions of participles and infinitives, for example, if you are not familiar with the functions of nouns, verbs, adjectives, and adverbs.

The tests in Unit Thirteen cover the essentials of grammar which you have been studying. These tests will give you an opportunity to apply your knowledge in a number of language situations. Your scores on the tests will show the degree to which you have mastered the problems presented. A careful analysis of your mistakes will reveal the types of errors that you still make and will identify the principles which you have not mastered.

The value of the tests lies in the use that you make of the results. If you analyze your mistakes carefully and do the follow-up work that is necessary, you will soon overcome the difficulties encountered in the tests. You will also remove any obstacles that might hinder your success in the study of the next twelve grammar units.

Mastery Test 1

IDENTIFYING THE PARTS OF SPEECH

Directions: Indicate the part of speech of each of the underlined words. Use the following abbreviations for noun, pronoun, verb, verb phrase, adjective, adverb, preposition, conjunction, interjection: **n., pro., v., v.ph., adj., adv., prep., conj., interj.** *(43 points)*

1. The <u>solution</u> of the <u>problem</u> seemed <u>hopeless</u>.

2. Mary looked <u>sadly</u> at the <u>old</u> pictures.

3. I <u>tasted</u> the medicine <u>cautiously</u>.

4. <u>One</u> of the boys <u>will take</u> you <u>to</u> the station.

5. The <u>students</u> <u>were studying</u> far into the <u>night</u>.

6. <u>Huge</u> bowls <u>of</u> rice <u>and</u> beans were placed <u>on</u> the table.

7. A <u>marker</u> <u>should have been placed</u> <u>there</u>.

8. <u>I</u> have <u>often</u> swum <u>across</u> <u>that</u> stream.

9. Have <u>you</u> signed the <u>necessary</u> papers?

10. A coin <u>had lodged</u> <u>in</u> the lining of his coat.

11. <u>Over</u> the road <u>arched</u> <u>tall</u> trees.

12. The city <u>is</u> <u>very</u> old and very <u>interesting</u>.

13. The library <u>contains</u> <u>many</u> books <u>about</u> animals.

14. Our <u>candidate</u> received a <u>large</u> <u>number</u> of <u>votes</u>.

15. <u>Oh!</u> <u>Look</u> at that rainbow!

Mastery Test 2

FINDING THE SUBJECT AND THE PREDICATE

Directions: Draw one line under the **simple subject** and two lines under the **simple predicate**. If the subject or the predicate is *compound,* indicate the *parts* of the **compound subject** or the **compound predicate** in the same way. *(34 points)*

1. Yesterday everyone in the plant started on a new project.

2. There are four people in the manager's office.

3. John walked across the room and picked up the papers.

4. Are you going to the opera next season?

5. How cold the wind is tonight!

6. We have seen that motion picture three times.

7. Oranges and lemons are grown in the valley.

8. The mayor addressed the group and presented the awards.

9. Raymond and I played tennis all day.

10. Away in the distance arose high walls and snow-capped mountains.

11. His father and his mother were born in France.

12. When do you expect the visitors from India?

13. Half of the street has been paved.

14. Working at night was distasteful to Raymond.

15. Nine-tenths of the money was invested in bonds.

Mastery Test 3

IDENTIFYING SENTENCE FRAGMENTS

Directions: If the group of words forms a complete sentence, write the word *complete* on the line at the right. If the group of words is not a complete sentence, write the word *fragment* on the line. *(15 points)*

1. A great many of the books about Roosevelt.   1. ....

2. There are several patients waiting in the office.   2. ....

3. Two tall candles in brass candlesticks.   3. ....

4. Every boy and every girl in the class.   4. ....

5. The vines creeping over the garden wall.   5. ....

6. The salesman had been demonstrating vacuum cleaners all day.   6. ....

7. During the night a terrific storm.   7. ....

8. All day long a wind blew through the pine trees.   8. ....

9. Repeating the terrible news over and over.   9. ....

10. Beyond the cottage, fields of fragrant clover.   10. ....

11. A large number of errors in his report.   11. ....

12. Always jumping to conclusions, always blaming someone.   12. ....

13. Every man in the plant received a bonus.   13. ....

14. Your report will be sent to the committee.   14. ....

15. A street of little bungalows.   15. ....

Mastery Test 4

IDENTIFYING THE KINDS OF SENTENCES

Directions: On the line at the right, indicate the kind of sentence: *declarative, imperative, interrogative,* or *exclamatory.* Supply the **end punctuation.** *(30 points)*

1. How many errors did you make in that report   1. ....

2. Turn left at the next corner   2. ....

3. She repeated the terrible news over and over   3. ....

4. What a fool I have been   4. ....

5. How are the men behaving in this crisis   5. ....

6. Have you made any progress on your new book   6. ....

7. Stop that noise at once, Junior   7. ....

8. Was the letter for Susan or for me   8. ....

9. Please close the window and lock it securely   9. ....

10. Give the coat to whoever can wear it   10. ....

11. What a sensation she made   11. ....

12. What a wonderful time we had at the banquet   12. ....

13. She would sit there by the hour and do nothing but read   13. ....

14. The manager interviewed several candidates for the position   14. ....

15. Jane, please serve the refreshments   15. ....

Mastery Test 5

MAKING THE VERB AND THE SUBJECT AGREE

Directions: Select the form of the **verb** in parentheses that agrees with the *subject*. Cross out the incorrect form of the verb. *(15 points)*

1. The jury (is, are) casting their ballots.

2. Some of the guests (has, have) left.

3. Ten miles (seems, seem) a long distance.

4. The class (has, have) been dismissed.

5. Part of the roof (was, were) blown off.

6. All (is, are) in order for the meeting.

7. Many a town (has, have) often been in danger of inundation.

8. There (are, is) ten thousand men in camp.

9. Half of the cake (is, are) left.

10. The student or the teachers (are, is) to blame for the accident.

11. Our cook and housekeeper (has, have) left.

12. There (was, were) no errors in his paper.

13. My cousin, with her children, (has, have) sailed for Italy.

14. Every man, woman, and child (has, have) left the hall.

15. Fresh air and exercise (build, builds) a strong body.

Mastery Test 6

DISTINGUISHING BETWEEN ACTION AND LINKING VERBS

Directions: Cross out the word in the parentheses that would be used incorrectly in the sentence. On the line at the right, indicate whether the verb expresses *action* or has a *linking* function. *(30 points)*

1. The flowers smell (sweet, sweetly).   1. ....

2. Our costumes looked very (curious, curiously) to the natives.   2. ....

3. The officer seems very (arrogant, arrogantly).   3. ....

4. Brush your teeth (good, well).   4. ....

5. A shower feels (good, well) on a hot day.   5. ....

6. That piano sounds (terrible, terribly).   6. ....

7. The medicine tastes (bitter, bitterly).   7. ....

8. The child appears (sick, sickly).   8. ....

9. Don't feel too (bad, badly) about the accident.   9. ....

10. The captain spoke very (angry, angrily).   10. ....

11. The milk turned (sour, sourly).   11. ....

12. The tailor felt the material (careful, carefully).   12. ....

13. John appeared (prompt, promptly) when I called him.   13. ....

14. The cake kept (fresh, freshly) in the container.   14. ....

15. I tasted the food (cautious, cautiously).   15. ....

Mastery Test 7

USING VERBS CORRECTLY

Directions: Cross out the **verb forms** that are used incorrectly. Write the correct form above the incorrect form. One sentence is correct. (*15 points*)

1. A peculiar smile come over her face.

2. Have you ever drunk such delicious cocoa?

3. Mother laid back in her chair and went to sleep.

4. A pipe in the cellar has bursted.

5. The church bell has rang.

6. Stocks have rose several points this week.

7. The tired old man set down to rest.

8. Yesterday I laid on the beach for several hours.

9. Some of the men had rode into the camp on horseback.

10. She has wore that red hat for two years.

11. Has the dough raised yet?

12. Was you home when the message came?

13. Someone lay a note on my desk.

14. I seen some of his famous animal pictures.

15. He has raised rapidly in his profession.

Mastery Test 8

USING PRONOUNS CORRECTLY

Directions: Correct the errors in the use of **pronouns** in the following sentences. Cross out the wrong form, and write the correct form above it. Two sentences are correct. (*38 points*)

1. To who did I give the examination questions?

2. Her and him led the singing.

3. Who's report was sent to the president?

4. They invited several guests and myself.

5. We boys like skating better than skiing.

6. Many had forgotten his credentials.

7. One must pass a test before you can enter college.

8. Give the money to Martha and he.

9. The tree was beautiful. It's branches were heavy with ice.

10. You will soon hear from we boys.

11. Everyone helped themselves.

12. It should have been us, but it was them who received the honor.

13. One likes to do what they can do well.

14. David and myself served as ushers.

15. Her and me attended the lecture.

16. Is that yellow sweater hers?

17. Each of the oarsmen did their best.

Mastery Test 8 (continued)

18. Neither of the men brought their tools.

19. Who did you invite to the exhibition?

20. Every ship has it's own officers.

21. All found his places at the stadium.

22. The secretary and the treasurer have outlined his plans.

23. These kind of shoes are always uncomfortable.

24. We recommended the plan to she and him.

25. Don't judge a person by their clothes.

26. If any girl wants the position, they should see Miss Smith.

27. The town built a memorial to their war veterans.

28. Martin's father became a general when he was three years old.

29. Her secretary and companion gave their account of the accident.

30. Those kind of grapes are sour.

31. You and him may enter the room next.

32. Nobody brought their lunch.

33. The audience rose to its feet.

34. Many a man wishes that they had studied harder.

35. The firm sent two salesmen, John and I.

Mastery Test 9

USING ADJECTIVES AND ADVERBS CORRECTLY

Directions: The problem in this test is to make a choice between *adjectives* and *adverbs,* and between the use of the *comparative degree* and the *superlative degree.* Cross out the **adjective** or **adverb** that is used incorrectly and write the correct form above it. One sentence is correct. (*16 points*)

1. Father doesn't feel badly today.

2. The apples are real good.

3. Do you think that Andrew drives good?

4. Those lilacs smell fragrantly.

5. The officer appeared prompt when we called him.

6. Jack sure is a good executive.

7. This medicine tastes bitterly.

8. My friend is acting very peculiar.

9. I have read both articles. This is the best of the two.

10. The child grew restless during the night.

11. Father worked steady all winter.

12. His machine runs easier than mine.

13. Of the two girls, Alice is the tallest, but Jane is the most beautiful.

14. I always report punctual at eight o'clock.

15. My son is doing very good at college.

Mastery Test 10

FORMING POSSESSIVES CORRECTLY

Directions: In the following sentences, supply the **correct possessive forms** of the *nouns* and *pronouns* in parentheses. Write the correct form above the word in parentheses. (*16 points*)

1. Tomorrow is (children) day at the theater.

2. (Who) coat did you take home with you?

3. We needed an (attorney) help to settle the estate.

4. The secretary asked for a three (month) leave.

5. I always enjoy reading (Dickens) "Christmas Carol."

6. Fred is going to Alaska with his (employer) son.

7. I asked for fifty (cents) worth of candy.

8. He married his (brother-in-law) sister.

9. We lost three (months) wages because of the strike.

10. I found (someone else) coat in my locker.

11. (Everybody) ticket was examined carefully.

12. Have you been invited to the (Higgins) new home?

13. (You) is a much more expensive car than (we).

14. May I borrow (father) car for the week end?

15. The (editor-in-chief) article was published in several papers.

Mastery Test 11

USING CAPITAL LETTERS CORRECTLY

Directions: Supply the necessary **capital letters** in the following sentences. Cross out the capital letters that are used incorrectly. Substitute small letters for them. (*47 points*)

1. The league of nations met in geneva, Switzerland.

2. The democrats are holding a convention in los Angeles.

3. I am going to the union league Club next friday for Lunch.

4. John eliot translated the bible from the english into the Indian language.

5. I am taking mathematics 102 at northwestern University.

6. He spoke to senator Lodge, a member of the united states senate.

7. That purse is made of spanish leather.

8. They saw queen Elizabeth enter Westminster abbey.

9. The senior class is having a Dance at the Edgewater beach hotel.

10. I work for Mandel brothers, and my sister works for Marshall Field and company.

11. Harvey is a Junior at North Park college. He is taking Physics, Economics, and english.

12. A Senator called on vice-president Barkley in washington.

13. Father prefers to play golf at a Country Club.

14. I live on Forty-Third street near fifth avenue in new York.

15. The speaker discussed the place of china in the far east.

Mastery Test 12

IDENTIFYING THE COMPLEMENTS OF VERBS

Directions: Underline the **simple subject**, the **verb**, and the **complement**. Write **S** under the subject, **V** under the verb, and **C** under the complement. On the line to the right, indicate whether the complement is a *direct object,* an *indirect object,* a *predicate noun,* a *predicate pronoun,* or a *predicate adjective.* Some verbs have two complements. Underline both. *(65 points)*

1. The radii of a circle are equal in length.   1. ....

2. We encountered gales and storms.   2. ....

3. I have laid the sticks in a row.   3. ....

4. Divide the favors among the guests.   4. ....

5. All of the pupils are present.   5. ....

6. He became her confidential adviser.   6. ....

7. Silas proved a hero during the flood.   7. ....

8. Whom did you see at the convention?   8. ....

9. The company gave the employees a bonus.   9. ....

10. Harvey proved eligible for the position.   10. ....

11. The stenographer gave the manager a copy.   11. ....

12. One member of the staff remained antagonistic.   12. ....

13. Lawrence should have been our adviser.   13. ....

14. The corn is growing ripe.   14. ....

15. That might have been he.   15. ....

Mastery Test 13

FORMING THE PLURALS OF NOUNS CORRECTLY

Directions: Write the **plural** of each of the following words on the line to the right of the word. (*40 points*)

1. grotto	1.	21. witness	21. ....
2. lady	2.	22. notary public	22. ....
3. shelf	3.	23. goose	23. ....
4. alibi	4.	24. contralto	24. ....
5. alumna	5.	25. Roman	25. ....
6. cactus	6.	26. appendix	26. ....
7. Charles	7.	27. phenomenon	27. ....
8. ally	8.	28. scarf	28. ....
9. dynamo	9.	29. forget-me-not	29. ....
10. belief	10.	30. Henry	30. ....
11. attorney	11.	31. half	31. ....
12. cupful	12.	32. valley	32. ....
13. Japanese	13.	33. Mr. Smith	33. ....
14. salmon	14.	34. Mary	34. ....
15. bus	15.	35. property	35. ....
16. Eskimo	16.	36. handkerchief	36. ....
17. chief	17.	37. lieutenant colonel	37. ....
18. life	18.	38. father-in-law	38. ....
19. ox	19.	39. leaf	39. ....
20. trade-union	20.	40. waltz	40. ....

Mastery Test 14

USING THE CORRECT FORMS FOR THE PLURAL

Directions: Fill in the blanks with the correct forms for the **plurals** of the nouns in parentheses. *(25 points)*

1. My uncle owns fifty (sheep) .... and ten (calf) ....

2. The (policeman) .... caught the two (thief) ....

3. Please send me six (tomato) .... and ten (potato) ....

4. I received two (handkerchief) .... for my birthday.

5. The (lady) .... baked thirty (loaf) .... of bread.

6. Jane will have two (maid of honor) .... at her wedding.

7. He did not realize that he had so many (enemy) ....

8. The (child) .... saw the (monkey) .... climb the trees.

9. His (6) .... look like (9) .... and his (k) .... look like (h) ....

10. There are several (man-of-war) .... in the harbor.

11. A (series) .... of lectures will be given this fall.

12. We have passed through several (crisis) ....

13. Three (soprano) .... sang several (solo) ....

14. A number of (hero) .... died during the war.

15. There are three (Mary) .... and two (Henry) .... in our office.

Mastery Test 15

CORRECT USAGE

Directions: Rewrite the following sentences, making any corrections that are necessary in **correct usage**, the use of **capital letters**, and the use of the **apostrophe**. Three sentences are correct. (*60 points*)

1. Each one wrote the story of their life.

2. Before a boy selects a college, you should know the requirements.

3. This apple tastes sour.

4. I feel better today. I felt badly yesterday.

5. Jack sure has gained weight this winter.

6. The dog frightened Ellen and I.

7. That pen is your's. Where is her's?

8. My uncle writes and speaks French fluent.

9. Who's going to plant the seeds?

10. Somebody has left their shoes in my locker.

11. Andrew is doing very good in his new position.

12. I stayed at the palmer house in chicago last Summer.

13. Both of the boys brought his golf clubs.

14. For who are you looking?

15. Ellen and her will ride in our car.

Mastery Test 15 (continued)

16. I grew tired of laying on the beach.

17. Have you ever seen these kind of flowers?

18. Book sales have raised recently.

19. David and myself read the book you recommended.

20. That might have been them.

21. Try to put yourself in anothers place.

22. The boys have ate all the melons.

23. Every ship had it's own orchestra.

24. Yesterday everyone begun a new project.

25. The house become unusual quiet.

26. Someones coat was left in Janes locker.

27. He hadn't scarcely time to get dressed.

28. Anthony is the best mechanic of the two.

29. She never enjoys these kind of pictures.

30. He has the littlest initiative of any worker in the plant.

31. The bell has already rang.

32. Both Ingrid and Jane forgot her skates.

Mastery Test 15 (continued)

33. Our familys estate was settled according to the judges ruling.

34. He looked frantically about the room.

35. Is this the more recent of the five copies?

36. Margaret always looks very handsomely.

37. This is the worse letter we have ever received.

38. I don't want none of these apples.

39. Has the dough raised enough?

40. Father always set in that large arm chair.

41. Martha laid on the couch all day.

42. He spoke to senator Lodge, a member of the United states senate.

43. Neither has finished their assignment.

44. This map is exceeding large.

45. We should respect others rights.

46. There isn't but one cake left.

47. I sure felt badly after that criticism.

48. How long has that money laid there?

49. I have always strived to do my best.

50. Harvey done his best to win the award.

ANSWER KEY

Grammar Unit Thirteen

KEY TO MASTERY TEST 1

1. The solution of the problem seemed hopeless.
      n.   n.   adj.

2. Mary looked sadly at the old pictures.
         adv.   adj.

3. I tasted the medicine cautiously.
  v.   adv.

4. One of the boys will take you to the station.
  pro.   v.ph.   prep.

5. The students were studying far into the night.
     n.   v.ph.   n.

6. Huge bowls of rice and beans were placed on the table.
  adj.   prep.   conj.   prep.

7. A marker should have been placed there.
   n.   v.ph.   adv.

8. I have often swum across that stream.
 pro.   adv.   prep. adj.

9. Have you signed the necessary papers?
    pro.   adj.

10. A coin had lodged in the lining of his coat.
      v.ph. prep.

11. Over the road arched tall trees.
  prep.   v. adj.

12. The city is very old and very interesting.
     v. adv.   adj.

13. The library contains many books about animals.
       v.   adj.   prep.

14. Our candidate received a large number of votes.
    n.   adj.   n.   n.

15. Oh! Look at that rainbow!
  interj. v.

KEY TO MASTERY TEST 2

1. Yesterday everyone in the plant started on a new project.

2. There are four people in the manager's office.

3. John walked across the room and picked up the papers.

4. Are you going to the opera next season?
   (You are going to the opera next season.) (*transposed order*)

5. How cold the <u>wind</u> <u>is</u> tonight! (The wind is how cold tonight!)

6. <u>We</u> <u>have seen</u> that motion picture three times.

7. <u>Oranges</u> and <u>lemons</u> <u>are grown</u> in the valley.

8. The <u>mayor</u> <u>addressed</u> the group and <u>presented</u> the awards.

9. <u>Raymond</u> and <u>I</u> <u>played</u> tennis all day.

10. Away in the distance <u>arose</u> high <u>walls</u> and snow-capped <u>mountains</u>.

11. His <u>father</u> and his <u>mother</u> <u>were born</u> in France.

12. When <u>do</u> <u>you</u> <u>expect</u> the visitors from India?
    (You <u>do</u> <u>expect</u> the visitors from India when?) (*transposed order*)

13. <u>Half</u> of the street <u>has been paved</u>.

14. <u>Working</u> at night <u>was</u> distasteful to Raymond.

15. <u>Nine tenths</u> of the money <u>was invested</u> in bonds.

MASTERY TEST 3

1. fragment
2. complete
3. fragment
4. fragment
5. fragment
6. complete
7. fragment
8. complete
9. fragment
10. fragment
11. fragment
12. fragment
13. complete
14. complete
15. fragment

MASTERY TEST 4

1. interrogative — question mark
2. imperative — period
3. declarative — period
4. exclamatory — exclamation mark
5. interrogative — question mark
6. interrogative — question mark
7. imperative — exclamation mark
8. interrogative — question mark
9. imperative — period
10. imperative — period
11. exclamatory — exclamation mark
12. exclamatory — exclamation mark
13. declarative — period
14. declarative — period
15. imperative — period

KEY TO MASTERY TEST 5

1. The jury **are** casting their ballots.
2. Some of the guests **have** left.
3. Ten miles **seems** a long distance.
4. The class **has** been dismissed.
5. Part of the roof **was** blown off.
6. All **is** in order for the meeting.
7. Many a town **has** often been in danger of inundation.
8. There **are** ten thousand men in the camp.
9. Half of the cake **is** left.
10. The student or the teachers **are** to blame for the accident.
11. Our cook and housekeeper **has** left.
12. There **were** no errors in his paper.
13. My cousin, with her children, **has** sailed for Italy.
14. Every man, woman, and child **has** left the hall.
15. Fresh air and exercise **build** a strong body.

KEY TO MASTERY TEST 6

1. The flowers smell **sweet.**	1. *linking*
2. Our costumes looked very **curious** to the natives.	2. *linking*
3. The officer seems very **arrogant.**	3. *linking*
4. Brush your teeth **well.**	4. *action*
5. A shower feels **good** on a hot day.	5. *linking*
6. That piano sounds **terrible.**	6. *linking*
7. The medicine tastes **bitter.**	7. *linking*
8. The child appears **(sick, sickly).** (Both **sick** and **sickly** are correct.)	8. *linking*
9. Don't feel too **bad** about the accident.	9. *linking*
10. The captain spoke very **angrily.**	10. *action*
11. The milk turned **sour.**	11. *linking*
12. The tailor felt the material **carefully.**	12. *action*
13. John appeared **promptly** when I called him.	13. *action*
14. The cake kept **fresh** in the container.	14. *linking*
15. I tasted the food **cautiously.**	15. *action*

KEY TO MASTERY TEST 7

1. came
2. correct
3. lay
4. has burst
5. has rung

6. have risen
7. sat
8. lay
9. had ridden
10. has worn

11. Has risen
12. Were
13. laid
14. saw
15. has risen

KEY TO MASTERY TEST 8

1. whom (not who)
2. She and he
3. Whose
4. me (not myself)
5. correct
6. their (not his)
7. he, or one (not you)
8. him (not he)
9. Its (not It's)
10. us boys
11. himself
12. we—they
13. he, or one (not they)

14. I (not myself)
15. She and I
16. correct
17. his (not their)
18. his (not their)
19. Whom (not who)
20. its (not it's)
21. their (not his)
22. their (not his)
23. These kinds or This kind is
24. her (not she)
25. his (not their)

26. she (not they)
27. its (not their)
28. Martin (not he)
29. her (not their)
30. Those kinds or That kind is
31. he (not him)
32. his (not their)
33. their (not its)
34. he (not they)
35. me (not I)

KEY TO MASTERY TEST 9

1. bad (not badly)
2. very (not real)
3. well (not good)
4. fragrant (not fragrantly)
5. promptly (not prompt)
6. surely (not sure)
7. bitter (not bitterly)
8. peculiarly (not peculiar)

9. better (not best)
10. correct
11. steadily (not steady)
12. more easily (not easier)
13. taller (not tallest) more beautiful (not most)
14. punctually (not punctual)
15. well (not good)

KEY TO MASTERY TEST 10

1. children's day
2. whose coat
3. attorney's help
4. three months' leave
5. Dickens' or Dickens's
6. employer's
7. fifty cents' worth
8. brother-in-law's
9. three months' wages
10. someone else's coat
11. Everybody's ticket
12. Higgins' or Higgins's
13. Yours—ours
14. father's car
15. editor-in-chief's article

KEY TO MASTERY TEST 11

Corrected capital and small letters are printed in **heavy type.**

1. The **L**eague of **N**ations met in **G**eneva, Switzerland.
2. The **D**emocrats are holding a convention in **L**os Angeles.
3. I am going to the **U**nion **L**eague Club next **F**riday for **l**unch.
4. John **E**liot translated the **B**ible from the **E**nglish into the Indian language.
5. I am taking **M**athematics 102 at **N**orthwestern University.
6. He spoke to **S**enator Lodge, a member of the **U**nited **S**tates **S**enate.
7. That purse is made of **S**panish leather.
8. They saw **Q**ueen Elizabeth enter **W**estminster **A**bbey.
9. The **S**enior **C**lass is having a **d**ance at the Edgewater **B**each **H**otel.
10. I work for Mandel **B**rothers, and my sister works for Marshall Field and **C**ompany.
11. Harvey is a **j**unior at North Park **C**ollege. He is taking **p**hysics, **e**conomics, and **E**nglish.
12. A **s**enator called on **V**ice-**P**resident Barkley in **W**ashington.
13. Father prefers to play golf at a **c**ountry **c**lub.
14. I live on Forty-**t**hird **S**treet near **F**ifth **A**venue in **N**ew York.
15. The speaker discussed the place of **C**hina in the **F**ar **E**ast.

KEY TO MASTERY TEST 12

1. The radii of a circle are equal in length.   1. *predicate adjective*
   <u>S</u>   <u>V</u>   <u>C</u>

2. We encountered gales and storms.   2. *direct objects*
   <u>S</u>   <u>V</u>   <u>C</u>   <u>C</u>

3. I have laid the sticks in a row.   3. *direct object*
   <u>S</u>   <u>V</u>   <u>C</u>

4. (You) divide the favors among the guests.
    S   V   C

4. *direct object*

5. All of the pupils are present.
    S   V C

5. *predicate adjective*

6. He became her confidential adviser.
   S   V   C

6. *predicate noun*

7. Silas proved a hero during the flood.
   S   V   C

7. *predicate noun*

8. You did see whom at the convention?
   S V   C

8. *direct object*

9. The company gave the employees a bonus.
       S   V   C   C

9. *indirect object and direct object*

10. Harvey proved eligible for the position.
    S   V   C

10. *predicate adjective*

11. The stenographer gave the manager a copy.
        S   V   C   C

11. *indirect object and direct object*

12. One member of the staff remained antagonistic.
     S   V   C

12. *predicate adjective*

13. Lawrence should have been our adviser.
    S   V   C

13. *predicate noun*

14. The corn is growing ripe.
    S V   C

14. *predicate adjective*

15. That might have been he.
   S   V   C

15. *predicate pronoun*

KEY TO MASTERY TEST 13

1. grottoes, grottos
2. ladies
3. shelves
4. alibis
5. alumnae
6. cacti, cactuses
7. Charleses
8. allies
9. dynamos
10. beliefs
11. attorneys
12. cupfuls
13. Japanese
14. salmon
15. buses, busses
16. Eskimos
17. chiefs
18. lives
19. oxen
20. trade-unions
21. witnesses
22. notaries public
23. geese
24. contraltos
25. Romans
26. appendixes, appendices

27. phenomena
28. scarfs, scarves
29. forget-me-nots
30. Henrys
31. halves
32. valleys
33. Messrs. Smith—the Mr. Smiths
34. Marys
35. properties
36. handkerchiefs
37. lieutenant colonels
38. fathers-in-law
39. leaves
40. waltzes

KEY TO MASTERY TEST 14

1. My uncle owns fifty **sheep** and ten **calves.**
2. The **policemen** caught the two **thieves.**
3. Please send me six **tomatoes** and ten **potatoes.**
4. I received two **handkerchiefs** for my birthday.
5. The **ladies** baked thirty **loaves** of bread.
6. Jane will have two **maids of honor** at her wedding.
7. He did not realize that he had so many **enemies.**
8. The **children** saw the **monkeys** climb the trees.
9. His **6's** look like **9's** and his **k's** look like **h's.**
10. There are several **men-of-war** in the harbor.
11. A **series** of lectures will be given this fall.
12. We have passed through several **crises.**
13. Three **sopranos** sang several **solos.**
14. A number of **heroes** died during the war.
15. There are three **Marys** and two **Henrys** in our office.

KEY TO MASTERY TEST 15

1. Each one wrote the story of **his** life.
2. Before a boy selects a college, **he** should know the requirements.
3. This apple tastes sour. (*correct*)
4. I feel better today. I felt **bad** yesterday.
5. Jack **surely** has gained weight this winter.

6. The dog frightened Ellen and **me.**

7. That pen is **yours.** Where is **hers?**

8. My uncle writes and speaks French **fluently.**

9. Who's going to plant the seeds? (*correct*)

10. Somebody has left **his** shoes in my locker.

11. Andrew is doing very **well** in his new position.

12. I stayed at the **Palmer House** in **Chicago** last **summer.**

13. Both of the boys brought **their** golf clubs.

14. For **whom** are you looking?

15. Ellen and **she** will ride in our car.

16. I grew tired of **lying** on the beach.

17. Have you ever seen **this kind** of flowers? (or **these kinds)**

18. Book sales **have risen** recently.

19. David and **I** read the book you recommended.

20. That might have been **they.**

21. Try to put yourself in **another's** place.

22. The boys **have eaten** all the melons.

23. Every ship had **its** own orchestra.

24. Yesterday everyone **began** a new project.

25. The house **became unusually** quiet.

26. **Someone's** coat was left in **Jane's** locker.

27. He **had** scarcely time to get dressed.

28. Anthony is the **better** mechanic of the two.

29. She never enjoys **this kind** of pictures. (or **these kinds)**

30. He has the **least** initiative of any worker in the plant.

31. The bell has already **rung.**

32. Both Ingrid and Jane forgot **their** skates.

33. Our **family's** estate was settled according to the **judge's** ruling.

34. He looked frantically about the room. (*correct*)

35. Is this the **most** recent of the five copies?

36. Margaret always looks very **handsome.**

KEY TO MASTERY TEST 15 (continued)

37. This is the **worst** letter we have ever received.

38. I don't want **any** of these apples.

39. **Has** the dough **risen** enough?

40. Father always **sat** (or **sits)** in that large arm chair.

41. Martha **lay** on the couch all day.

42. He spoke to **Senator** Lodge, a member of the United **States Senate.**

43. Neither has finished **his** assignment.

44. This map is **exceedingly** large.

45. We should respect **others'** rights. (**others'** —plural)

46. There **is** but one cake left.

47. I **surely** felt **bad** after that criticism.

48. How long **has** that money **lain** there?

49. I have always **striven** to do my best.

50. Harvey **did** his best to win the award.

HOW TO OBTAIN YOUR SCORE

The test totals 60 points. To obtain your score, divide the number of your correct answers by 60. The answer will be your score on this test. For example, if you have 54 points correct, your score is 54 divided by 60 which is 90 per cent. In other words, your score on this test is 90.

GLOSSARY OF TERMS

GLOSSARY OF TERMS

The following reference list contains definitions of the grammatical terms used in both volumes of this course. The terms are listed here so that you may quickly refer to them whenever necessary. You are not expected to memorize the definitions.

Active voice	A verb is in the active voice when it represents the subject as performing the action.
Adjective	An adjective is a word used to modify a noun or a pronoun.
Adjective clause	An adjective clause is a subordinate clause that functions as an adjective.
Adjective phrase	An adjective phrase is a prepositional phrase that functions as an adjective.
Adverb	An adverb is a word that modifies a verb, an adjective, or another adverb.
Adverbial clause	An adverbial clause is a subordinate clause that functions as an adverb.
Adverbial phrase	An adverbial phrase is a prepositional phrase that functions as an adverb.
Antecedent	The antecedent of a pronoun is the noun or pronoun to which it refers.
Appositive	An appositive is a word or a group of words that identifies or explains another word or group of words.
Article	The articles are *a, an,* and *the.* They are regarded as adjectives. *The* is the definite article. *A* and *an* are the indefinite articles.
Auxiliary verb	An auxiliary verb is one that helps the principal verb form a verb phrase.
Case	Case is that property of a noun or pronoun that shows the relation of the noun or pronoun to other words in the sentence.
Clause	A clause is a group of words having a subject and a predicate.

1

Collective noun	A collective noun is the name of a group or a collection of objects.
Comma fault	The comma fault is the use of a comma as the sole connection between two independent clauses. A comma should not be used for this purpose *unless* a coordinate conjunction is used with the comma.
Common noun	A common noun is the name of any one of a class of persons, places, or things.
Comparative degree	The comparative degree is used when a comparison is made between two persons or things. The comparative degree of *large* is *larger*. (My house is *larger* than yours.)
Comparison	Comparison is the change in the form of an adjective or an adverb to show a difference in degree. There are three degrees of comparison: *positive, comparative,* and *superlative.*
Complement	A complement completes the meaning of the verb.
Complete subject	The complete subject is the simple subject with all its modifiers.
Complete predicate	The complete predicate is the predicate verb or verb phrase with its complements and modifiers.
Complex sentence	A complex sentence is a sentence that consists of one independent clause and one or more subordinate clauses.
Compound complex sentence	A compound complex sentence is a sentence that consists of two independent clauses and one or more subordinate clauses.
Compound predicate	A compound predicate is made up of two or more connected verbs or verb phrases.
Compound relative pronoun	A compound relative pronoun is a pronoun formed by adding *ever* or *soever* to certain relative pronouns.

Compound sentence	A compound sentence is a sentence that consists of two or more independent clauses.
Compound subject	A compound subject is made up of two or more connected simple subjects.
Conjugation	The conjugation of a verb is the systematic arrangement of all its forms.
Conjunction	A conjunction is a word used to join words or groups of words.
Co-ordinate conjunction	A co-ordinate conjunction is a conjunction that connects words, phrases, and clauses of equal rank.
Dangling modifier	A dangling modifier is a modifier that does not refer to any word in the sentence. The word that it should modify has been left out of the sentence.
Declarative sentence	A declarative sentence makes a statement. A declarative sentence ends with a period.
Demonstrative pronoun	A demonstrative pronoun points out a specific person, place, or thing.
Dependent clause	A dependent clause (subordinate clause) is a group of words that has a subject and a predicate, but does *not* express a complete thought.
Direct address	A noun or pronoun that is used in addressing some person (or persons) is used in direct address.
Direct object	The direct object of a verb names the receiver of the action.
Emphatic form of a verb	The emphatic form of a verb is a form used to give greater emphasis to the idea expressed by the verb. The auxiliaries *do, does,* and *did* are used to give this emphasis.
Exclamatory sentence	An exclamatory sentence expresses strong feeling or sudden emotion. An exclamatory sentence ends with an exclamation mark.

Expletive	An expletive is an introductory word which fills in the place of the grammatical subject. The real subject appears after the verb. An expletive has no grammatical connection with any part of the sentence. The words *it* and *there* are commonly used as expletives.
Future perfect tense	The future perfect tense denotes action that will be completed at some definite time in the future.
Future tense	The future tense denotes future time.
Gerund	A gerund is a verb form (verbal) that is used as a noun.
Gerund phrase	A gerund phrase is a gerund with any complement or modifier that it may take.
Imperative mood	The imperative mood is the mood which expresses a command or a request.
Imperative sentence	An imperative sentence gives a command or makes a request. An imperative sentence ends with a period or an exclamation mark.
Indefinite pronoun	An indefinite pronoun does not point out a definite person, place, or thing.
Independent clause	An independent clause (main clause) is a group of words that has a subject and a predicate and expresses a complete thought. An independent clause is the equivalent of a simple sentence.
Independent element	An independent element is a word or group of words that has no grammatical connection with the rest of the sentence.
Indicative mood	The indicative mood is the mood that is used to make a statement or ask a question.
Indirect object	The indirect object of a verb tells to or for whom something is done.

Infinitive	An infinitive is a verb form (verbal) that is used as a noun, an adjective, or an adverb. An infinitive is usually preceded by the word *to,* which is commonly called the sign of the infinitive.
Infinitive phrase	An infinitive phase is an infinitive with any complement or modifier that it may take.
Interjection	An interjection is a word that expresses strong feeling or sudden emotion.
Interrogative adverb	An interrogative adverb introduces a question and modifies the verb.
Interrogative pronoun	An interrogative pronoun asks a question.
Interrogative sentence	An interrogative sentence asks a question. An interrogative sentence ends with a question mark.
Intransitive verb	An intransitive verb is a verb that does not have an object.
Inverted order	The sentence is in inverted order when the predicate, or part of the predicate precedes the subject.
Linking verb	A linking or copulative verb is one that is used to connect the subject with a word that explains or describes the subject. The explanatory word, which may be a noun, a pronoun, or an adjective, follows the verb.
Misplaced modifier	A misplaced modifier is a modifier that is incorrectly placed in the sentence. It seems to modify the wrong word because it is placed nearer to this word than to the correct word.
Modifier	A modifier is a word or group of words that limits or qualifies the meaning of another word.

Mood	Mood is the form that the verb takes to show the manner in which the action or state of being is to be regarded—as a *fact,* a *command,* as a *wish, doubt, uncertainty,* etc.
Nominative case	The nominative case is the case of the subject. A predicate noun is also in the nominative case. Nouns have no special form to indicate the nominative case.
Non-restrictive clause	A non-restrictive clause is a subordinate clause that is *not* essential to the meaning of the sentence. A non-restrictive clause is usually set off by commas.
Normal order	The normal or grammatical order of a sentence is subject first, followed by the predicate.
Noun	A noun is a word used as the name of a person, place, thing, idea, or action.
Noun clause	A noun clause is a subordinate clause that is used as a noun.
Objective case	The objective case is the case of the direct object of a verb or a preposition. Nouns have no special form to show the objective case.
Participial phrase	A participial phrase is a participle with any complement or modifier that it may take.
Participle	A participle is a verb form (verbal) which is used as an adjective.
Parts of speech	Words are classified as parts of speech according to the work they do in sentences. The eight parts of speech are: *nouns, pronouns, verbs, adjectives, adverbs, prepositions, conjunctions,* and *interjections.*
Passive voice	A verb is in the passive voice when it represents the subject as receiving the action.

Past perfect tense	The past perfect tense denotes action that was completed at some definite time in the past.
Past tense	The past tense denotes past time.
Person	The *first person* is the person speaking. The *second person* is the person spoken to. The *third person* is the person or thing spoken of.
Personal pronoun	A personal pronoun shows by its form whether it refers to the person speaking, the person spoken to, or the person or thing spoken of.
Phrase	A phrase is a group of words, without a subject and a predicate, that is used as a part of speech.
Positive degree	The positive degree is used when there is no suggestion or comparison. It is the simple form of the adjective or the adverb. The positive degree of the adjective *large* is *large.*
Possessive case	The possessive case shows ownership. Nouns have special forms to show the possessive case.
Predicate	The predicate is the part of a sentence that makes a statement about the subject.
Predicate adjective	A predicate adjective is an adjective that completes the verb and modifies the subject. A predicate adjective is found in the predicate.
Preposition	A preposition is a word that shows the relation between its object and some other word in the sentence.
Prepositional phrase	A prepositional phrase is a group of words which consists of a preposition and its object. The object of the preposition may have modifiers.
Present perfect tense	The present perfect tense denotes action that is completed at the time of speaking or writing.

Present tense	The present tense denotes present time. The present tense is also used to express habitual action, and to express an idea which is generally accepted as true.
Progressive form of a verb	The progressive form of a verb is the form which shows that the action is continuing at the time indicated by the particular tense.
Pronoun	A pronoun is a word used in place of a noun.
Proper noun	A proper noun is the name of a particular member of a class.
Reflexive pronoun	A reflexive or intensive pronoun is a pronoun formed by adding *self* or *selves* to some form of a personal pronoun.
Relative adjective	A relative adjective is a relative pronoun that is used as an adjective. A relative adjective refers to an antecedent in the main clause.
Relative adverb	A relative adverb is an adverb that refers to an antecedent in the main clause and modifies some word in the subordinate clause.
Relative pronoun	A relative pronoun is a pronoun that joins a clause to its antecedent.
Restrictive clause	A restrictive clause is a clause that is essential to the meaning of the sentence. A restrictive clause is *not* set off by commas. A restrictive clause defines, limits, or identifies the word it modifies.
Run-on sentence	A run-on sentence is a sentence in which two independent clauses are written as a single sentence, without the use of a conjunction or any mark of punctuation to separate them.
Sentence	A sentence is a group of words that expresses a complete thought. A sentence must have both a subject and a predicate. Sentences are classified into the following four groups, according to the purpose they serve: *declarative, interrogative, imperative,* and *exclamatory.*

Simple predicate	The simple predicate is the verb or verb phrase.
Simple sentence	A simple sentence is a sentence having one subject and one predicate, either or both of which may be compound.
Simple subject	The simple subject names the person, place, or thing that is talked about.
Subject	The subject of a sentence is the part about which something is said.
Subjunctive mood	The subjunctive mood is the mood that is used to express doubt, wish, uncertainty, or a condition that is contrary to fact.
Subordinate conjunction	A subordinate conjunction is a conjunction that is used to connect a subordinate clause with the main clause.
Superlative degree	The superlative degree is used when more than two persons or things are compared. The superlative degree of *large* is *largest*. (My house is the *largest* house in the block.)
Tense	The tense of a verb is the change in the form of the verb to show the time of the action or state of condition.
Transitive verb	A transitive verb is a verb that has an object. The action expressed by the verb passes over to a receiver.
Verb	The verb is a word that expresses action or state of being. Verbs that express state of being are called linking verbs, or copulative verbs.
Verbal	A verbal is a verb form that is used as another part of speech. Participles, gerunds, and infinitives are verbals.
Verb phrase	A verb phrase is a verb that consists of more than one word. It is composed of a principal verb and one or more auxiliary verbs.
Voice	Voice is that property of a verb which shows whether the subject is performing the action or is receiving the action.

COMPREHENSIVE INDEX

COMPREHENSIVE INDEX

Bold-faced numbers (**8**: **21**: etc.) indicate the unit numbers as given on the index tabs. Numbers in regular type (5–7; 19, etc.) indicate the page number within the unit.

Bold-faced numbers (**8: 21:** etc.) indicate the unit numbers as given on the index tabs. Numbers in regular type (5–7; 19, etc.) indicate the page number within the unit.

Bold-faced numbers (**8: 21:** etc.) indicate the unit numbers as given on the index tabs. Numbers in regular type (5–7; 19, etc.) indicate the page number within the unit.

Bold-faced numbers (**8: 21:** etc.) indicate the unit numbers as given on the index tabs. Numbers in regular type (5–7; 19, etc.) indicate the page number within the unit.

Bold-faced numbers (**8: 21:** etc.) indicate the unit numbers as given on the index tabs.
Numbers in regular type (5–7; 19, etc.) indicate the page number within the unit.

Bold-faced numbers (**8: 21:** etc.) indicate the unit numbers as given on the index tabs. Numbers in regular type (5–7; 19, etc.) indicate the page number within the unit.

Bold-faced numbers (**8: 21:** etc.) indicate the unit numbers as given on the index tabs. Numbers in regular type (5–7; 19, etc.) indicate the page number within the unit.

Bold-faced numbers (**8: 21:** etc.) indicate the unit numbers as given on the index tabs. Numbers in regular type (5–7; 19, etc.) indicate the page number within the unit.

Bold-faced numbers (**8: 21:** etc.) indicate the unit numbers as given on the index tabs. Numbers in regular type (5–7; 19, etc.) indicate the page number within the unit.

Bold-faced numbers (**8: 21:** etc.) indicate the unit numbers as given on the index tabs. Numbers in regular type (5–7; 19, etc.) indicate the page number within the unit.

Bold-faced numbers (**8**: **21**: etc.) indicate the unit numbers as given on the index tabs. Numbers in regular type (5–7; 19, etc.) indicate the page number within the unit.